TEN OUT OF TEN

Other collections from
the Young Playwrights Festival

SPARKS IN THE PARK

HEY LITTLE WALTER

TEN
OUT OF
TEN

TEN WINNING PLAYS

SELECTED FROM

THE YOUNG
PLAYWRIGHTS FESTIVAL
1982–1991

PRODUCED BY
The Foundation of
the Dramatists Guild

■

Edited by
Wendy Lamb

Preface by
Wendy Wasserstein

Introduction by
Nancy Quinn

**Delacorte
Press**

Published by
Delacorte Press
Bantam Doubleday Dell Publishing Group, Inc.
666 Fifth Avenue
New York, New York 10103

Library of Congress Cataloging in Publication Data

Ten out of ten : ten winning plays selected from the Young Playwrights Festival, 1982–1991, produced by the Foundation of the Dramatists Guild / edited by Wendy Lamb ; preface by Wendy Wasserstein ; introduction by Nancy Quinn.
  p.   cm.
  Contents: The birthday present/by Charlie Schulman—Third Street/by Richard Colman—Sparks in the park/by Noble Mason Smith—Fixed up/by Patricia Durkin—Twice shy/by Debra Neff—Remedial English/by Evan Smith—The Ground Zero Club/by Charlie Schulman—Hey Little Walter/by Carla Debbie Alleyne—I'm not stupid/by David Rodriguez—Women and Wallace/by Jonathan Marc Sherman.
  ISBN 0-385-30811-6
  1. Youths' writings, American. 2. American drama—20th century. 3. One-act plays, American. [1. Plays—Collections 2. Youths' writings] I. Lamb, Wendy. II. Young Playwrights Festival. III. Dramatists Guild. Foundation.
PS628.C55T46 1992
812'.0410809283—dc20   92-7944 CIP AC

Manufactured in the United States of America

November 1992

10 9 8 7 6 5 4 3 2 1

BVG

The ten plays in this anthology were selected from those given full productions or staged readings in the Foundation of the Dramatists Guild's Young Playwrights Festival. Information on the Young Playwrights Festival is available from the Foundation of the Dramatists Guild, 321 West 44th Street, Suite 906, New York, New York 10036. Phone: (212) 307-1140.

YOUNG PLAYWRIGHTS FESTIVAL STAFF

Nancy Quinn, *Producing Director*
Sheri M. Goldhirsch, *Managing Director*
Paul Selig, *Director of Education Programs*
Ben Pesner, *Marketing Associate*
Kristina Borovicka, *Administrative Assistant*

YOUNG PLAYWRIGHTS FESTIVAL COMMITTEE

Stephen Sondheim, *Chairman**
Andre Bishop
Christopher Durang*
Charles Fuller
Ruth Goetz*
Micki Grant
A. R. Gurney
Carol Hall*
Murray Horwitz
David Henry Hwang*
Albert Innaurato

Marshall W. Mason
Eve Merriam
Marsha Norman*
Gail Merrifield Papp
Nancy Quinn*
Mary Rodgers*
Alfred Uhry*
Wendy Wasserstein*
John Weidman*
Richard Wesley
George C. Wolfe*

*Denotes current membership.

THE FOUNDATION OF THE DRAMATISTS GUILD
BOARD OF DIRECTORS

Alfred Uhry, *President*
Stephen Sondheim, *Executive Vice President*
Mary Rodgers, *Vice President*
David E. LeVine, *Administrative Vice President*
Tom Margittai, *Treasurer*
Stephen Graham, *Secretary*
Nancy Quinn, *Executive Director*

Major support for the Young Playwrights Festival is currently provided by American Express, Educational Foundation of America, Samuel Goldwyn Company, Stephen Graham, M. A. and Josephine Grisham Foundation, Irving B. Kahn Foundation, George Link Jr. Foundation, National Endowment for the Arts, New York City Department of Cultural Affairs, New York State Council on the Arts, Helena Rubinstein Foundation, and Shubert Foundation. To all of the above, and to all of the many corporations, foundations, and individuals who have supported the Young Playwrights Festival over the past ten years, the Festival extends its thanks.

The Young Playwrights Festival is the recipient of the Obie, the New York Drama Critics Circle Award, the Alliance for the Arts Schools and Culture Award, eight George Oppenheimer/*Newsday* Playwriting Awards, the Margo Jones Award, and the Jujamcyn Theaters Award.

Nine of these plays appeared in anthologies published by Dell: *Meeting the Winter Bike Rider* (plays from the 1983 and 1984 Festivals), *The Ground Zero Club* (plays from the 1985 and 1986 Festivals), *Sparks in the Park* (plays from the 1987 and 1988 Festivals), and *Hey Little Walter* (plays from the 1989 and 1990 Festivals). The writers' original autobiographical notes are reprinted here, with an update for this collection. One play, "I'm Not Stupid" by David E. Rodriguez, is from the 1991 Festival, and appears in print for the first time.

—Editor

CONTENTS

PREFACE

This book is the definitive answer to every panel debating "The Death of the American Theater" or "Where Are Our Playwrights?" Anyone who reads these plays collected from ten years of the Young Playwrights Festival would immediately know that the American theater is alive and well, thank you very much, and secure in the hands of these astonishingly gifted young writers.

I love these plays. Of course, frankly, I've always believed that any reviewer or preface writer can never be accused of being too positive. But the truth is, I really do love these plays. They are funny, sad, bitter, hopeful, ironic; and like the best art, they are acute reflections of our times. Taken separately, they are impressive; and together, they demonstrate a remarkable range. Most important, however, each play is the work of a young theater artist with an individual voice. And it is these new voices, clear and distinct, that make the plays so eminently theatrical.

Happily, I have the pleasure of knowing most of the writers in this volume. Some of them, like Charlie Schulman, Tish Durkin, Evan Smith, and Debra Neff, I met when I was the dramaturge, or literary adviser, for the Festival production of their play. Others, like Noble Smith, David Rodriguez, Carla Alleyne, and Jonathan Marc Sherman, I first encountered on the page, when I served on the selection committee that initially read their plays. Richard Colman's play, as directed for the Festival by the late Michael Bennett, was one of the best-produced one-act plays I'd ever seen. Opening night I rushed backstage to meet the author.

Like any other group of writers, these playwrights, all of whom wrote their plays before turning nineteen, are quite diverse. They are men, women, short, tall, funny, intense, shy, and outrageous. But what they have in common is that each one, even years after the initial submission, continues to write. In other words, these plays were not written by young men and women looking for a cool credential for a college application. They were at the time of their production, and continue to be, true artists with unique visions.

When I was in high school I knew of no Young Playwrights Festival. Actually, I didn't even know that girls could seriously grow up to be playwrights. Yes, there was an artsy crowd, but they mostly wore black and were pretentious and intimidating. My greatest hope is that after reading this book young people who dream about writing plays, whether they wear black or not, will simply pick up a pen—all right, a processor—and begin. As evidenced by these ten, there is nothing as satisfying as creating an original life in the theater.

I love these plays because they make me very proud of growing up to be a playwright.

WENDY WASSERSTEIN
New York
December 7, 1991

INTRODUCTION

Ten years ago, though a mysterious disease had begun to kill healthy young people, almost no one knew its name. Ten years ago, though drugs were destroying lives, no one had ever heard of a crack baby. Ten years ago, though there was desperate poverty everywhere, no one spoke of a class of people called the homeless.

Ten years ago the Young Playwrights Festival leapt from idea ("Plays by kids? You mean children's theater? *Gasp.* You don't mean children's theater?") to reality. The Young Playwrights Festival recognizes what young people can be and listens closely to what they think, to how they see the world. The Young Playwrights Festival celebrates their talent and imagination.

Ten years ago a group of prominent American writers, led by Stephen Sondheim, became increasingly concerned at the lack of training and professional support available to young writers. Sondheim et al. feared that the creative impulse, unacknowledged and unsupported, could not survive until the potential artist was old enough for the programs that did exist. While in London in 1979, Sondheim saw the Royal Court Theatre's Young Writers Festival. He found the work extraordinary and returned to the United States convinced of the need for a program specifically geared to younger writers. He persuaded the late Gerald Chapman, the heart and soul of the Royal Court's program, to help start the Young Playwrights Festival. Ten plays, selected from over seven hundred, were presented in the first Young Playwrights Festival, held at the Circle Repertory Company in 1982. Since then, the Festival has received over eight thousand scripts from writers aged eighteen and younger. We've brought sixty-one of them to New York for design meetings, auditions, rehearsals, and opening nights. At last count, fifty-three are still writing.

The idea was, and is, to introduce talented young writers to the professional theater by putting them exactly where they should be: at the center of the production of their plays, working with the best teachers available—top professional actors, directors, and designers who are all there to serve them. Most important, they work with playwrights like Wendy Wasserstein, David Henry Hwang, Christopher Durang, Marsha Norman, Stephen Sondheim, Carol Hall, Alfred Uhry, Mary Rodgers, and George C. Wolfe, who help their younger colleagues struggle with rewrites, explain the role of the playwright in the rehearsal process, and become friends for life.

To quote one of our young playwrights, John McNamara, whose *Present Tense* was produced in the 1982 Festival: "What the Young Playwrights Festival does is overcome prejudice: the prejudice of being young and being a playwright at the same time."

Today, there are forces working to change the definition of art from a creation of wo/man that transcends, uplifts, confuses, angers, and, above all, moves us to that which may be pretty to look at but elicits few emotions from the viewer. Artists themselves are in danger of losing a basic right, freedom of speech. I suspect that the ability of artists to make us see the suffering behind the convenient labels—AIDS, drug addiction, homelessness—might have a great deal to do with the current repressive climate.

There are those who say artists must be controlled and silenced in order to protect the "innocent," which in this case means young people. This idealized view of a childhood that has never existed is appealing, though untrue. And while it is certainly laudable to want to protect the young from the ugliness and harshness of life, it is better to acknowledge that what they see and feel is real, is true. It is even better to show them that art is the creative expression of complicated thoughts and feelings.

Our work with children has taught us a lot. Kids, we learned, suffer because of the poor quality of inner-city public schools, the dearth of cultural programs, the continuing erosion of family life, and the exclusion of the poor and the disabled from anything that could inspire them to succeed. We learned, too, that only privileged children were encouraged to create and that most kids had never even met an artist. To change this, we sent professional playwrights into the schools to lead our WRITING ON YOUR FEET! workshops. Writing a play requires the development of analytical skills, an understanding of human relationships, the ability to see the connection between cause and effect. These skills, of course, transcend playwriting, transcend writing, transcend school. They are necessary for communication. They are necessary for young people to learn if they are to survive, if they are to grapple with the problems in their lives and perhaps even to solve some of those problems.

Both Carla Alleyne *(Hey Little Walter)* and David Rodriguez *(I'm Not Stupid)* first learned about playwriting in our workshops. Both submitted many scripts to our New York City High School Playwriting Contest year after year, determined to win. Both did win, first in New York City and then nationwide, and went on to have their plays produced in the Festival.

Teachers were amazed by our success in the classroom and asked, insisted, demanded that we share our secrets with them. In response, we created the YPF Teacher Training Institute to give teachers a way to use our methods in their daily classroom activities. By the end of their training, teachers have actually written a scene, if not an entire play, and know firsthand what it means to stare at a blank page.

The Young Playwrights Festival's mission to represent and serve the culturally diverse world we live in extends beyond ethnic boundaries. There are children who are so poor that they cannot afford subway fare to the theater and children with physical disabilities who are excluded from trips and special events. Since they can't come to the Festival, the Festival goes to them, complete with sign language interpreters when needed. The children get to meet and talk with the actors and, best of all, with young playwrights like Carla Alleyne, Richard Colman, and Jonathan Sherman, whose plays are among those we've toured.

More and more kids spend the greater part of their day away from home. Families spend little or no time together, have little to talk about and little to share. YPF's TAKE A GROWNUP TO THE THEATER! program offers free tickets to students who bring an adult family member with them to Festival performances. This program shows kids that theater can be part of their lives and something they can share with their families. Our plays directly touch the lives of young people and offer adults insight into what it means to be young in these very difficult times.

This volume of plays is meant to be shared in the same way. It is a multigenerational multicultural resource—a guide to what our young people are feeling, thinking, and accomplishing. We salute Dell/Delacorte for publishing these plays exactly as we produced them. You may find some language and ideas you're not used to hearing from kids. You may find that these writers know exactly what you're feeling. You may remember being desperate to be heard and understood. Listen to these writers. Listen to what they're saying.

NANCY QUINN
Producing Director
Young Playwrights Festival

THE YOUNG PLAYWRIGHTS FESTIVAL

Writers under the age of nineteen (on July 1) are invited to submit their plays to the Foundation of the Dramatists Guild's annual Young Playwrights Festival. Selected playwrights will participate in casting and rehearsals of their plays which will receive professional productions in New York City. Playwrights will also receive transportation, housing, royalty, and membership in the Dramatists Guild, Inc.

All entrants will receive detailed written evaluations of their plays.

Guidelines:

- The choice of subject, style, and length is up to you.
- Scripts must be original. Collaborations are acceptable, but all writers must be under the age of nineteen on July 1. Scripts must be typed and securely fastened—no loose pages.
- Scripts must be submitted by the author, not by a teacher or parent.
- Submit one copy of your play and keep the original at home—scripts will not be returned. Receipt of plays will be acknowledged.
- You may submit more than one play.
- Screenplays and musicals are not eligible, nor are adaptations of other authors' work.
- On the title page of your play, please type your name, date of birth, home address, and telephone number. You may be asked to submit proof of age.

Some Points to Remember:

- In plays, the story is told through speech and action rather than description. Avoid using a narrator if possible.
- Stage directions are useful, but cannot take the place of information conveyed through dialogue. Avoid too many

characters—try to limit the number of actors to no more than
ten.

- In the theater, unlike film or television, you cannot switch from
  one elaborate setting to another. What you write has to be
  acted out on a stage.
- Look at a printed playscript to see how a play is typed.

DEADLINE: Scripts must be POSTMARKED on or before OCTOBER
1. It is not necessary to send scripts by express or overnight mail.
Scripts sent by FAX will not be accepted.

Mail scripts to: Young Playwrights Festival
The Foundation of the Dramatists Guild
321 West 44th Street, Suite 906
New York, New York 10036

OTHER YOUNG PLAYWRIGHTS FESTIVAL PROGRAMS

WRITING ON YOUR FEET!: Presents intensive improvisatory workshops in
playwriting in schools throughout the New York metropolitan area.
Workshops are led by professional playwrights.

YPF School Tour: Presents YPF plays in schools and youth centers
throughout New York City free of charge; discussions with the playwrights and cast follow all performances.

YPF Teacher Training Institute: Prepares educators to teach
playwriting to their classes. Available annually to New York City
public high school teachers and upon request to schools and
school districts nationwide.

YPF Student Matinees: Offers special performances of the annual
Young Playwrights Festival to school groups at a reduced price; discussions with the playwrights, directors, and cast follow each performance.

New York City High School Playwriting Contest: Selects best plays
submitted by students in New York City's public high schools; an
annual event.

TAKE A GROWNUP TO THE THEATER!: Offers free tickets to the annual
Young Playwrights Festival to any New York City public school student who attends the Festival with an adult.

If you have any questions, please contact the Foundation of the
Dramatists Guild at (212) 307-1140.

*This book is dedicated to those who have
lost the fight against AIDS and to those
for whom the fight continues.*

THE BIRTHDAY PRESENT

by
CHARLIE SCHULMAN
(age sixteen when play was written)
New York, New York

■

The Birthday Present was performed at the Circle Repertory Company in New York City, April 12 through May 1, 1983. The director was John Ferraro, and the dramaturge was A. R. Gurney, Jr. The production stage manager was Kate Stewart. John Arnone designed the set, Patricia McGourty the costumes, Mal Sturchio the lighting, and Chuck London Media/Stewart Werner the sound. Richard Weinstock composed the music.

The cast:

WALLACE	*Christopher Durang*
MARY	*Jean DeBaer*
SHEILA	*Deborah Rush*
HENRY	*Bill Moor*
HOPP	*Burke Pearson*
LUCY	*Kim Beaty*
NEWSCASTER	*Novella Nelson*
JOE FLANAGAN	*Edward Power*
TV HOST	*Brian Tarantina*

Scene One

The Coopers' living room.

Today is WALLACE COOPER*'s tenth birthday and nobody has shown up for his party yet. The room is decorated for a party. Down right is a small round table with five chairs, each of which has a helium balloon tied to the back. On the table is a paper tablecloth patterned with fire engines or anything else that might be of interest to a group of ten-year-olds. On the table the paper plates, cups, and napkins all match the tablecloth. The party hats can be of any type. Up left and facing the audience diagonally is a very warm, cushy armchair. In front of the armchair is an end table with a drawer and a telephone on it. Behind the armchair is a swinging door leading into the kitchen. Down center is the front door. In between the front door and the party table, facing the armchair, is the couch. As the lights come up,* WAL-LACE *is sitting on the floor, in the middle of the stage. He is wearing his party hat and sobbing quietly. To his immediate right is a Monopoly set with a game already in progress.*

WALLACE: *(still crying)* What time is it, Mom?

MARY: *(from the kitchen)* It's almost time, dear.

WALLACE: *(crying louder)* How many more minutes?

MARY: *(entering)* Actually, Wallace, everybody's five minutes late. But you've got to give them time.

WALLACE: They're not coming! It's gonna be just like last year. Why do things like this always have to happen to me?

(SHEILA, *Wallace's twelve-year-old sister, enters the room from the kitchen, eating a piece of cake. She flops down on the armchair; her feet dangle over the side.*)

MARY: We can still have the party. There is plenty of food and Daddy will be here soon.

WALLACE: Will Daddy bring me a present?

MARY: Sure, he will.

WALLACE: He will?

MARY: Well, he might.

WALLACE: He won't. *(He starts sobbing again.)*

MARY: *(to* SHEILA*)* I'll go and call him at the office and see if I can catch him there before he leaves. Why don't you try and make Wallace feel a little better? *(She exits into the kitchen.)*

SHEILA: Looks like we are going to have lots of leftover cake. And we can use all the hats and plates from the party you didn't have this year for the party you're not going to have next year. It's your turn to roll the dice.

(WALLACE *picks up the dice from the board.*)

WALLACE: I'm all through not having parties.

(*He rolls the dice and moves his piece.* SHEILA *slowly slides off the armchair headfirst until she is sitting on the floor.*)

SHEILA: That's Park Place with four houses, that comes to . . .

WALLACE: It doesn't matter. I lose.

SHEILA: You can't quit, I've told you that before. Once you start a game, you have to finish it. Besides, I'm supposed to cheer you up.

WALLACE: But, Sheila, you own all the property, you have all the money; it's not that I want to quit, it's just that I lose.

SHEILA: I'll lend you a thousand bucks. If you have a thousand bucks you're still in the game.

WALLACE: But that's not the way you're supposed to play. I don't have a chance, you're slaughtering me. I quit.

(SHEILA *jumps on top of* WALLACE; *straddling his chest, she grabs him by the collar.*)

SHEILA: You quitter, that's the last time I'm gonna let you play with me.

WALLACE: C'mon, Sheila, let's do something else. Anything you want.

SHEILA: (*Her eyes light up.*) Anything? (*She loosens her grip.*)

WALLACE: Sure.

SHEILA: (*jumping to her feet*) Okay, we're going to play Berlin Wall. I'll go get the mop.

(*Pause.*)

Loser cleans up.

(*She points to the Monopoly game and runs into the kitchen.* WALLACE *starts to clean up the game but stops after a few seconds when* SHEILA *reappears with the mop.*)

All right, the couch is the wall, and the chair is freedom.

(WALLACE *gets behind the couch.* SHEILA, *who has become the guard, walks back and forth with the mop on her shoulder, singing the "Volga Boatman." When her back is turned,* WALLACE *leaps over the couch and dashes toward the chair.* SHEILA *whirls around and stops him with the mop, pushes him down on the couch, and starts to pummel him.*)

WALLACE: Sheila, stop!

SHEILA: Kill the traitor.

WALLACE: Let's play Monopoly.

SHEILA: Kill, kill, kill.

WALLACE: Mom!

(SHEILA *gets off* WALLACE *and sits down next to him.*)

MARY: *(from offstage)* What's going on in there?

SHEILA: Nothing, Mom! All you had to say was stop.

WALLACE: I did, I said stop.

SHEILA: You don't have to be a little squealer. I hate squealers.

WALLACE: I'm sorry, Sheila.

SHEILA: Oh, that's okay.

WALLACE: What do you want to play now?

SHEILA: How about boot camp?

WALLACE: No, not boot camp.

SHEILA: How about gestapo?

WALLACE: How does that go?

SHEILA: You sit here . . .

(She points to the armchair.)

because you are the prisoner.

WALLACE: What are you?

SHEILA: I'm the gestapo, stupid.

WALLACE: Why do you get to be the gestapo?

SHEILA: Because someone has to do it.

WALLACE: But, but—

SHEILA: Shut up! The game is starting.

(She puts on a German accent.)

What is your name?!

WALLACE: You know my name, Sheila.

SHEILA: C'mon, if you're gonna play, play right.

(She puts on the accent again.)

What is your name?!

WALLACE: Wallace Cooper.

SHEILA: You lie! You lie! *(She slaps him twice, each time on the word "lie.")*

WALLACE: I don't think I want to play this game.

SHEILA: You sure? I kinda like it. . . . All right, I know what we can do now. You can help me practice my kissing.

WALLACE: Can't we play something else?

SHEILA: I'll tell you what, I'll give you a dollar. But I can't give it to you now, I'll just spend an extra dollar on your birthday present. I haven't gotten it yet.

WALLACE: Nobody has.

SHEILA: All right, so you want to play or not?

WALLACE: Okay.

SHEILA: Sit over here.

(WALLACE walks back to the couch and sits down next to SHEILA.)

Okay, here goes.

(She starts caressing Wallace's face with both hands.)

WALLACE: What are you doing?

SHEILA: That's what you're supposed to do. It's called foreplay.

WALLACE: *(as if a tremendous revelation has hit him)* Ohhh.

(Suddenly SHEILA pulls away and looks in the other direction.)

What are you doing now?

SHEILA: I'm playing hard to get. Girls don't want boys to think that they're cheap.

WALLACE: I don't think you're cheap.

SHEILA: That's exactly what you're supposed to say. You're gonna make a terrific boy someday.

WALLACE: How can you be cheap when you just gave me a dollar?

SHEILA: Okay, Wallace, now you have to pay off.

(She grabs him and gives him the kiss of his life.)

WALLACE: Arrrggghhhh! Arrrggghhhh! You stuck your tongue out!

(He wipes his mouth off with his sleeve.)

Mom! She stuck her tongue out! Disgusting. Disgusting.

(MARY enters.)

MARY: Sheila! Don't stick your tongue out at your brother. You're too old for that kind of silliness. Now, why can't you two play something quiet like charades.

(MARY sits on the couch.)

SHEILA: That's a good idea, let's play charades. But let's have a theme. Ummmmm. How about famous deaths?

(To WALLACE.)

Get out of that chair!

(WALLACE scampers over to the couch. SHEILA kicks off her sneakers and sits on the back of the chair with her feet on the seat. With a broad grin she starts waving to an imaginary crowd. Suddenly she pretends to get shot and slumps down into the chair.)

MARY: John Kennedy!

WALLACE: Let me go now, let me go now. I've got a good one.

(WALLACE goes over to the table where the party wasn't, and using a knife and fork, he pretends to eat. He starts choking and gagging and finally falls to the floor. Then he sits up.)

Doesn't anyone get it?

(Pause.)

I'm Grandpa Cooper.

MARY: Wallace! If your father heard you say that.

SHEILA: That's disgusting, Wallace, don't you have any class? But that reminds me of a good one.

(SHEILA *picks up the mop and, holding it like an ax, starts to pretend to strike her mother with it.*)

WALLACE: Lizzie Borden! Everyone knows that.

WALLACE and SHEILA: *(singing)*

Lizzie Borden took an ax
and gave her mother forty whacks.
When she saw what she had done,
she gave her father forty-one.

MARY: I think playing this game was a big mistake.

SHEILA: Just one more. I've got a great one.

MARY: All right, one more, but that's it.

(SHEILA, *using a mop, imitates Jesus on the cross and walks around the room in a way that could be mistaken for flying.*)

MARY: Amelia Earhart!

(After a pause the front door flies open. DR. HENRY COOPER *stares in wonderment at his crucified daughter.)*

SHEILA: *(turning toward her mother)* Dad's home.

(SHEILA *walks back to the armchair.*)

(HENRY *stands in the doorway. In his right hand he carries a rolled-up newspaper. Today he is more depressed than usual.*)

MARY: Henry!

(She kisses him.)

Step inside and stay awhile.

(She laughs at her little joke. HENRY *steps inside and closes the door.)*

Let me take your coat.

(She pulls off his right sleeve as HENRY *passes the newspaper from his right hand to his left. She then pulls off his left sleeve as he passes the newspaper back to his right hand.)*

How was your day, dear?

HENRY: *(in a low monotone)* I've decided not to be cremated.

MARY: What?

HENRY: I'll burn when I get there.

MARY: That isn't a very pleasant thing to say.

(HENRY *starts to cry.* MARY *puts his coat on the back of an armchair and guides him to the couch where he sits down.)*

What is it? What's the matter?

HENRY: *(He opens the newspaper and folds it back.)* Read this.

(He hands her the paper.)

MARY: What's this all about, Henry?

HENRY: Read it.

MARY: *(reading)* "The Personal Practices Committee of the American Medical Association has revoked the license of Dr. Henry Cooper, connecting him with fifteen cases in which Dr. Cooper performed unauthorized experiments on patients at City Hospital. Dr. Cooper—"

HENRY: *(interrupting) Mr.* Cooper.

(MARY *is startled but regains her composure.)*

MARY: "Dr. Cooper claims that his experiments in the area of germ resistance may prove to be a great contribution to the medical world, especially with the growing reality of germ warfare. Cooper's methods, in which the patient undergoes a series of inoculations, were rejected by the AMA in the fall of last year . . ." Is this some kind of joke?

HENRY: No. It's not a joke.

MARY: Then it's a lie, some terrible, filthy lie. You can never believe what this paper says. Oh, it was once a good paper until that horrible Australian bought it.

SHEILA: Sometimes they tell the truth.

HENRY: I was so close.

(He starts crying again.)

So close. It only takes eight weeks to finish. Then I could have proved to them that they were wrong about me.

MARY: It says here that you said even if you completed the procedure it might take years before we could find out if it really worked.

HENRY: Don't you understand that I'm sitting on something really big?

(He thinks about that for a few seconds.)

I'm the only one that believes in it, the only one. Some people only get one really good idea in their whole lives and this is mine. Can you understand that?

SHEILA: Dad, did you get Wallace a present? It's his birthday, you know.

WALLACE: He didn't, he forgot; everyone forgot.

(He starts crying again.)

SHEILA: Did you forget to buy Wallace a present?

HENRY: A present?

(He starts to space out.)

MARY: Sheila, can't you see that your father is very upset about something?

HENRY: Of course I did. Of course I got Wallace a present.

WALLACE: You did?

HENRY: Yes, I did.

WALLACE: Can I have it?

HENRY: Sure . . . but not today.

WALLACE: Not today?

HENRY: Tomorrow. Tomorrow morning.

WALLACE: Are you sure you have it?

HENRY: Yes, I have it. Now, be patient and I'll give it to you in the morning.

MARY: *(becoming very upset)* Why couldn't you tell me about all this before? Why did you have to wait until it came out in the papers? I don't understand how you could throw away your whole career like that. I don't understand what those experiments were all about, but doing them after you were not supposed to is wrong. Can't you understand that it's wrong?

SHEILA: But Daddy is always right and Mommy is always wrong. Didn't you know that?

MARY: Be quiet, Sheila.

SHEILA: Daddy was right when he married Mommy, but Mommy was wrong when she married Daddy.

HENRY: That's enough out of you, Sheila. Now finish that article, Mary.

MARY: There's more?

HENRY: That's right, there's more.

MARY: *(looking back at the newspaper)* It says—it says, "Dr. Cooper is also facing criminal charges."

(They all look around at one another.)

SHEILA: *(skipping around the room and singing)* Daddy is going to jail, Daddy is going to jail.

HENRY: Shut up, Sheila!!!

BLACKOUT

Scene Two

The Coopers' living room.
   It is the next morning. HENRY *is sitting in the armchair talking on the telephone to his lawyer. He is in a bathrobe and slippers.*

HENRY: The twenty-third? It is just not long enough. I need more time. But, Burt, I'm not asking you to win this case for me. I just want you to get me another postponement. I need the time.

*(*WALLACE *enters in his pajamas.)*

WALLACE: Dad?

*(*HENRY *gives* WALLACE *the "be quiet" sign and puts his hand on the boy's shoulder.)*

HENRY: July seventeenth? . . . Perfect.

(He circles the wall calendar just above the telephone.)

That's in exactly eight weeks. . . . You don't think there'll be any problem, do you? . . . Great. . . . Forget this case, Burt, it's a lost cause. I just needed the postponement. Okay, thanks a lot. Sorry for calling so early in the morning. Good-bye.

(He hangs up the phone.)

Hi, Wallace. I was thinking about you a lot last night.

WALLACE: You were?

HENRY: Yes, I was. I guess you're pretty upset about your party yesterday, so I made this sign for you.

(He opens the top drawer of the end table and takes out a small cardboard sign with a piece of string attached at both ends.)

You can wear it to school. It says, "My name is Wallace Cooper and I would like for someone in this class to be my friend. Thank you."

(He hangs it around Wallace's neck.)

WALLACE: Thanks, Dad. . . . This isn't my present, is it?

HENRY: *(laughing)* No, it isn't.

WALLACE: Do you have my present?

HENRY: *(smiling)* Yes, I do, son.

WALLACE: Can I have it?

HENRY: *(seriously)* You have to promise me one thing first. You won't tell anybody about this present—not Mommy, not Sheila, not anybody. That's why I waited until we could be alone before I gave it to you.

WALLACE: I promise.

HENRY: Now, Wallace, the present I'm about to give you isn't a toy.

WALLACE: It isn't?

HENRY: No. As a matter of fact it's going to take two months to give it to you.

WALLACE: Two months?

HENRY: I know this is hard for you to understand, but this present hurts.

WALLACE: It hurts?

HENRY: Then it helps.

WALLACE: It hurts?

HENRY: Yes, but when you grow up you'll thank me, I promise.

(HENRY takes out a syringe from the drawer, fills it up with a liquid, and spurts a little out through the needle.)

WALLACE: Is that my present?

HENRY: Yes.

WALLACE: I think I'm late for school.

(WALLACE *backs away.*)

HENRY: Wallace, I'm not going to chase after you. . . . Come here, Son, it will only take a second.

WALLACE: I don't want to.

HENRY: If you don't do this for me, if you don't come over here, you'll be no son of mine.

(WALLACE *walks over to his father and puts his hand on the arm of the chair.*)

You're going to have to trust me, Wallace. It might take ten, fifteen, even twenty years, but one day you'll thank me.

(HENRY *rolls up the boy's sleeve. The lights fade to black as he injects him.*)

Scene Three

Wallace's apartment.
   Twenty years have passed. Today is Wallace's thirtieth birthday. The stage is now in two parts. On the left side is Wallace's apartment. All the furniture has been taken out of the apartment by Wallace's wife, LUCY, *and her lawyer,* ALFRED HOPP. *Strewn about the room are boxes filled with books, records, etc. All that is left in the room is a small television set on the floor; it faces* HOPP. *Down left, up against the side wall, is a window with a small cactus on the sill. On the other side of the TV sits the* NEWSCASTER *in the dark. Behind him is a screen for slides to be projected on. As the lights come up on Wallace's apartment, both* LUCY *and* HOPP *are sitting on boxes.* HOPP *has his briefcase open on his lap.*

HOPP: *(taking out a sandwich wrapped in tinfoil)* I hope you don't mind if I eat my lunch while we're waiting for your husband?

LUCY: Not at all. Do what you like.

HOPP: Thank you.

(*He takes a light beer and a can opener out of his briefcase. With some difficulty he opens the beer, puts the can opener back in the briefcase, and takes out a piece of chocolate cake wrapped in cellophane. Balancing the sandwich on one knee, the cake on the other, and the beer between his legs, he takes out a paper napkin that has been folded sixteen times, and carefully unfolds it. Using his briefcase as a table, he meticulously smooths the napkin and then strategically places his food on it.)*

Lately I've been eating on the run most of the time. No time for peace and quiet. Always another miserable marriage to attend to. People paying me to help them get away from each other. It just doesn't seem right.

(He looks deeply into his roast beef sandwich.)

I like my roast beef rare. If you cook it too much it stops bleeding.

(He tears into his sandwich viciously.)

I could never be a vegetarian, couldn't imagine spending my whole life just eating plants. As for me, if I don't eat meat for a couple of days, I get irritable. I gotta sink my teeth into something bloody every once in a while or I just don't act myself.

LUCY: I guess that makes for a good divorce lawyer.

HOPP: I guess so.

(He laughs uproariously.)

LUCY: I wonder where Wallace is? I hope he hasn't forgotten.

HOPP: *(unwrapping his cake)* That would be pretty funny.

(WALLACE enters.)

He'd walk in here and we'd say "Surprise!"

WALLACE: I—I don't know what to say. I am surprised. A party, beer, cake, guest. I never expected this in a million years. Thanks, Lucy; thanks, Lucy. Thanks for remembering my birthday.

LUCY: Today is your birthday?

WALLACE: I've never had a birthday party before.

LUCY: I'm sorry, Wallace, I've made a terrible mistake. Didn't I tell you that I was coming over with my lawyer to have you sign the divorce papers?

WALLACE: No, you didn't.

LUCY: I feel so foolish.

WALLACE: It's okay.

LUCY: I'm such an idiot.

WALLACE: No, it's okay, really, I'm used to it. What happened to the furniture?

LUCY: It's gone. I've taken back everything that was mine. And, well, everything was mine, except for the TV. This is my lawyer.

HOPP: *(interrupting)* Alfred Hopp at your service

(He shakes hands with WALLACE.)

or should I say at your wife's service. Have you gotten yourself a lawyer, Mr. Cooper?

WALLACE: No, I haven't. But I guess I should.

HOPP: Well, here's my card just in case you ever get divorced again.

WALLACE: Divorced again?

LUCY: We brought the papers. I signed them; now we need you to.

HOPP: I have them right here.

(He stands up, puts his food down on a box, and takes the papers from his briefcase. With a pen that he has removed from his breast pocket, he presents them to WALLACE who doesn't respond in any way.)

LUCY: *(whispering)* Wallace?

(HOPP and LUCY look at him, then at each other.)

WALLACE: You took all the furniture?

LUCY: Except the TV.

(WALLACE turns on the TV, sits down on a box, and starts to watch. LUCY and HOPP look at the TV and around the room; they don't know what to do.)

WALLACE: The TV?

LUCY: You can't do this, Wallace.

WALLACE: I wasn't expecting to get divorced today. I'm really not up for it.

LUCY: Wait a second, when I asked you to marry me last year, I told you we'd get divorced in a year, and you agreed.

WALLACE: I know, but . . .

LUCY: I offered you four thousand dollars, that was the going rate; but you said you'd marry me as a favor and wouldn't accept any money. I should have made you take it.

WALLACE: I couldn't take any money from you.

LUCY: That's very nice of you, Wallace, but just because you like me doesn't mean I owe you anything. I don't want to hurt your feelings, but you wouldn't want to force me to be married to you, would you? I wanna go out and be on my own. I'm a citizen now. I have my green card.

(Looking at the audience.)

Yugoslavia seems so far away. Please sign these papers, Wallace, please?

WALLACE: I don't think I should.

LUCY: What do you mean, you don't think you should? This is pathetic, this is really pathetic.

WALLACE: Could you step out of the way? You're blocking the TV.

HOPP: May I have a word with you alone, Mrs. Cooper?

(They walk to the other side of the room.)

Of course, you do realize that your husband deciding not to sign the divorce papers is an unexpected development, and since it will take quite a bit of coercion on my part to change his mind, I must inform you that my fee is no longer fixed.

LUCY: You told me last year that I would have no problem.

HOPP: I believe that I said you *should* have no problem. But really, Mrs. Cooper, surely you must know that not even a lawyer can predict the future. Now, if you would just leave me alone with your husband for a few minutes, I'm sure I could convince him to change his mind.

LUCY: If you think I should.

HOPP: Believe me, I've dealt with these kind of guys before.

(He picks up her coat and hands it to her. LUCY puts it on and he guides her to the door, which he opens.)

Now say good-bye to your husband.

(She doesn't say anything.)

Say good-bye!

LUCY: Good-bye, Wallace.

(WALLACE waves good-bye without looking away from the TV screen.)

HOPP: I'll let you know how everything works out.

(He closes the door.)

Well, Mr. Cooper, it seems we have a little problem here. Your wife has made it clear that she wants a divorce.

WALLACE: It's just a misunderstanding.

HOPP: This is not a misunderstanding, believe me; I've been divorced before.

WALLACE: Maybe she'll change her mind.

HOPP: Listen to me, son. You're young, single, and mildly attractive. You're too young to be tied down for the rest of your life. You should follow my example, Wallace. Divorce has been the best thing that ever happened to me in my life. Look, you seem like a nice young man. I'm sorry to do this to you. You don't think I do this job because I like it, do you? It makes me feel guilty whenever I go to a wedding. As a present, I refer them to a good marriage counselor; it's the least I can do. The truth is that I do my job for the money. I'm not ashamed to say it; I need the money.

NEWSCASTER: *(The lights come up.)* We interrupt this program so that we can bring you a special report.

WALLACE: Hey, a special report. I love those.

NEWSCASTER: We have just received word from reliable sources in Morocco that no births have been reported in that country for the past two days.

HOPP: Turn up the volume.

(As WALLACE turns up the sound, the NEWSCASTER begins to speak louder.)

NEWSCASTER: Other countries in North Africa have reported a major decrease in pregnancies and births. A search of the region for pregnant women is getting under way. Specialists are now being flown in to Rabat, Morocco's capital city, in the hope of combating this dreadful epidemic which may be threatening the existence of mankind. We repeat, a major wave of infertility has been reported to be sweeping most of North Africa. We will keep you informed of the latest developments coming out of the area.

(WALLACE presses the off button and the lights fade on the NEWSCASTER.)

WALLACE: *(after a pause)* So that's why Ingrid Bergman left Humphrey Bogart in *Casablanca*.

HOPP: Now I get it! How could I have been so stupid? I know what you're doing, you're holding out for a cash settlement, right?

WALLACE: Well, uh, I—actually, no.

HOPP: C'mon, don't kid me. I know you're out of a job, and I also know that there's no great demand for pipe fitters either.

WALLACE: I don't need your money.

HOPP: Don't give me that! Everybody needs money! You look like you could use some new furniture around here. How about if I fix you up with my sister. If you ever decide to get married, I'll do the divorce for free.

WALLACE: But I really like Lucy. She can be a lot of fun when she's not divorcing you. Haven't you ever heard of love?

HOPP: Love!? Well, if you're going to be like that, Mr. Cooper, I'm afraid that I will have to settle this in court.

BLACKOUT

Scene Four

Lights come up on the NEWSCASTER.

NEWSCASTER: Ladies and gentlemen, one week after first reporting to you of the wave of infertility in North Africa, we regret to inform you that no pregnancies have been reported on the continent of Africa today. Scientists are still baffled by the cause of this epidemic. What they do know is that whatever this disease is, it is very contagious. They have also determined—

(Looks up.)

and this is a major point—that infertility is occurring in males only. To make matters worse, births and pregnancies are down in the United States as well as in many other countries. On a good note, this disease has had no effect on livestock or wildlife. The reason for this—well, your guess is as good as mine. The big question in the world today is, What or who is the cause of this problem? Fingers are being pointed at the United States and the Soviet Union.

(A slide of the United States is projected on the screen behind the NEWSCASTER; *the word* oops! *is written across it.)*

It is believed that both of these countries have been experimenting with germ warfare, and perhaps one of them has made a mistake which has triggered this worldwide catastrophe. The State Department has issued a statement claiming that they have not experimented with germ warfare since the forties and that this is probably some misguided Soviet plot aimed at the destruction of the free world. The Kremlin said today that they, too, have not experimented in this area since the forties, and claimed that this is an imperialist plot from the West which, at the beginning, was aimed at the destruction of the Third World but somehow got out of hand. Said one official from the State Department who wished to remain unidentified, "We believe that aliens from another planet may be responsible, and we will look seriously into this possibility." The president has asked that all male American citizens and noncitizens, "who should not fear deportation," comply with a nationwide semen evaluation by bringing a personal sample to their local hospital.

BLACKOUT

Scene Five

Wallace's apartment, one week later.

    WALLACE *is sitting on a box, reading a copy of* Field and Stream. LUCY *opens the door with her key and enters.*

WALLACE: Lucy, what brings you here?

LUCY: I've come to take back my boxes.

WALLACE: Have a seat; would you like something to drink?

LUCY: No, thanks, I'm in kind of a hurry.

(She starts collecting the boxes.)

WALLACE: Want me to help you with those boxes?

LUCY: No, that's okay.

(JOE FINNEGAN enters.)

Joe is gonna help me.

WALLACE: Joe?

LUCY: Joe, this is my husband, Wallace Cooper. Wallace, this is Joe Finnegan.

WALLACE: Hi.

(The two men shake hands; JOE*'s grip hurts* WALLACE.*)*

LUCY: Joe used to work for the Secret Service.

JOE: Shhh!

LUCY: Sorry, I forgot.

JOE: I used to protect the president, but they fired me when he got shot.

LUCY: They said it was his fault. It wasn't, Joe; it wasn't your fault.

JOE: I was way out of position, never even got a chance to throw myself in front of a bullet, so now I'm out of a job, and to make matters worse, I have to worry about being sterile. Ya know, Wallace, all my life women have fallen all over me like I was going out of style. But just yesterday I was rapping with this chick and she wasn't interested. That's never happened to me before. It was like she could tell that I was sterile. I don't know, maybe I'm losing my confidence. Maybe I'm losing my scent. Can you see what I'm trying to get at?

LUCY: Joe?

*(*JOE *looks at* LUCY *as if he just noticed that she was in the room.)*

LUCY: I think we should be bringing those boxes downstairs.

JOE: I got 'em.

WALLACE: So I see that you're running around with unemployed bodyguards.

LUCY: It's a free country, isn't it?

WALLACE: You may have forgotten, but we are still married.

LUCY: Just call my lawyer and we can change all that.

*(*LUCY *exits. The lights dim. A slide appears behind the* NEWSCASTER. *It shows a naked man with his arms extended and his groin area blacked out. The word "Infertility" is written in large letters at the bottom of the slide.)*

NEWSCASTER: The feeling is one of helplessness and despair in America and all over the world today. No pregnancies have been reported anywhere. All birth control manufacturers and distributors have folded, leaving thousands jobless. Abortion is no longer an issue. For a short time it was believed that sperm banks held the answer to this predicament. However, scientists have confirmed that there is no defense against contamination from bacteria causing sterilization.

(Lights come up on Wallace's apartment where WALLACE *is sitting on the floor watching TV. Then lights come up on* HENRY COOPER *Stage Right. He is lying on a fold-up beach chair. He is bare-chested and is drinking a Bloody Mary with a celery stalk in it.* HENRY *picks up the telephone and starts to dial. The phone rings in Wallace's apartment.)*

WALLACE: Hello?

HENRY: Hello, Wallace?

WALLACE: Yeah?

HENRY: This is it.

WALLACE: What do you mean this is it? Who is this?

HENRY: I've waited a long time for this day to come. Now your birthday present starts to pay off.

WALLACE: Dad?

HENRY: That's right, it's me.

WALLACE: Dad, where have you been? We haven't seen or heard from you in ten years, not since you broke out of prison. Where are you?

HENRY: Somewhere in South America. I can't tell you where. I'm still wanted, you know. How's your mother?

WALLACE: She divorced you, Dad.

HENRY: Yeah, I figured she would.

WALLACE: She married a dentist and moved to Arizona.

HENRY: A dentist! I thought the woman had more class than that. I guess you never really know a person. What about your sister?

WALLACE: Sheila? She went to Africa seven years ago. She's teaching the finer points of guerrilla warfare to the Tanzanian army.

HENRY: Sounds like something Sheila would do. Have you been paying attention to the news lately?

WALLACE: Who hasn't . . . it's pretty strange.

HENRY: Did you do what the president told you to—I mean, go down to the hospital?

WALLACE: Sure I did. Everybody has.

HENRY: Did you get your results back?

WALLACE: No, not yet, but I figure I—

HENRY: *(interrupting)* Good! Good! I'm glad I got to you first. Now listen to me, Wallace, this may be hard for you to believe, but . . .

(Long pause.)

you are the last fertile man in the whole world.

WALLACE: *(looking down at his crotch)* Are you kidding me?

HENRY: *(very distinctly)* I am not kidding. *(He starts to laugh.)*

WALLACE: You mean those shots you gave me before you went to jail?

HENRY: Yes, happy birthday, Son.

WALLACE: D-dad, you didn't do the procedure with anyone else, did you?

HENRY: What?! No! I wouldn't do something like that and spoil all your fun. Of course, I tried to before they put me in jail. So you're the only one. You know, I have the cure for this little problem the world is having.

WALLACE: That's great, Dad, you'll be a big hero. You'll go down in history as the greatest man in history.

HENRY: I know, I know, but why so fast? What's the big hurry? Look, they'll make the connection between you and me immediately, but what good will it do them? Nobody knows where I am. I could be dead.

WALLACE: What are you trying to say?

HENRY: Say I resurface. I show everyone the cure, and the world returns to normal, no big deal. *(Pause.)* But let's say that I stay right here in South America. Imagine it: You're the only man in the world that can impregnate women. The whole goddamn world. Think of the power you'll have. It'll be up to you to keep the human race going. And this is the part I like most of all. You get to start the world over, Wallace, and in eighty years every single person will be one of our descendants. Talk about a family operation.

WALLACE: Do you think people will be better off?

HENRY: I don't know if they'll be better off, but at least they'll be better looking. *(He laughs very loudly.)*

WALLACE: Dad?

HENRY: Yes?

WALLACE: How can we be sure that my son will be fertile?

HENRY: I'm glad you asked that question. Hopefully, you'll be able to genetically pass on your immunities to your sons. It worked with drosophila, mice, and even chimpanzees, so if it worked with them, it should work with you. Of course, there is a possibility that it won't work. But that's what makes life interesting, right?

WALLACE: I guess so.

HENRY: Well, good-bye, kid. I expect the CIA will be out looking for me soon, so I've got to keep one step in front of them. *(He sips his Bloody Mary.)* Good luck, Wallace, and watch out for those European women.

WALLACE: I haven't been having very much luck with them lately.

HENRY: I'm sure you haven't been having very much luck with any women lately. But all that's going to change now, because of what I've done for you.

WALLACE: I hope so.

HENRY: Good-bye, I've really got to go. *(He hangs up.)*

WALLACE: Good-bye. *(He hangs up. A big smile comes across Wallace Cooper's face.)*

(Lights come up on NEWSCASTER.)

NEWSCASTER: Word has just reached the newsroom that a fertile man has been found in New York City.

(A slide of WALLACE appears.)

His name is Wallace Cooper. Now, you all must be wondering why Mr. Cooper has not fallen victim to this strange epidemic which has already had a devastating impact upon the people of this planet. It seems that Mr. Cooper's fertility may be connected with experiments performed by his father over twenty years ago. A worldwide dragnet is now getting under way in the hope of finding Dr. Cooper, who is still at large. So, Dr. Cooper, if you're out there listening, please, sir, make yourself known, the world needs you. Until then, Wallace Cooper, the fate of the human race is in your hands.

(Focus shifts to Wallace's apartment. SHEILA enters. She is dressed in an African robe and is holding two large suitcases.)

SHEILA: Hi, Wallace, it's me, Sheila, your sister. Remember me?

WALLACE: Well sure, yeah, of course I remember.

SHEILA: That's not a very enthusiastic welcome. Aren't you glad to see me?

WALLACE: Sure I am, but I'm kind of, well, ah, I'm . . .

SHEILA: Speak up, Wallace. *(She puts down her suitcases.)*

WALLACE: I said I've been kinda overwhelmed by everything that has happened today.

SHEILA: Took the first flight out of Dar es Salaam as soon as I heard.

WALLACE: I just talked to Dad on the phone.

SHEILA: Oh, yeah, how is he?

WALLACE: Fine.

SHEILA: Is he still in jail?

(She opens her suitcase and starts replacing the paintings on the wall with African wall hangings.)

WALLACE: No, Sheila, he escaped ten years ago.

SHEILA: Oh, yeah, I forgot. What about Mom?

WALLACE: She married a dentist and moved to Arizona.

SHEILA: Oh . . . *(Pause.)* You know I always thought that Dad was a really sick guy who didn't know what he was doing, but I guess I was wrong. Either that or he was very lucky.

WALLACE: So what are you doing while you're in town?

SHEILA: I've decided to become your agent. You need one, don't you?

WALLACE: Well, I . . .

SHEILA: Don't mention it, that's what sisters are for. Now, what I need to know is what exactly is our policy going to be about artificial insemination?

WALLACE: I don't think we should. I mean, that way it could fall into the wrong hands, and we don't want that. Personal delivery seems to be the best way.

SHEILA: I agree. I've already scheduled you for two appointments tomorrow. Mrs. Hilton was sitting next to me on the plane, and we have her scheduled for nine A.M.

(WALLACE starts doing push-ups.)

I took the liberty of charging her a million dollars without asking you first. Is that okay? What are you doing?

WALLACE: Getting in shape.

SHEILA: Are you listening?

WALLACE: Yeah, Hilton at nine, and a million is fine.

SHEILA: At ten-thirty we have the wife of the oil minister of Kuwait. We're charging her two million; her husband can afford it. Of course, later you're gonna have to do some freebies so we don't get poor people angry at us. After all, we can't just have a society of rich people. I mean, what's the point of being rich when there is no one around to be poor. And I almost forgot, we are having a press conference at twelve.

(The phone rings and SHEILA *answers it.)*

Hello. . . . Wallace, it's the president. Would you hold on a minute, please.

(She hands him the phone. WALLACE *speaks into the phone.)*

WALLACE: No, Mr. President, I haven't decided whether I'd sleep with communists. . . . No, I don't think that it would mean I was a traitor if I did. In fact, I think it would improve relations. . . . No, sir, I haven't decided about the Third World either. Isn't this a free country? . . . Oh, I see. Your wife? Isn't she kind of old? How about your daughter?

(The doorbell rings.)

Okay, speak to my agent.

*(*WALLACE *hands the phone to* SHEILA *and goes to open the door.* JOE FINNEGAN *stands there in his three-piece suit; he is wearing sunglasses and carries a walkie-talkie.)*

What are you doing here?

JOE: The president has assigned me to protect you.

SHEILA *(speaking into the phone):* We can fit your daughter in at eleven. *(She hangs up the phone.)*

WALLACE: What do I need to be protected from?

JOE: Have you looked outside?

*(*WALLACE *goes to look out.)*

Stay away from that window.

(JOE *jumps in between* WALLACE *and the window. Phone rings and* SHEILA *answers it.*)

You can look over my shoulder.

(WALLACE, *on tiptoe, peeks over* JOE'S SHOULDER.)

WALLACE: Wow! There's thousands of women out there.

(SHEILA *hangs up the phone.*)

Who was that?

SHEILA: *Time* magazine. They want you for next week's cover, a picture of you next to a picture of George Washington, with a caption reading "The future father of our country."

WALLACE: Future father of our country. I like that, it has a nice ring to it. I cannot tell a lie; it was I who got your wife pregnant.

SHEILA: *(noticing* JOE*)* Who's that?

WALLACE: Oh, Sheila, this is Joe Finnegan, my bodyguard and my wife's lover. Joe, this is my older sister and agent, Sheila Cooper.

(They shake hands, but SHEILA *doesn't let go.*)

SHEILA: *(to* WALLACE*)* Your wife? What's all this about a wife?

WALLACE: Lucy? She's from Yugoslavia. She married me so that she could get her green card. Now she wants a divorce, but I wouldn't sign the papers.

SHEILA: You wouldn't sign the papers?

(She starts shaking him back and forth.)

Of all the stupid. I should have realized that you're still an imbecile. Some things never change. *(She lets go.)*

(ALFRED HOPP *enters and* JOE *frisks him.*)

Who's that?

WALLACE: That's Lucy's lawyer, Alfred Hopp.

(LUCY *enters and waves a brown paper bag in* JOE*'s face.*)

LUCY: I brought you some lunch.

JOE: *(to* LUCY*)* Could you raise your arms in the air, I'm going to have to frisk you.

SHEILA: *(smiling)* Hello, Mr. Hopp. I'm Sheila Cooper, Wallace's agent.

HOPP: Nice to meet you.

(They shake hands.)

JOE: Mr. Cooper, can I have my lunch break?

WALLACE: Sure.

SHEILA: Well, Mr. Hopp, I've talked to Wallace and I've been able to convince him to sign those divorce papers.

HOPP: I'm afraid that will be impossible.

*(*JOE *is still frisking* LUCY.*)*

LUCY: Not here, Joe.

HOPP: My client has informed me that she is no longer solely interested in obtaining a divorce.

*(*JOE *starts kissing Lucy's neck; he makes animal noises.)*

WALLACE: What does that mean?

SHEILA: It means she wants your money.

WALLACE: But I just got it. I mean I was just about to get it. That's not very nice.

HOPP: Adultery isn't very nice either, Mr. Cooper.

WALLACE: Adultery? I haven't done anything yet. She wanted the divorce in the first place. Besides, what about her? She's the one committing adultery.

*(*JOE*'s animal noises become louder.)*

HOPP: That will be very hard to pin on them. Mr. Finnegan is undercover and you are an international figure. Everyone knows about you and Mrs. Hilton, it's all over the news. Frankly, I think what you're planning to do is disgusting and immoral. It's unfortunate that it had to come to this, but you leave me no choice. I'm afraid the next time we meet will have to be in court.

SHEILA: You really got us into a mess this time.

BLACKOUT

Scene Six

A TV studio.

It is ten months later. The stage is set up for a talk show. Four black swivel chairs are lined up next to one another. The talk show HOST *sits on the chair on the far left. About ten feet to the left of the* HOST *a curtain hangs from the ceiling creating an offstage onstage. Standing by the talk show* HOST *are* JOE FINNEGAN *in full bodyguard attire,* SHEILA, *and* WALLACE.

HOST: Ladies and gentlemen, today history will be made on this show. As some of you may know, last night authorities found Dr. Henry Cooper in Peru. The doctor, who is being heavily guarded backstage, has consented to come out on stage and tell us a few things, like where he has been all this time and how come he didn't turn himself in. Immediately following this show Dr. Cooper will be whisked away to City Hospital where he will explain to a jam-packed lecture room of specialists the cure to this wave of sterility which struck the world a little over ten months ago. Also joining us this evening are two other members of the Cooper family. May I introduce to you a woman who has unselfishly stayed behind the scene because, well, she's just that kind of person, and boy, do we need some of them. Wallace's sister and press agent, Sheila Cooper.

*(*SHEILA *walks in. The* HOST *gets up and steps one chair to the right. They shake hands.* SHEILA *kisses him on the cheek. They laugh and smile. She kisses him again; they sit down.)*

Tell me, Sheila, what was your first reaction to finding out that your brother was the last fertile man?

SHEILA: Well, I was in Africa when Wallace called me. He told me that he needed me to help him. We've always been a close family, so of course I dropped everything and flew here to be with him.

HOST: I must ask you this question, Sheila.

SHEILA: *(smiling)* Please do.

HOST: How did the divorce case affect you and Wallace?

SHEILA: Let's just say that it was unfortunate that the divorce had to be so nasty and bitter. Of course, it was emotionally draining, not to mention all the money we lost. But I would like to say—and I'm sure I speak for Wallace—that we think Lucy is a fine young lady and we wish her all the best.

HOST: *(interrupting)* Um, ah, let's bring Wallace in now.

SHEILA: Certainly.

HOST: And now a man who needs no introduction, a man who as a ten-year-old had no friends but has plenty now . . . let me introduce Wallace Cooper.

(WALLACE *enters; the* HOST *stands and moves one seat over.* WALLACE *shakes his hand but does not acknowledge his sister. They both sit down.*)

Tell me, Wallace, how do you feel about having thirty-six girls and no boys?

WALLACE: Well, of course, it's depressing. It puts a lot of pressure on me, but that has eased up now that my father has shown up to save the world. . . . But yes, people are getting angry about that.

HOST: How do you explain it?

WALLACE: How do I explain it? Well, I can't really. I'm pretty sure that it's just a coincidence. I'm still expecting to have a son any day now.

HOST: And on that note let's break for a commercial and come back with Wallace Cooper's father.

(HOST *looks up to the lighting crew.*)

MEMBER OF THE LIGHTING CREW: We're off the air. Two minutes, everybody.

(ALFRED HOPP *runs onstage.*)

HOPP: Wallace.

(WALLACE *walks over to him.*)

Miss America just had a baby.

WALLACE: Yeah, so what is it?

HOPP: It's a . . . girl.

WALLACE: A girl?

HOPP: Sorry.

WALLACE: Thirty-seven? I can't believe it.

HOPP: Miss America is a client of mine, and we are suing you for breach of contract.

WALLACE: What!! I got her pregnant, didn't I?

HOPP: That's true, you did. But the reason you impregnated these women was to keep the race going. But that can't happen if there aren't any boys.

WALLACE: I don't guarantee boys.

HOPP: I know, but you've had thirty-seven daughters; obviously there's something wrong with you and you can't spawn males.

WALLACE: But if you sue me and win, then everyone will sue me. I'll be right back where I started.

HOPP: Sorry, Wallace, this time you lose.

(He exits through the back way.)

MEMBER OF THE LIGHTING CREW: One minute!

(HENRY COOPER runs onstage.)

HENRY: Wallace, I've got to talk to you. *(He takes him aside.)* I have something to confess.

WALLACE: Well?

HENRY: I—I don't know the cure.

WALLACE: What!

HENRY: Shhhhh!

WALLACE: What are you talking about?

HENRY: I don't know the cure. I just know the prevention. There's a big difference.

WALLACE: Why did you wait till now to tell me?

HENRY: I wanted to be a big hero. I didn't want to let the world down.

WALLACE: God damn it, Dad, we are on international television.

MEMBER OF THE LIGHTING CREW: Ten seconds.

HENRY: Don't worry, I'll talk my way out of it.

WALLACE: You've got to be kidding. This is crazy!

(WALLACE walks back to his seat and sits down with his head in his hands. SHEILA makes him sit up straight.)

MEMBER OF THE LIGHTING CREW: Five, four, three, two, one. You're on.

HOST: And now the moment you've all been waiting for. The most respected man in the world. May I introduce Dr. Henry Cooper.

(SHEILA, HOST, FINNEGAN, *all give* COOPER *a standing ovation.* WALLACE *stands up late and claps along.* HENRY *waves to crowd, shakes* HOST*'s hand and sits down.*)

It's a pleasure to meet you, Dr. Cooper.

HENRY: Not at all.

HOST: No really, the world is happy to see you.

HENRY: Is that so? They didn't seem very happy twenty-one years ago when they took away my license and sent me to jail. That wasn't a very happy experience.

HOST: That may be true but—

HENRY: But nothing. That's what's wrong with people today, they don't take you for what you are. Only after you do something great do they treat you with any respect. I'm the same person as I was before. Only now I'll be accepted in the scientific world. I hate those people who, when you're young and unknown, won't listen to a word you say, treat you like a nobody. But they're the same guys who kiss your ass when you finally make it. I've got it all up here. *(He points to his head.)* It's not written down anywhere, and now after everything it's done to me, the world is now dying for my knowledge. Well, let me tell you something, I don't owe the world anything and I don't feel like telling them a damn thing.

HOST: But you can't do that, sir, we're talking about the survival of mankind. The world won't let you get away with it. We'll beat it out of you.

(HOST starts to roll up his sleeves.)

DR. COOPER: I've already thought about that, but the world does not deserve to live. They'll probably blow themselves up anyway. Having the race just get old and die seems the best way . . . that's why I've decided to take this cyanide pill.

(He holds up the pill. They all lunge for him, but he eats it and dies immediately.)

SHEILA: Oh, my God.

WALLACE: *(taking his pulse)* He's dead. *(Looking at his father.)* I can't believe you did this.

HOST: That's it, ladies and gentlemen, the future of mankind has just ended and you saw it right here on *The Bill Johnson Hour*. Well, everybody, this is your host, Bill Johnson, saying good-bye for myself

(He looks at HENRY COOPER.*)*

and my guests. See you

(He points to the audience.)

next week.

(He holds this pose.)

Are we off?

CREW MEMBER: Yep.

HOST: *(jumping out of his seat)* Jesus Christ! Jesus Christ! Goddamn son of a bitch!! I wonder if this will have any bearing on my career. On the other hand, maybe this could help. I mean all the exposure. But this isn't what I want to be known for! I don't want to become a trivia question!

WALLACE: I think we should move the body.

HOST: *(whirling toward* WALLACE*)* You shut up! This is very confusing. *(To* JOE.*)* Hey, you! Come over here and make yourself useful! Help me get this stiff out of my studio! Of all the rotten luck.

*(*JOE *takes the arms and the* HOST *takes the legs, and they start to carry* HENRY*'s body off.* ALFRED HOPP *runs onstage.)*

HOPP: Wallace, that wife of the Brazilian coffee plantation owner just had a baby!

WALLACE: And?

HOPP: It's a bouncing baby boy!

WALLACE: It's a boy!

*(*WALLACE *walks over to his father's body and, standing between the* HOST *and* JOE *who are carrying* HENRY*, reaches into his pocket and pulls out a cigar.)*

Have a cigar, Dad!

(He puts the cigar between Henry's lips.)

BLACKOUT

CHARLIE SCHULMAN

(1985) Then . . .

I'm a native New Yorker currently attending the University of Michigan where I have been the recipient of the Avery Hopwood Award for Drama in 1984 and 1985. I've had two plays produced in the Young Playwrights Festival: *The Birthday Present* at Circle Rep in 1983 and *The Ground Zero Club*, a comedy about nuclear war, at Playwrights Horizons in 1985. At the University of Michigan I am a member of Streetlight Theater (a student-run theater group committed to producing short works by its members). I think that acting, directing, and play writing are all part of the same thing, and in Streetlight Theater I have been able to pursue them all.

About the Play

It was exciting and somewhat overwhelming to have a professional production of my play at the age of seventeen, and I was very happy to get another chance with a new play two years later. During the second, *The Ground Zero Club*, I had more of an idea of what I wanted for the production. I was able to assert myself better and disagree when I had to. I hope to continue writing for the theater and I also hope to continue writing comedy.

. . . And Now

Since my two productions with the Young Playwrights Festival I have continued pursuing my interest in writing for the theater. In 1991 I became a founding member of The Playwrights Collective, a nonhierarchical, democratic theater-producing organization committed to realizing the vision of the playwright. I received an M.F.A. from New York University and teach playwriting workshops in New York City public schools. My play *Angel of Death* was presented at the Eugene O'Neill National Playwrights Conference, where it received the Charles McArthur Award. It was produced at the Magic Theater in San Francisco and the American Jewish Theater in New York.

A short monologue, "The Happy Camper," will be published in *Best Monologues of the 90's*.

THIRD STREET

by
RICHARD COLMAN
(age eighteen when play was written)
Brooklyn, New York

∎

Third Street was performed at the Circle Repertory Company in New York City, April 12 through May 1, 1983. The director was Michael Bennett, and the dramaturge was Michael Weller. The production stage manager was Kate Stewart. John Arnone designed the set, Patricia McGourty the costumes, Mal Sturchio the lighting, and Chuck London Media/Stewart Werner the sound.

The cast:

RON . . . . *Keith Gordon*
JOHN . . . . *Robert Alan Morrow*
FRANK . . . . *Brian Tarantina*

SETTING: *Twilight in a Brooklyn graveyard that is not visited anymore. The tombstones are old and faded and crowded together. In the distance we can see elevated train tracks.*

Three youths are leaning and sitting on the tombstones. It is the summer after they have graduated from high school.

They have been friends since their earliest memories. They work in the neighborhood and come to the graveyard to get away from their houses, families, and Brooklyn in general.

They used to cut school on the nice afternoons to sit and talk and get high. It is a private place. Once in a while somebody's girl tags along, but this is distinctly their spot.

An especially prominent tombstone stands at center stage. They have put graffiti on it for years; they can trace their history on it.

As the scene opens, RON *is leaning against a marker, cleaning and rolling dope. He enjoys this activity and puts a lot of care into it.*

JOHN *is seated with his back to the audience, staring out toward the train tracks.*

FRANK *is sitting on a large tombstone; he is drinking.*

A few six-packs of beer sit on a tombstone. There is a slow pace through-out the beginning minutes. There is no rush to say anything, because they've played this scene before, in years of minor variations.

RON: Nice dope . . . really nice.

JOHN: *(distantly)* Yeah.

FRANK: It's not bad. I took it from my brother. *(He laughs.)* My brother! In junior high school! Remember how afraid we used to be we'd get caught when we used to go out in the backyard to get high? It's funny, y'know? I mean, it's just kinda funny.

JOHN: Yeah, that was funny. What were we so nervous we were gonna get caught for?

FRANK: I dunno. I just thought I shouldn't encourage little Tony, y'know? He's still kinda little, right? So I figure it's in his best inter-est. *(A smile lights up* FRANK's *face. He loves this story. Whenever he tells it,* JOHN *and* RON *pretend they have never heard it—or perhaps they really don't remember it that well. In any case, they love to hear old stories.)* Remember . . . Remember . . . Re member when . . . *(*FRANK *bursts out laughing just thinking about it. The beer and dope add to the quality and duration of everybody's laughter.)*

JOHN: What is it, Frankie? Huh? Spit it out! *(The laughter progresses until the end of the story, at which point they can barely breathe.)*

FRANK: Remember—*(He is constantly going off on laughing jags that infect* JOHN *and* RON.*)* Remember after ninth grade graduation, we snuck over to that storage shed in Rosen's backyard to get stoned? And we're sitting there smoking away, and Rosen's dad sees all that smoke comin' out the crack by the door? And he calls the fire department and we hear those sirens coming from way off and Ronnie says, "They're comin' to get us," and you said, "Don't be so paranoid," and the sirens just kept getting closer and closer and we hear them pull up in the driveway! And we're all pissing in our pants! And we ate all the shit we had left! And the firemen pull open those doors and they're standing there with that! That hose! And we're just sitting there in the dark, out of our minds! *(The laughter lasts a long time.)*

JOHN: That was so fucking funny!

RON: You didn't think so at the time.

JOHN: I didn't think it was so funny?! You should've seen your face, your eyes was like a frog!

RON: Man, you were trying to burrow under those rusty old beach chairs.

FRANK: I was pretty cool about the whole thing. (RON *and* JOHN *laugh.)*

JOHN: Oh yeah, real cool, except for that big lump of shit in your pants!

FRANK: Bullshit!

RON: Oh come off it, Frankie, saying your Hail Marys is not exactly an indication of cool! *(They all laugh.)*

FRANK: I guess I was a little nervous . . . we thought they were gonna lock us up for life. *(He reads off the graffitied tombstone.)* Rosen's garage. June twenty-eighth, 1986. Shit, what was that—three, four years ago. Doesn't seem that long.

JOHN: Nice dope.

FRANK: Yeah, my brother gets better dope than I do. 'Course, he gets an allowance. *(They begin to laugh again, but it passes more quickly. Silence.)* Got me a vacation comin' up in two weeks.

RON: Still goin' down to Florida?

FRANK: Naaah. Gonna stay home and lie out on the porch. Use the money I'll save to put in one of those aboveground pools, y'know. For Tony and Rocco's little friends. Right in the backyard so they don't have to go all the way down to Coney Island so my ma don't have to worry.

JOHN: Nice . . . when I get me a house, I'm gonna put one of those in for sure.

FRANK: I'm taking it out on time payments—it's real cheap.

RON: Real cheap for a loooooooooong time. *(They laugh.)*

FRANK: *(slightly annoyed—defensive)* It's gonna be nice, though. *(They are quiet.* FRANK *plucks a beer. They smoke some more.* JOHN *lights a cigarette. The quiet lasts maybe fifteen, maybe thirty seconds. They are taking care of the business of getting their brains into a condition they feel comfortable in.)*

FRANK: *(speaks for no apparent reason)* Half past a cow's ass. *(At first* JOHN *and* RON *are caught off guard. Then they remember and laugh! laugh! laugh!)*

RON: *(through his laughter)* It's half past a monkey's ass!

JOHN: *(through his laughter)* Hey Frankie, what time is it?

FRANK: Half past a monkey's ass, quarter to his balls.

JOHN: *(still laughing)* Remember when you said that to Mr. Kahn during that final exam—I thought I'd bust a fucking gut! That was so fucking funny! *(The laughter passes. There is quiet. They continue to smoke dope. Suddenly* FRANK *starts to giggle—a little at first. It gets harder and harder, till he's rolling on the floor.* JOHN *and* RON *start to giggle, too, till they're all out of control. It fades. It starts up again for a second and finally passes. Some moments pass.* FRANK *takes a beer. He has asked* RON *this question before.)*

FRANK: So—when's that college start?

RON: Twenty-third of August. Leave in about a week and a half.

FRANK: What's that school of yours called again? Flintstone?

RON: Princeton.

FRANK: Ohh.

JOHN: *(odd tone)* Sign up for classes?

RON: Yeah, usual boring stuff, math, English . . .

FRANK: Huhh. *(Everyone is getting more and more stoned—*FRANK *bursts out laughing again.)* Remember—at graduation—when you won that math award or something, me and John and that geek Millman started that chant for you? (*Mimicking an old teacher*) And the winner of the 1990 Nathaniel Phipps Mathematics Award is . . . Ronald Crane! (FRANK *and* JOHN *begin to chant, softly at first and building.*)

FRANK *and* JOHN: Crane the brain, Crane the brain, Crane the brain, Crane the brain. Crane the brain, CRANE THE BRAIN! (JOHN *and* FRANK *are hysterical.* RON *is not amused, though he pretends to be.*)

FRANK: Man, everyone was doin' it!

RON: No, it wasn't everyone.

JOHN: Aw, g'wan, we must've had at least twenty people.

FRANK: Anyone that mattered, anyway.

RON: My parents felt really retarded. (JOHN *and* FRANK *continue to laugh, though not as hard. They refuse to notice when* RON *won't partake in group jokes. Silence for a while. They drink and smoke and gather strength.*)

RON: So Frankie, what's it gonna be? You gonna stay on at Mario's Primo Meats or what? When you gotta let him know?

FRANK: Yeah, I figure I'll do him a favor and stay on there. I got the payments to keep up on the Corvette. Probably stay there till something better comes along. My dad's old boss says all the time, "Maybe soon, maybe soon I get a job for you in the garage," but—Ahhhh, fuck him. The old bastard.

JOHN: He fuckin' owes it to you, all the time your dad put in there.

FRANK: Damn fuckin' right. Lot more'n a job he owes my family. My dad was a fuckin' institution. Anyway, I kinda like the butcher business.

RON: Beats office work any day of the week.

JOHN: (*suddenly*) You know what I was thinking about this morning at work? I was lifting those forty-pound boxes of loose-leaf paper for that fuckhead Greenbaum and I got to thinkin' about how we always used to say we were going to take off in a van right after high school and go see something. Just scout around, check out America.

FRANK: Hey, maybe we can go next year.

JOHN: Yeah, for two weeks in July. It's different for you, you got your family at home to support. Me, I got shit.

FRANK: Hey, don't say that, John, you got Elise.

JOHN: I got too fuckin' much Elise. (*They all laugh nervously.*)

FRANK: When'd she get so fat?

JOHN: Pregnant, you asshole, not fat!

RON: The minute they get married they fuckin' expand anyway. Like all the tension is just *re*leased! Sure, being married's got its good points—you're getting laid whenever you want! *(They all laugh.)*

FRANK: When's the kid due?

JOHN: I dunno, couple of months. Elise is like a fuckin' beached whale around the house. Whining and groaning—Jesus Christ, it could make ya puke! "Get me this, get me that." She's all right, though.

RON: She's a nice girl.

FRANK: Yeah, she's real nice.

JOHN: Like a beached whale. Like deadweight.

FRANK: Gonna be a good-looking kid, your kid. Nice kid. I'm gonna be the godfather—me and Ronnie; you can leave him with us anytime you want to go somewhere with Elise.

JOHN: She's always sittin' around watchin' TV and eatin'.

FRANK: She's supposed to eat a lot, she's eatin' for two.

JOHN: She's eatin' for twenty! *(Nervous laughter.)* Like an infantry unit. The kid's gonna come out a middleweight, for chrissakes!

FRANK: *(as if trying to make it true by saying it)* You can't shit me, I know you love her.

JOHN: Oh yeah, we're married; don't get me wrong, she's a great girl. It's just that sometimes I feel like I need her, sometimes I can't stand to look at her. Sometimes I feel like I know her, but sometimes I feel like I could leave her ten thousand miles behind and forget her name by the time I passed Newark.

RON: When I found out she was pregnant, I thought, Wow, that's terrific.

FRANK: Yeah, definitely, it's like we're all gonna be one big family, y'know? It's gonna be real cool! Picnics and shit! Cub Scouts! Zoos! Bring him up to college to see Uncle Ronnie! You're gonna be tops in the pops department!

JOHN: *(suddenly)* Maybe I'll go up to school with you for a while. I wouldn't bother you. Maybe I could just get an apartment and see you once in a while. We could catch a movie. *(FRANK laughs ner-*

vously.) Then Frankie could come up. We could get jobs while you study and then when summertime rolls around we could drop a down payment on a customized van and take off!

FRANK: For points unknown!

JOHN: Yeah, what do you say?

RON: *(laughs)* Oh yeah, all of us and that kid, and Elise.

JOHN: But . . . oh shit . . . forget about them. *(Laughs.)* Shit.

(FRANK *laughs.)*

FRANK: My ma said I was the man of the house now, and you got that kid to bring up. Adults like us, man, we don't go running around in no van—no way! For us, it's total and complete luxury. One year cruise down to the Bahamas! Puerto Rico! Las Vegas! Anything, man!

JOHN: But a customized van . . .

RON: Sounds real good, John.

FRANK: Yeah, and when you're a big hotshot college graduate, you'll fly us down in your plane, private jet, and we'll parachute right onto the beach! *(Long silence.)*

JOHN: *(ever so slightly accusatory)* What are you going to do about Diana?

RON: What about her?

JOHN: Gonna marry her?

RON: Naaah. Don't think so. She's working at that office. In downtown, near Wall Street. Probably write her when I get to school.

FRANK: Wanta have space on that social calendar for those rich women, huh?

RON: Damn right!

JOHN: *(laughing nervously)* How long's it been since you've been seeing Diana? Like ninth grade or something?

RON: Yeah. *(To JOHN)* Remember the first time I laid her? It was at that party at your house—in your parents' bedroom under all those coats piled up.

FRANK: *(smiling incredulously)* You laid her there? Under all those coats? On his parents' bed?

RON: Yeah!

JOHN: I think I remember that party. Jeez. I didn't realize you laid her that long ago.

RON: Yeah, I did. *(Beat.)* She's all right. It's just, y'know, compatibility. We're just not compatible.

JOHN: Yeah. I kinda like her, though. She's real pleasant.

RON: Yeah, she is.

JOHN: I remember in fifth grade I once loaned her these crayons for this art project she was doing. A big box of sixty-four with a sharpener and everything. She was drawing this big house with, like, ten thousand windows on it. And all these people in the windows smiling out. And she was gonna color all the people all different colors. And she was so happy, man, when I said I'd loan her my crayons. I couldn't believe it. She was so nice. Real nice.

RON: Yeah, I like her too.

JOHN: How come you're so mean to her sometimes?

RON: Hey, what's the problem?

JOHN: You should be nice to her, she really likes you—

RON: Yeah, yeah. *(FRANK senses a confrontation.)*

FRANK: My brother said the damnedest thing at dinner today—

JOHN: You asshole! She cares about you!

RON: Hey, you don't have to marry a girl just 'cause you fuck her, you know.

JOHN: Yeah, well, fuck you, Ronnie. Fuck you. I don't know what's with you, man. You think you're some kind of hot shit. A real god. But you're just an asshole. Ass-hole. Know how to spell that, spelling-bee champ? *A-S-S* and a tight little *O!*

RON: *(overlapping from "A real god")* Hey, calm down, John. Don't get all worked up.

JOHN: I'm just saying be nice to her. That's all—be nice. . . .

RON: Yeah, I'm nice. I am nice. We're all a bunch of fucking nice guys, remember?

FRANK: Hey, wanna do some shots? Whaddaya say, John? You wanna do some shots?

JOHN: *(softly)* No. No, thanks. Hey, I'm sorry. *(Silence.)*

FRANK: You're not mad, are you, John? Ronnie didn't mean nothin' by it.

JOHN: No, really, it's all right. I'm all right. I'm sorry.

RON: John, all I meant to say was—

JOHN: I gotta go. I gotta go call Elise. She said to call, tell her where I am. I gotta go. *(JOHN darts off. Silence. RON is on the ground. FRANK is perched on a tombstone. FRANK's bottle is on the ground.)*

(RON surveys the sky.)

RON: Nice Saturday night.

FRANK: Yeah. Hand me that bottle. *(RON hands him the bottle.)* Thanks. *(He drinks and chases with a beer. He smacks his lips.)* Good. *(He hands the bottle back down.)*

RON: We should've went with John to the phone. It's a long walk.

FRANK: Naah . . . Elise just gets lonely, tells John to come home early. She drinks, y'know. Even though she's preggo.

RON: *(changing the subject)* You learning anything in that butcher shop of yours?

FRANK: I'm learnin' a lot. A shitload. There's a lot more to the butcher business than just hacking away.

RON: I'm sure.

FRANK: Last week I learned how to chain-saw an entire cow. They come in practically whole and we just keep cuttin' 'em up into smaller and smaller pieces. It's cool—makes me feel like a madman murderer or somethin'. *(They laugh.)* Sometimes I get to feelin' a little sad, like Old MacDonald's farm's all dead. Like Old MacDonald just couldn't make the payments on his Corvette and had to sell off his little farm friends. Mostly it's cool, though—and the refrigerator place we work in is better than air conditioning. Gonna learn that business good.

RON: Definitely.

FRANK: My sister, Marianne? She's graduating in two years from high school. Says she wants to go to college. I want to pay, y'know?

RON: *(Nods his head.)* That's great.

FRANK: Everything's gonna be different when you're gone, man.

RON: It's different anyway. School's over and all.

FRANK: Hope you come back once in a while.

RON: I will, you know I will.

FRANK: You get off for Christmas and all that.

RON: Yeah, yeah, of course—Christmas, Thanksgiving, everything.

FRANK: It's just that John, he's gonna miss you. A lot, man. You don't know how much. You . . . you'll be all right. But John . . . he needs you.

RON: He'll be all right. It'll be good for him.

FRANK: Damn right it'll be good for him. Good man. Gets up at five thirty every morning, six days a week, to toss that heavy shit around for old Greenbaum. Plus his kid. I think it'll be good for him . . . make him, you know, grow up.

RON: I think so.

FRANK: Said he was gonna name the baby Ronald, after you.

RON: No kidding.

FRANK: Even if it's a girl. *(He laughs.)* You got to be more understanding with him, Ronnie, he really respects you.

RON: Yeah, I know. (FRANK *looks as if he might say something, but doesn't.*)

FRANK: Shit, I don't know. You got to write John once in a while.

RON: Sure.

FRANK: You can skip me, but John—

RON: Yeah I will, I said.

FRANK: I never told you this before, now I'm sure it's nothing weird, but . . . in a way, he sort of loves you.

RON: Yeah I know there's nothing weird.

FRANK: Right, it's just that he needs you . . . like . . . sort of a role model, y'know?

RON: No, I know. Right. Definitely.

FRANK: He loves you in a positive way and he needs your support, so sometimes you have to set him straight. Hey—how'd that visit to your school go? How's it look?

RON: Nice. Big. Scary. Cool.

FRANK: Got ivy?

RON: Yeah, it's the real thing. They're not just screwin' around.

FRANK: Damn right.

RON: You know, I was thinking, maybe I'd take Chinese.

FRANK: Chinese? What the fuck for?

RON: I don't know. What the hell, it would be cool to speak it.

FRANK: *Chingfang shaw maitai ling shoooo.* You gotta get that singsong voice down. That's the tricky part. If you can get that part, the rest of that shit should be a snap. It's just like the whole thing is a song, you gotta have that kinda voice, y'know?

RON: Yeah.

FRANK: Probably be easy for a smart guy like you.

RON: Maybe I'll even go over to China for a while.

FRANK: No shit. When?

RON: Maybe a year from now.

FRANK: No shit. Wow. We'll miss you.

RON: I'll send you some jade or something.

FRANK: Send me a geisha. Yeah. Wow. That's some faraway place.

RON: Yeah, I figure it'll be a change of pace.

FRANK: Yeah, like culture differences, right. Customs and stuff . . . Uhhh, I wasn't supposed to tell you this, but John is having this going-away dinner for you. I mean, I just thought I'd tell you, so when he asks, you'll know.

RON: Yeah, sure. That'll be great.

FRANK: It's his first big party as man of his house—he's definitely doin' it up big. Bought champagne, fancy pastries, everything.

RON: Yeah, sure. Definitely.

FRANK: Elise's mom's comin' over, too, 'cause Elise don't cook so hot yet. Big fat thing, isn't she?

RON: She is one immense motherfucker . . . think Elise'll be like that someday?

FRANK: Naah. . . . No way. . . . Couldn't be. . . . Although she's kinda wide . . .

RON: She's got the frame.

FRANK: Sometimes I think John's not too crazy about her. You ought to tell him what a great girl she is, why it's great he married her right away.

RON: I try. *(A train starts to go over the tracks. It gets louder and louder. FRANK's next line is audible but partially masked by the passing train.)*

FRANK: Johnnie said he loved you more than anybody in the world. *(A long pause as the train recedes.)*

RON: There's definitely nothin' faggy about us . . . I hope you know that.

FRANK: Nobody said that, don't be a fuckin' idiot. Shut up. Forget about it. Shut up. *(Time passes. They cannot speak.)*

RON: Why the fuck did he have to marry that stupid cunt Elise, anyway? *(Silence. There is nothing to say.)* What time is it?

FRANK: Nine seventeen.

RON: Hey—when'd you get the digital watch?

FRANK: Birthday. My little brother. Check it out. *(He shows it proudly.)* Got a lot of functions, but I don't use 'em. Hey . . . I hope we don't change too much. *(JOHN reenters, with a six-pack.)* Löwenbräu! Now all we need's the fuckin' yacht. *(JOHN is a little too quick and cheerful and bright throughout the scene.)*

JOHN: Only the best for my friends. I'm a lucky guy.

FRANK: Hey, we're all lucky, we are lucky as hell. We're all doin' all right. How's Elise?

JOHN: Oh, she's fine. Can't wait for me to get home. She's so horny, she's rubbin' up against the furniture. She makes me call her when I'm at work, too, just to hear my voice.

FRANK: Keep it up, man. *(He laughs at his own joke.)*

JOHN: Yeah.

RON: You know, I was on the subway comin' home today. I saw this old guy dressed real snappy, and I remembered the magic act we used to do.

JOHN: I remember, man, we used to put on that clown makeup, and I did that juggling, and that rope trick. That was a fuckin' amazing rope trick.

FRANK: Yeah, and Irving the Dove? Poor Irving the Dove. Had to die. Christ, that was fun.

JOHN: Man, you never told me how you did that rope trick. Come on, how'd you do it? *(RON's smiling, not telling.)* I mean, I don't see any way possible you could've done that because I remember inspecting the ropes before and after. Come on, spill, how'd you do it?

RON: What trick? Which of my tricks are we talkin' about?

JOHN: You know which trick I'm talkin' about—the one with the three ropes. How the hell did you do it?

RON: Come here. *(He motions to JOHN to come closer so FRANK can't hear. Whispers in JOHN's ear.)*

JOHN: Hmmm. Wow.

FRANK: So? How'd he do it?

JOHN: Says it was really magic. . . . I saw Janie at the superette.

RON: Janie who?

JOHN: Janie Quinn, she was in our bio class; she had long black hair, lotsa makeup, nice ass.

RON: How's she doin'?

JOHN: She's great.

RON: I know she's great, I mean how's she doin'?

JOHN: She's workin' at an office in downtown Brooklyn. Filing and typing. I took her phone number.

FRANK: I think her little sister comes over to play with my little brother.

JOHN: She ain't got no little sister. Don't you think she's pretty, Ron?

RON: Yeah, she's pretty.

JOHN: Maybe I'll give her a call sometime. No, Ronnie, you should give her a call. She remembers you. She was asking about you.

RON: Naaah.

JOHN: Why not? *(He tries to force the number on RON.)* I thought she would be good enough for you, at least for a little date, like a movie or something. You can even borrow my car and fuck her in the back. It'll be easy to clean up, too, I got vinyl seats. Here, take it.

RON: No, what would I say to her?

FRANK: Go on, you idiot, you'll think of something.

RON: *(laughing)* Yeah, I guess I will, let me have it.

JOHN: No, no, I think you were right, you really wouldn't have anything to say.

RON: Gimme it.

JOHN: Yeah, my cousin's coming in from Cleveland next weekend . . .

RON: Come on!

JOHN: Frankie! Frankie, you want Janie's number?

RON: John, please—I'm begging you.

JOHN: All right, here you go . . . enjoy. *(RON smiles when he receives the number; the smile spreads to JOHN, then to FRANK.)*

FRANK: I propose a toast. To three friends whose friendship can never end. Just like the Three Musketeers. Brave. Gallant. Gorgeous. Only cooler! May their friendship last longer than any pair of Levi's—and may they live to see many more stitches. *(They clink beer bottles.)*

JOHN: *(in a whisper)* Hey Frankie, do you think now would be a good time to ask him?

FRANK: Yeah, sure. Go ahead.

JOHN: You want to come to dinner next Saturday at my place?

RON: Yeah, sure—Elise is gonna cook?

JOHN: Yeah—her mother's comin' over too. She's a regular sideshow attraction. Got a voice like an ambulance siren. *(They all laugh.)*

RON: Yeah, it should be a good time—

JOHN: Seven—

RON: *(suddenly remembers)* Next Saturday? I've got my Princeton alumni dinner I have to go to next Saturday. Oh fuck. I'm sorry. Oh God, I'm sorry.

FRANK: Hey . . . no problem . . . it's no big deal . . . right, John? Just a little dinner and a little talk.

RON: Could we do it another night?

JOHN: Nah. Don't worry about it. Don't worry about it. Look, I gotta be gettin' home. Elise wanted me to help her move some furniture up from the basement. I gotta go. Look, gimme a call before you leave if you can. (JOHN *runs off.*)

FRANK: Hey, Flintstone. You gotta go. (*Silence.*)

RON: Hey—you wanna get out of here? Let's go get Kate and Diana and go see a movie?

FRANK: Sure.

RON: Let's move.

FRANK: Hey, wait. Hold on a second. (FRANK *takes out a big black Magic Marker. He writes something on the center tombstone that has all the writing on it.*)

RON: What did you write this time?

FRANK: Just the date. (*They leave slowly, walking toward the train tracks. Lights dim and out.*)

RICHARD COLMAN

(1985) Then . . .

I was raised in Brooklyn and graduated from Dartmouth in 1984. At college I had a senior fellowship and won a 1985 Reynolds fellowship to go to Europe and write. I am working on my book "The Fish and the Axe" now. My hobbies are insane people and finding patterns. I was unpopular in high school. I plan to go to the New York University drama school.

About the Play

Third Street was written in one afternoon. I did it in the commons room of my dorm during the winter of 1982. The story had been on my mind for a while, but there was no particular inspiration to write it at the time. To be honest, I was probably avoiding writing a term paper. I finished by dinnertime and stuffed it into my desk. Several weeks later I typed it up and sent it off to Gerald Chapman, who'd encouraged me the year before in a playwriting workshop at E. R. Murrow High School in Brooklyn, New York. When he called me up that summer and told me that the play was being considered for the Festival, I had forgotten all about it (honestly!). I had been certain it couldn't be any good because the writing itself had been so effortless and angst-free. That

winter, it was performed in a reading and I met Michael Bennett, who
directed it the following spring. Some improvements in the script happened during rehearsal, but the bulk of the play was identical to what I
had scribbled the year before.

There's a valuable lesson here, I think, one that I am constantly
forgetting and that I will probably have to keep relearning for the rest
of my life: Stop thinking about it and go for it!

. . . And Now

Having my work showcased in the Festival was one of the worst things
that ever happened to me. Because my work was phenomenally well
received by critics and the theatrical community, I felt compelled to be
a writer. I've met with varying degrees of success with my work over the
years, but nothing would ever again be as spontaneous as *Third Street,*
which I don't even remember working on. I was sitting in the commons
room in French Hall at Dartmouth, there was lots of noise and pizza
flying. I remember doing some typing, but no writing.

Now I sit at a desk and write words for sale. It is a hell of a way to try
and make a living—right up there with bank robber, contortionist,
prostitute.

The jobs I've had along the way to fill the gaps? Methadone counselor, Wall Street paralegal, au pair, film critic, poker player, direct
mail copywriter, scholarship winner, law school admission test teacher.

I have written a number of screenplays that I'm proud of, including
G. I. Jill, for Donald P. Borchers (*Two Moon Junction, Angel*), about a
pacifist woman in the postapocalyptic future who discovers that some
things are worth fighting for; and *Don't Touch That Dial,* for Neal Moritz
(*Juice*), about two wheeler-dealer high school kids who discover a re-
mote control that makes people disappear temporarily inside TV sets.
And *Real Money,* a comedy set in Cleveland, about a guy from the
Italian Mafia who falls in love with a girl from the Jewish mafia.

And much, much more. Anybody out there looking for a seasoned
screenwriter? I'm listed in L.A.

SPARKS
IN THE
PARK

by
NOBLE MASON SMITH
(age eighteen when play was written)
Yakima, Washington

■

Sparks in the Park was performed at Playwrights Horizons in New York City, September 15 through October 11, 1987. The director was Gary Pearle. The playwright adviser was Alfred Uhry. Sets were designed by Derek McLane, and costumes by Michael Krass. Nancy Schertler designed the lighting, and Lia Vollack designed the sound. Fights were staged by Bjorn Johnson, and original music was composed by John McKinney. Mary Fran Loftus was the production stage manager.

The cast:

LOUIS REYNOLDS	*John Vennema*
JANICE ENGLISH	*Nancy Giles*
INDIAN WAITER	*Oliver Platt*
AGENT 4-H	*Stephen Mellor*
BARRY DANIELS	*Todd Merrill*
STEPHANIE ECKERT	*Cynthia Nixon*
BARRY'S MOM	*Nancy Giles*
CHUCK HOLLISTER	*John Vennema*
DR. RUDOLPH SCHMEER	*Stephen Mellor*
DR. RENEE SCHMEER	*Susan Greenhill*
BUDDY HOLLISTER	*Oliver Platt*

BEN ECKERT	*Doug Hutchison*
FRENCH WAITER	*Oliver Platt*
CRAIG STRONGMAN	*Stephen Mellor*
GUY RICHMONT	*Stephen Mellor*
BART	*Oliver Platt*

For Dinky and Dad

And special thanks to:

Gary Pearle, Nancy Quinn, and everyone at the Young Playwrights Festival. Andre Bishop and the crew at Playwrights Horizons. The incredible New York cast. Alfred and Jolly.

And . . . Kendra.

Scene One

The Zim Zam Café, a seedy little dive off Queen Victoria Street, Bombay, India. Center stage is a small, dilapidated table with two chairs. A MAN, *tan shirt, ascot, and pith helmet, sits at another table, up right. He is reading a book and smoking a pipe. The room is illuminated by a single, exposed bulb. Christmas tree lights surround various religious posters and plaster deities. Outside, the sounds and voices of the city can be overheard: The whiny whistle of a pipe and the tinny beat of a drum play dully on the street. Car horns honk constantly, followed by shouts of anger. A* MAN *selling his wares comes closer, then fades into the oblivion of voices.*

A WOMAN *enters the room. She is dressed like a tourist; dumpy clothes, straw hat perched upon her head. She walks hesitantly up to the table at center stage and looks around nervously. Her eyes come to rest on the filthy table and the sticky chair. From her shoulder bag she takes out a butt-protection sheet and sets it on the chair. She maneuvers herself over the chair and plops down carefully, as if sitting on a toilet.*

An INDIAN WAITER, *wearing Punjabi pants and a long collarless white shirt, comes up to the table. The* WOMAN *does not notice him. She is reading the menu, running her finger down the list of confusing names. The* WAITER *becomes impatient. He scratches his butt. He glances at the* MAN *in the corner. He peeps at his watch. He taps his pencil on his notepad. The* WOMAN *takes off her hat. The* WAITER *looks at the top of her head. Suddenly he smacks her head with his notepad.*

WAITER: *(His voice thick with accent. He shouts.)* Big Scary Bug! *(The* WOMAN *jumps and lets out a little gasp.)* Whad wood you luk?

JANICE: *(She is American. Her voice is typical West Coast. She looks up and points to an item on the menu.)* I would like the cantaloupe and—

WAITER: *(interrupting)* Whad do you say?

JANICE: Cantaloupe. *(She holds her hands in a ball shape.)*

WAITER: *(Shaking his head from side to side, he yells offstage.)* Salim! Kandy Loop?

OFFSTAGE VOICE: No!

WAITER: *(Beat. Bellowing.)* Out of seazun!

JANICE: *(pointing to another item)* All right. What about the dahl and rice with chutney—

WAITER: *(Starts to write.)* One dahl and rice with . . . *(He stops, a frustrated look on his face.)* Oh, pleaze! Dat is onely on da dinna menu. *(He crosses his arms, purses his lips, and wags his head even faster.)*

JANICE: *(becoming impatient)* Okay. How about oatmeal?

WAITER: *(throwing up his arms)* Ahhh. . . . Dat iz brakefast!

JANICE: *(upset)* Well, how am I supposed to tell. They are all mixed up. *(Pause.)* Just give me an orange juice.

WAITER: *(Sighs, turns to exit stage left.)* One cheeze sandawich—*(He says with relief, not quite understanding the order.)*

JANICE: *(with bewilderment)* What!? No. I said one orange juice!

WAITER: *(An equally puzzled look. He repeats himself.)* One cheeze sandawich. *(JANICE holds up a hand and gestures for the WAITER to read her lips. JANICE and the WAITER at the same time:)*

JANICE: Orrr-annn-juice!

WAITER: Orrr-annn-cheeze sandawich! *(JANICE screams and jumps up. The MAN in the pith helmet crosses down to the table.)*

LOUIS: *(in a prim British accent)* Excuse me. May I be of some assistance?

JANICE: *(slumping down in her chair)* Oh, good. You speak the language?

LOUIS: *(to the WAITER)* Ravi.

WAITER: Yes, Mister Loowy?

LOUIS: The mem-sahib would like one or-dranz-goozie. *(He says the word putting stresses on consonants, stretching vowels, until it sounds like a completely "foreign" word.)*

WAITER: *(Raises his eyebrows.)* Well, if she wanted one or-dranz-goozie, why did she not just ask for one!? *(He sulks off, muttering under his breath.)* Stupid American cow . . .

JANICE: I can't seem to say anything they understand. Hindu English is like . . .

LOUIS: *(continuing her sentence)* Like a completely different language. Yes, I know all too well. *(He stares at something on the floor.)* It's slurred and mixed up and jumbled about. *(He stomps on a bug.)* Quite annoying, really. *(Pause.)* Oftentimes it's like . . . talking to an American.

JANICE: *(peeved)* Thank you.

LOUIS: *(Sits down.)* I'm only kidding of course. *(Snickering at his little joke.)* My name is Reynolds, Louis Reynolds.

JANICE: Mine's English, Janice English.

LOUIS: Oh, English! How delightful. *(Pause.)* Quite a dismal city, you know. Sometimes I feel as if I were going mad myself.

(From up right, a MAN *dressed in a dark "G-Man" suit and sunglasses enters and crosses to the table up right, unnoticed by* JANICE *or* LOUIS.*)*

JANICE: Yes, I know the feeling. *(Pause.)* So, what do you do here in Bombay, Louis?

LOUIS: I work at the embassy, British, that is. If you think it is trouble ordering orange juice, try making them understand the procedure for granting a Pakistani visa. Why, once—

JANICE: *(She notices the* STRANGER, *who is standing staring intently at her. She interrupts* LOUIS *and grabs his arm.)* Louis! *(She leans forward. He stops and stares at her curiously.)* Louis. Do you see that man standing over there? *(She points to the corner.)*

LOUIS: *(staring at her)* Excuse me?

JANICE: Listen to me. There is a man standing in the corner. Pretend to wipe your forehead on your sleeve or something. (LOUIS *shrinks back, stares at* JANICE, *then pretends to wipe his forehead on his sleeve, still staring at her.)* No . . . no. Pretend to sniff under your arm or something, then take a peek at the man.

LOUIS: *(His eyes grow wider.)* Oh, I see . . . a trick! *(He fingers his nose. Then, he slowly, awkwardly sniffs under his arm and glances under his shoulder at the man. He turns back around with an excited look.)* Oh, my! I do believe that man was watching me.

JANICE: *(Grabs his arm, pulling him close.)* Listen, Louis. I have to tell you something. A dangerous secret . . . about me.

LOUIS: Yes . . . yes . . . do tell.

JANICE: *(Fumbles with her sunglasses and puts them on. She takes a deep breath.)* Louis . . . I'm a spy!

LOUIS: *(A long pause as he leans back, then laughs aloud.)* Ripping! Absolutely ripping.

JANICE: *(growing impatient)* Listen to me. I really am a spy.

LOUIS: How delightful. A prankster like myself.

JANICE: *(extremely serious)* I have a gun in my purse!

LOUIS: *(Stops snickering, leans toward her.)* A what?

JANICE: A gun! *(She thrusts her bag under the table and opens it for him.)*

LOUIS: My God. What are you doing here? What in God's name is a spy doing in Bombay?

JANICE: Actually, I'm just passing through. My plane was shot down over the Himalayas . . . my pilot killed. I've spent the last month trying to get to Tibet. I was supposed to meet a contact here—

LOUIS: *(Shudders with excitement.)* And you think that man over there is—

JANICE: Either my contact or an agent sent to kill me. He has trailed me since I left the hotel.

(The MAN walks over to the table. JANICE and LOUIS sit completely still.)

MAN: Good afternoon, miss. *(He pulls on one of his earlobes.)*

JANICE: Good afternoon.

MAN: I don't mean to intrude . . . *(He jerks his head to the left.)* but I overheard you asking for some orange juice. . . . *(He puts both hands under his chin and wiggles his fingers.)*

JANICE: Yes . . . *(She sticks out her tongue and touches her nose.)* orange juice would be nice for this climate . . . *(She pulls back her coat and squeezes one of her breasts.)* Would you enjoy a cigarette? *(Holds out a pack.)*

MAN: Dunhills . . . *(He stresses the Dun part.)* My favorite. Would you enjoy a breath mint . . . a Certs perhaps? *(Holds out a pack.)*

JANICE: *(Sighs.) Cert-ainly . . . (She says, completing the code.)*

MAN: *(Sits down, wipes his forehead.)* I am Agent Four-H. I have been trying to find you for the past three days— *(He stares at LOUIS.)*

JANICE: *(to 4-H)* He's okay.

AGENT 4-H: *(Nods.)* Do you have the plans?

(Unseen, the WAITER comes onstage holding a small tray covered with a napkin.)

JANICE: Yes, I have them . . .

WAITER: *(He stops.)* Here is your— *(He pulls off the napkin. On the tray is a German Luger.)* cheeze sandawich! *(He takes the gun and points it at JANICE.)*

LOUIS: Oh, my God. . . . He's got a *gun!*

(Suddenly JANICE *swings her purse and knocks the* WAITER *into a spin.* 4-H *lunges across the table, flipping the cigarettes he's been holding into the* WAITER*'s face. The* WAITER *jumps on a chair.* 4-H *grabs his arm. The gun swings back and forth.* JANICE *and* LOUIS *hold on to each other, screaming. The gun is pointed at the ceiling. A shot is fired. Blackness. Music erupts as the stage is cleared. A special light comes up on a* YOUNG MAN, *who appears downstage out of nowhere. He stares at the audience.*)

BARRY: Aren't plays amazing? I think I love writing more than anything in the world. You sit down at a typewriter, stare at that empty, white page . . . and pretty soon . . . voices start talking in your head.

(Voices offstage.)

WAITER: Now I have you and I'm not going to let you go.

JANICE: *(screaming)* Loooouuuuuiiiiisss!

AGENT 4-H: Don't move, waiter . . . or your ass is chutney.

LOUIS: Oh MY!

BARRY: *(listening)* Amazing! Once they get started, they just don't stop.

(Voices offstage.)

JANICE: The doooooooor!

LOUIS: Whooaoaooaoa.

WAITER: I've got a hold on you!

LOUIS: Those are my privvies you're groping.

WAITER: I thought dey were da kandy loops.

AGENT 4-H: Outta season, pal!

BARRY: There is one thing I don't like about writing, though. I don't like it when I write something that I think is really great *(pause)* and my best friend thinks it's stupid.

(Lights up. We are now in BARRY*'s room. A futon chair sits stage right. A desk and bookshelf are up center. A small wastebasket is placed next to the desk. Sitting on the chair in front of the desk is* STEPHANIE ECKERT. BARRY *stares at her. She stares back.*)

BARRY: *(softly)* What do you mean, "plot manipulation"?

STEPH: Well . . . I mean . . . *(She chooses her words carefully.)* it was okay, kind of funny almost . . . until . . . it turned out that . . .

ummm . . . Louis Reynolds was a double agent working for the KGB, and that he just happened to have that private jet on that . . . island or whatever.

BARRY: He didn't just happen to have it there. It was all planned out by the Taoist Terrorists!

STEPH: But you didn't explain that!

BARRY: Well . . . it was obvious. *(Pause.)* Wasn't it?

STEPH: *(looking away)* No.

BARRY: Hey, I didn't ask you over here to criticize my play to little shreds.

STEPH: It was lame. What am I supposed to say? *(He doesn't answer.)* I think I'd better go. *(She gets up.)*

BARRY: No . . . stay. You're right. It's worthless trash.

STEPH: Well, for comedy adventure, it was pretty good.

BARRY: No . . . no. *(Slumps his shoulders.)* My fate is incurable. I'm destined to be an insurance agent like my father.

STEPH: *(angry)* Don't you ever say that again.

BARRY: Listen, Steph, I'm serious. I cannot write anymore. I'm a literary loser. I used to put out some great stuff, but now . . . *(raspberry)*

STEPH: Don't be pretentious.

BARRY: *(Repeats the word.)* Pretentious.

STEPH: Barry, you are one of the most *(pause)* talented guys I know. But your best stuff comes when you don't try so hard. Your poems are some of the most beautiful things I have ever—

BARRY: *(interrupting)* POEMS! Po-ems. Poems are for weenies. I want to write something that people will go to and cry and laugh at. I want to sit in the back row of my play and watch real live people live my words. Poems are hollow. I can't explain.

STEPH: Look. People know when a writer is lying. Tell about something you know. Write about something true.

BARRY: You want true! Watch *Wild Kingdom*. This is the Theater.

STEPH: But you have so much in your life—

BARRY: *(cutting her off)* I have nothing. I'm boring. This world is boring. My room is boring. *(Pause.)* And you are boring.

STEPH: I'm leaving. *(She exits.)*

BARRY: *(screaming)* I CANNOT TAKE IT ANYMORE!!!

MOM: *(Offstage. She has a loud, ear-splitting voice.)* Barry! Barry, what are you doing?

BARRY: *(Moans.)* Nothing, Mom.

MOM: *(offstage)* Listen, Barry . . . are you writing plays again? I thought I told you not to write anymore. If you can't write without screaming every five minutes, I don't want you doing this at all. You are giving me an ulcer.

BARRY: Okay.

MOM: *(offstage)* Barry? What did you say?

BARRY: All right. God . . . give me a break. *(Pause, then to the audience:)* I really think I'm going insane. Do you want to know why I'm going insane? Well, I'll tell you anyway. *(He pulls off a poster that is tacked to his bookcase.)* It's all because of this. *(Holds it up for the audience to see.)* Can you read it? It says, "Write a play and see it produced by top professionals in New York City in America's Annual Young Playwrights Festival." Pretty neat. My English teacher gave it to me just before school was out for the summer. *(Beat.)* Just the kind of thing an English teacher would give you right before summer. This thing has been like a curse. It's killing me. Don't get me wrong. It's not like I have to do this or anything. It's just become like a quest. I always thought . . . hey, I could write a play. I mean . . . listen. I have been to so many bad plays in my life. Stupid, idiotic plays . . . plays that make you say, "My God, what kind of madman wrote this?" And do you know why there are so many bad plays? *(Yells:)* BECAUSE THEY ARE IMPOSSIBLE TO WRITE! *(Pause, waiting for his MOTHER's voice.)* I have been sitting in this stupid room all month. It's not that I don't have anything to say. That's just it. I have too much to say. I'm too incredibly smart. Write a play . . . write a play. *(Pause.)* Have you ever gone to a play and sat through about the first ten minutes, maybe even up to intermission, without having any idea what was going on? People are sitting around you, laughing, or crying their brains out, and you're just sitting there thinking, "God, my tongue hurts." *(Beat.)* What's worse is when you go to a play, one you really like, and they give it this completely moronic ending. I hate them. I have decided that I hate plays more than anything in the world. That's it. I give up. *(He sits down on the futon couch.)* No more plays for me. *(He leans back.)* Hey . . . what's this? *(He reaches behind his back and pulls out a rolled-up script. Inside is a toy helicopter.* BARRY *takes out the helicopter, unrolls the script, and stares at it. Recognition comes into his face.)* Hey . . . this is one of my best works. *(Flips the pages.)* The Karma Cowboy. *(Pause.)* Great name, isn't it? *(Sits on the edge of the couch.)* It's all about this guy, Buddy Hollister, who flew helicopter gun ships in Vietnam. *(He turns a page.)* Ahhh . . . here it is, scene three. Vienna, Austria. A creepy mental institution.

(As BARRY *is speaking, the lights dim. Weird string music plays. A bust of Freud appears from stage left and rolls across the stage behind the scrim and stops. A special comes up on* BARRY.*)*

BARRY: Buddy's been locked up 'cause everyone thinks he's insane. When the curtain comes up, Chuck, Buddy's older brother, is coming to visit him for the first time . . . all the way from El Paso.

*(*BARRY *looks at the script. From stage right,* CHUCK *enters. He is wearing cowboy boots, a cowboy hat, old Wrangler jeans, a beat-up corduroy jacket, and a bolo tie. He looks around the stage and stops by the desk. He takes off his hat and sets it down.)*

BARRY: *(flipping through the papers)* Uhhh . . . Chuck is nervous. He is tired and worn out from the flight. Every so often he looks about the room. He glances at the door in anticipation.

*(*CHUCK, *following* BARRY*'s directions, glances about the room.)*

BARRY: Chuck reaches into his pocket and . . .

*(*CHUCK *reaches into his pocket—)*

BARRY: He reaches for a . . .

*(*CHUCK *fumbles in his pockets for some time. Finally he looks at* BARRY *and opens his mouth as if to speak.)*

BARRY: For a . . . *(Flips a page.)* For a gun!

*(*CHUCK *shakes his head, then starts to pull a Colt .45 from his jacket.)*

BARRY: No, wait. Not a gun . . . a pack of cigarettes.

*(*CHUCK *rolls his eyes, puts the gun back, and pulls out a pack of cigarettes.)*

BARRY: They are Dunhills.

CHUCK: *(Squints at* BARRY.*)* Now hold it right there, you little—

BARRY: No, wait! They are Marlboros.

CHUCK: That's betta. *(He puts one in his mouth. From another pocket,* CHUCK *takes out a huge box of wooden kitchen matches.)*

BARRY: Chuck lights the match—

*(*CHUCK *lights the match with his thumb.)*

BARRY: *(reading the script)* —on his shoe.

*(*CHUCK *sighs, blows out the match, and lights another one off the bottom of his shoe.)*

BARRY: *(looking up)* Marlboros. The real man's cigarette.

CHUCK: You said it.

BARRY: Okay . . . ummmmm. *(Pause.)* Suddenly from the hallway come several screams.

(We hear several weak, toneless utterances.)

BARRY: *(upset)* They are creepy, demented screams. . . . Obviously the utterances of deranged individuals. *(*BARRY *lets forth a deranged scream. The offstage voices match his intensity.)*

CHUCK: My God . . . what in the Holy Moses . . . where in the hay-eck . . . *(*CHUCK *stops as a particularly strange laugh erupts stage right.)*

*(*DR. RUDOLPH SCHMEER, *deranged psychiatrist, enters the room backward, talking to someone offstage.)*

SCHMEER: —and den, zee strudel fell on his lap and he screamed, "Oh, my . . . last time it was banana cake!" *(Offstage voices laugh.)*

CHUCK: *(He takes a step toward* SCHMEER.*)* Hello, Dr. Uhhh—

SCHMEER: *(Whirls around and stares wide-eyed, looking* CHUCK *up and down.)* Dr. Schmeer, Dr. Rudolph Schmeer—

*(*OFFSTAGE VOICES, *everyone at the same time, building to a hysterical crescendo:)*

VOICE ONE: Crying in a demented fashion.

VOICE TWO: Repeating, "Schmeer, Schmeer, Rudolph Schmeer . . ."

VOICE THREE: Laughter, strange and twisted.

VOICE FOUR: Repeating, "Who is it? Who is that? Who is it? What is he doing . . . ?"

SCHMEER: *(raising his voice until the last word,* clinic*)* I am in charge of THIS CLINIC!! *(The voices stop. He stares at* CHUCK.*) And you must be?*

CHUCK: I'm Chuck Hollister from El Paso, Texas. *(He reaches out his hand to shake* SCHMEER*'s.* SCHMEER *looks disdainfully at* CHUCK*'s hand, and daintily touches* CHUCK*'s fingers in a half handshake.)*

SCHMEER: Ahhhh . . . Tex-ass. *(Motions for* CHUCK *to sit on the futon couch.* BARRY *gets up and moves to the box, down right.)* Texas is a very beautiful place, Meester Hole-ister . . . quite luffly . . . rolling-ga heels . . . very attractive cowz unt sheeps. *(Sneering.)* But it's a long way from Owstria now, isn't it!?

CHUCK: Well, uhhhh . . .

SCHMEER: So. What do you think of our little country, Meester Hole-ister?

CHUCK: Uhhh . . . well, I haven't had much time to look around much. But I mean . . . it's nice and all—

SCHMEER: Nice, only nice!? *(His words are biting.)*

CHUCK: *(taken aback)* Uhhh . . . well, real nice.

SCHMEER: Real nice. . . . *(He stares at* CHUCK.*)* I would say it iz beautiful, Meester Hole-ister, the most beautiful place in the world perhaps *(pause, then with contempt),* probably even more beautiful than El Paso!

CHUCK: *(standing up)* Now what are you gettin' at?

SCHMEER: What am I getting at, Meester Hole-ister . . . what I am getting at iz that I don't think you know what you are doing here. I don't think you know, using a Tex-ass fa-raize, your ass from axle grease!

CHUCK: Listen, Schmoo—

SCHMEER: *(screaming)* SCHMEER!

CHUCK: Whatever. *(Crosses to* SCHMEER.*)* I think I know what you're tryin' ta do. I may be just a dumb shitkicker from Texas, but no fancy high-tootin' doctor is goin' ta tell me what ta do. I know why I'm here. I'm here ta git my little brother . . . Buddy!

SCHMEER: *(Completely changing his attitude. He smiles meekly.)* You must know that Butty is a fairy *(pause)* zick man.

CHUCK: I know, but—

SCHMEER: He has one of the worst kisses *(beat)* of schizophrenic sarcosis I have ever vitnessed.

CHUCK: Well, where I come from, out on the range and all, you can be pretty weird and get away with it. Sometimes it's all a man has ta do ta pass the time. Why, I remember this one time, we took this sheep and three gallons of halla-pana peppers an—

SCHMEER: *(interrupting)* Listen to me!

CHUCK: I'm a-listanen.

SCHMEER: Your brother was shot down over the Chang Mai Peninsula in 1973. He says he was rescued by a Chinese fisherman. He shpent the last nine years with this man shtudying the ways of Toyism.

CHUCK: My Gawd! I didn't imagine it was that awful.

SCHMEER: Oh . . . yes . . . it get vorse. We have reason to believe he is lying. We believe that he was brain-vashed by the Red Army, forced to shmuggle weapons back and forth between Thailand, captured by communist agents, and then eshcaped through East Berlin—

CHUCK: How do you know all this?

SCHMEER: It's just a hunch *(beat)*, but I know he's lying. He has this crazy fantasy that this Chinese man found him, took him to live in this Shangra-la-la land, then sent him back to shpread this massage of eternal piss.

CHUCK: *(overcome with grief)* Oh, my Lord! I never knew he could've become so twisted. The poor little sonofaseabiscuit!

SCHMEER: Yes, it is quite sad, I know.

(Lights suddenly go out. A special comes up on BARRY. CHUCK and SCHMEER freeze in their positions—CHUCK sobbing with hands covering his head, SCHMEER looking forlornly toward the audience.)

BARRY: *(to audience)* God . . . this is beautiful. Wait a minute. How about a little love interest, though? *(Pencils in on his script.)* This is beautiful. *(A slender WOMAN dressed exactly like SCHMEER comes onstage and walks up behind SCHMEER. She taps him on the shoulder. He hands her the clipboard. She takes his place.)* That's the thrill of being an author . . . total control, I love it.

(Lights out on BARRY. Lights back up on the new SCHMEER and CHUCK.)

CHUCK: *(not looking up)* Oh, Doctor. What in the world am I gonna do?

BARRY: *(pointing to the ceiling)* Red gel.

(A steamy red gel appears over CHUCK*'s head. Slinky lounge music plays.* DR. RENEE SCHMEER *pulls a barrette from her hair, which falls into a cascading mane about her shoulders. She takes off her lab coat and drops it on the floor. She is clad in a sexy red nightie. She removes her glasses . . . walks over and stands behind* CHUCK, *massaging his shoulders.)*

CHUCK: *(head down)* Oh, Doctor. I feel like my guts are dying inside. Like a dull knife is diggin' into my very innards. I feel all hot and cold, like the mist that rises off the desert in the early mornin'— blood red, deep and yearning like the sky was on *fire.*

(He looks up at her, surprised by her sudden change. She straddles him. They kiss madly. Suddenly, BUDDY *steps onstage. The music stops. The lights come on.* CHUCK *pulls away from* SCHMEER *and stares in disbelief.)*

CHUCK: Oh, my God! It's Buddy.

*(*BUDDY *walks up to the desk. He is wearing cowboy pajamas and has a white Ace bandage wrapped around his head. He looks at the two in bewilderment. In one hand he holds a Japanese geisha doll.)*

BUDDY: *(with Texas drawl)* Chang dow? *(Pause as he stares at the two.)* Dee oo may? *(Pause.)* Chu . . . chy . . . ch . . . (CHUCK *spits in the palm of his hand, slaps his thigh, and points his hand in the shape of a gun at* BUDDY. BUDDY *immediately recognizes the old "hello" sign.* BUDDY *drops the doll into the wastebasket. His voice cracks with sudden realization.)* Chucky! It is you. (CHUCK *rushes forward to hug* BUDDY. *At the last moment,* BUDDY *brings his hands together in the traditional Oriental sign of namaste, poking* CHUCK *in the neck.* CHUCK *glances at* SCHMEER. *He licks his lips, then punches* BUDDY *playfully in the shoulder.)*

CHUCK: It's been too darn long, little brother!

BUDDY: *(shaking his head)* Ahhh, Chuck. I've missed ya, man. I never stopped thinking about you and Ma, not once, no sir—

CHUCK: I just can't believe it, pal. You look great. A little pale maybe, but that desert sun will tan your hide in no time!

BUDDY: *(somber, dropping his head)* Chuck, I have to tell you something.

CHUCK: Yeah, what is it, little brother?

(Both men stare at SCHMEER. *She nods encouragement for* BUDDY *to continue.)*

BUDDY: I can't go back with you.

CHUCK: *(Looks from* BUDDY *to* SCHMEER *with a frantic smile on his lips.)* What do ya mean? You look fine. I expected ta find ya with your head shaved and lectrodes stickin' out of your brain and all, and rantin' in a room with pillows all over the wall, but you're doin' just fine!

BUDDY: *(putting a hand to the side of his head)* It's not that, Chuck, I'm a different man now. A lot has happened to me over the years . . . a lot I can't explain.

CHUCK: Well, ya gotta come back, Buddy. I mean, that's partly why I'm here. It's the ranch, Buddy.

BUDDY: Yes.

CHUCK: We need ya, Buddy. You were one of the best cowhands ever in those parts, maybe even the world. The boys and me, well, we need your inspiration. We lost that special something that makes us real cowboys . . . call it guts, call it love. . . . But I need ya, Buddy, the boys need ya, Ma needs ya . . . the dog needs ya!

BUDDY: *Whiskers?! (Pause.)* I don't know what to say. Oh, God . . . how can I tell you this—

CHUCK: Tell me what, little brotha?

BUDDY: I'm . . . I can't . . . I can't be a cowboy no more . . .

CHUCK: *(slapping* BUDDY's *hands)* Well, durn, boy, what do ya mean?

BUDDY: I'm . . . I mean . . . well . . . I can't . . . I can't . . . I'm a—

CHUCK: You're a what, for Chrissakes!?

SCHMEER: *(screaming)* He is a VEGETARIAN!!

BUDDY: *(nodding)* I'm a vegetable.

CHUCK: *(Falls to his knees.)* Jesus H. Christ . . . *(Pause, then he looks at* BARRY.) This is the silliest durn plot I have ever heard.

BARRY: What do you mean?

CHUCK: I mean . . . as far as writing goes, you have about as much potential as a gelded calf.

SCHMEER: He iz right.

BUDDY: *(in a dreamy, mellow voice)* I think you should write with honesty and love. *(He takes out a slip of paper from his shirt pocket and unfolds it.)* Your poems are some of the most beautiful—

BARRY: *(He runs up and furiously snatches the poem from* BUDDY's *fingers.)* Give me a break. My poems are some of the cheesiest pieces of crap—

SCHMEER: No, zay are goot . . . unt do you know why?

CHUCK: Because they are honest and true, like the desert in the evening when—

BARRY: *(yelling)* Shut up!

(The THREE *come up and stand several feet behind* BARRY, *encompassing him.* BARRY *looks at the script in his hand, facing the audience.* SCHMEER *puts her hand on* BARRY's *shoulder.)*

SCHMEER: *(wrapping her leg around his waist)* Young man, you have one of the vorst kisses of penile frenzy I have ever vitnessed.

CHUCK: *(Gooses him.)* That means ya need a girl.

BARRY: *(The* THREE *are practically breathing down his neck.)* AHHHHHH! Get out of my brain—

MOM: *(offstage)* Barry? What are you doing?

THE THREE CHARACTERS: He's writing a play!

BARRY: *(eyes wide open)* I'm writing a play. *(BARRY jumps away from the group and holds the script out in front between two hands as if he is going to rip it in half. The* CHARACTERS *cower away, shaking their heads.* BARRY *speaks resolutely.)* I am writing a play.

(He rips the script in half. BUDDY, SCHMEER, *and* CHUCK *fall dead on the floor. Blackout.)*

Scene Two

The park at night. Lights come up slowly. The stage is empty except for a park bench. BARRY *is sitting on the bench. He still has the ripped-up script in his hands. In the distance thunder rumbles.*

BARRY: I like thunder . . . I think. I like being outside, especially when it rains . . . just sitting. *(Pause.)* People tell you to write about what you know, but sometimes you don't even want to think about what you know. There is this room at the back of my house. It has windows all around and this high ceiling above. I'll just lay there at night . . . and the moon will be out . . . and all these creepy shadows will start swaying in the backyard. I get this desperate feeling . . . when I'm alone like that. I want to call my parents or my dog . . . or someone. But I don't. I just sit there until I start to shake and feel as if I'm going to scream.

(As he is speaking, BEN ECKERT *comes onstage, unseen by* BARRY. *He is dressed in shabby skateboarder clothes. He sneaks up behind* BARRY.*)*

BARRY: I think I just like to scare myself. I'm pretty good at it.

*(*BEN *leans over and jabs his fingers into* BARRY's *waist.)*

BEN: *(screeching)* BEGAW! *(*BARRY *jumps.* BEN *leaps over the bench and starts to dance, singing a few lines from "Fashion" by David Bowie. He pauses, then lifts his hand up, sort of waves.)* Sorry if I scared you.

BARRY: Yeah. No. It's okay.

BEN: You all right?

BARRY: Yes. I'm great.

BEN: *(Sits down next to him. Both stare at the sky.* BEN *takes out a Pez dispenser.)* Pez?

BARRY: I hate Pez.

BEN: I think it's gonna rain.

BARRY: *(Nods.)* Yes. I think it might.

BEN: *(gesturing at the ripped script in* BARRY's *hand)* What's that?

BARRY: A play. I read it to you a couple of months ago.

BEN: *(naming a play) Lacerations?*

BARRY: No.

BEN: *Byzantium Revisited?*

BARRY: Nope.

BEN: *Brunch with the Devil?*

BARRY: *Breakfast with the Devil!* No, not that one either. *(Holds up the script and sighs.)* It's *The Karma Cowboy.*

BEN: Is that the one about the two gay cowpokes?

BARRY: What?

BEN: Those two guys. The one that became a Hindu and the other one— *(He stops, trying to remember.)*

BARRY: It was that memorable, huh?

BEN: I can't remember. *(Pause.)* You know, Barry, you should try writing something different for a change. You know . . . like a short story or something . . . variety.

BARRY: I don't want variety. I want to be bland and contrived, like every other writer in the world.

BEN: *(leaning back, holding up his hands)* O-kay. *(Pause.)* Did you call Stephanie's house?

BARRY: Yes, but she wasn't home. *(Looks at Ben.)* Hey?

BEN: What?

BARRY: How long have her parents been like—

BEN: About to kill each other? Gosh, how long have they been married? Ten, twenty . . . twenty years.

BARRY: Why didn't they do this a long time ago?

BEN: Some people like to torture themselves. I don't really know. I really think they both love Stephanie . . . maybe that's the only reason they ever tried . . . but God . . . she's lucky she turned out as great as she did.

BARRY: Yeah!

BEN: *(Laughs.)* Yeah.

BARRY: What's so funny?

BEN: I was thinking about the day you moved into the neighborhood. I was in those bushes. *(Points.)* Right there.

BARRY: What were you doing?

BEN: I was butt-rubbing with Billy Boner.

BARRY: *(laughing)* What?

BEN: In those bushes. We used to come over here every day. We'd take off all our clothes, then sort of dance around a little. *(He dances.)* Then we'd rub our butt-cheeks together. God it was fun! I can still remember the way his skin felt. He had this weird dermatitis . . . his skin was all rough . . . it felt like I was rubbing up against an elephant or something. (BEN *smiles, laughing with* BARRY. *He loves this story. He loves telling it passionately.)* It was so . . . primal . . . you know? God, I loved that. One day I came home and my shirt was on inside out. My mom freaked. She thought I was being molested by some creep in the park. I said, "Nope, Mom . . . just Billy Boner."

BARRY: How old were you?

BEN: We must have been in the third grade. One wonderful year. Wow, I love this park. It's got something ancient about it.

BARRY: Yeah. *(The two laugh.)*

BEN: *(becoming serious)* I have to ask you something. *(They try not to laugh.)* Since Billy moved away, and you're really the only friend I've got . . . will you?

BARRY: *(bursting with laughter)* Butt-rub with you!? No, I don't think so.

*(*BEN *bites* BARRY'*s shoulder.* BARRY *jumps up, and* BEN *chases him downstage.* BEN *starts doing a little dance, singing a funny nonsense song, such as "Papa Oo Mau Mau" or "The Bird's the Word," joined by* BARRY. *They rub butt-cheeks madly. In the midst of this enters* STEPHANIE. *She stands for some time and stares at the two. They see her and stifle their laughter. Silence.)*

BEN: Hey, I'm sorry about your mom and dad. *(Pause.)* I gotta go. *(He looks at the two awkwardly, then exits.)*

BARRY: I'm sorry, too. *(They both sit on the bench.)*

STEPH: I feel like crapola.

BARRY: It's all right, you deserve to feel like crapola.

STEPH: No, I feel worse than I ever have in my entire life.

BARRY: Your mom and dad will—

STEPH: No! They won't, thank God, they won't get back together. But it's not just that. Everything has been building for a couple of months. This just sort of finally broke me.

BARRY: *(putting his arm around her shoulder)* What is it?

STEPH: *(throwing up her hands)* Everything! It's everything!

BARRY: Oh, my . . . that is a problem.

STEPH: I'm serious, Barry. Sometimes I feel as if someone is squeezing my lungs, just sort of pushing all the air out of me.

BARRY: I know that feeling too.

STEPH: I really think I'm going insane sometimes.

BARRY: Everyone does.

STEPH: No, everyone doesn't. A lot of people do, but the majority doesn't.

BARRY: Have you been taking secret polls again?

STEPH: I just know. Sometimes I wish I were a little kid again. I think it was the only time when I was ever really happy.

BARRY: You mean . . . oblivious.

STEPH: Is there a difference? *(Pause.)* When I was a little kid, I remember this one time I went out in front of our house with this colored chalk. I sat down on the sidewalk and just started drawing this . . . this mural thing. I worked from like twelve noon to nine at night. When I got done, I was so proud. I ran inside and told Mom. She came out and looked at this . . . this glob of chalk thing. She said, "Uhhh . . . it's good." I was so happy. I went to bed, but I couldn't sleep. I sat by the window all night. I just kept thinking about it. I was so worried something would happen to it, like it would blow away or something. When I woke up, it was all mooshed . . . and, well, they had left the sprinklers on, and people had walked on it. It was ruined.

BARRY: Were you devastated?

STEPH: No, I forgot about it in a couple of days. I can move on to things pretty fast.

BARRY: Oh . . . not me. I'm just the opposite. When I was a little kid, I would spend hours, days on some stupid project I was making. And then I would get done, and I would look at it . . . scream and rip it up because I thought I had ruined it or something.

STEPH: I wasn't that way at all. I was such an easy kid to satisfy.

BARRY: I like to torture myself.

STEPH: That's not good. *(Pauses, then blurts out:)* I always wanted a horse!

BARRY: *(Nods his head.)* I always wanted a treasure chest. I used to pray for one. I would tell God that if he gave me a treasure chest, I would use all the money to save all the poor little kids and starving animals in the world. I wanted to start this home for stray dogs and cats. All of them would come and live in this big field, and I would set up troughs and feeding bins for them. One day me and my two friends took this old wagon and went all over the neighborhood searching for strays. And you know what?

STEPH: What?

BARRY: There wasn't one single stray!

STEPH: No—

BARRY: Yes! All we found were dead ones. A dead poodle, two dead birds, and a hamster. We put them all in the wagon and set up this little cemetery in my backyard.

STEPH: That's pathetic.

BARRY: I know.

STEPH: This one Christmas Eve, I wanted to stay up until twelve sooo bad. I cried and cried to get them to let me stay up. I sat on the stairs and bawled. Finally my dad came up and sat down next to me and said, "What do you want more than anything in the world?" And of course, I said to stay up until twelve, and he said, "Okay . . . you can." I was so happy. I just sat there smiling. Then all of a sudden I jumped up and screamed, "No, wait . . . a HORSE . . . I WANT A HORSE!" and started crying all over again. *(They both laugh.)* You know, the greatest thing about being a little kid is that if something wasn't working out, you could always change it.

BARRY: Yeah . . . I guess.

STEPH: And when something you had always hoped for finally did happen, it was always a letdown.

BARRY: I don't know about that.

STEPH: *(Stares at him.)* Barry, I have this one great fear, and I can't stop thinking about it.

BARRY: What?

STEPH: You will think I'm stupid.

BARRY: No more than I already do.

STEPH: Thanks, but—

BARRY: Go ahead. I'm in a listening mood.

STEPH: *(after a pause)* I'm afraid of the future . . . my future.

BARRY: What do you mean?

STEPH: I'm afraid, Barry. I'm afraid I will never be satisfied. I don't think I will ever be truly happy with anything.

BARRY: I don't think you can be happy. My God, look at the world we live in. It's demented.

STEPH: Don't you ever think about it?

BARRY: Of course, but I've sort of trained myself to realize that the greatest lesson a human being can discover is he is living in a ridiculous world, and happiness is something only found by . . . brain donors!

STEPH: Don't you think we were put on this planet for some purpose? Don't you think there is something to change?

BARRY: Yes, I think I'm here for a reason. I'm going to live my life to the fullest, but in the back of my mind this little voice will always be saying, "This isn't it."

STEPH: So—

BARRY: So . . . this is how I see it. God, or whatever, sends us to live in these bodies. We are like trees, and we have these incredible roots which tie us down. Our egos, vanities, desires—anything physical—dig into the ground, and keep us here. My goal is to pull out all those roots, one by one, so that there is nothing left to tie me down.

STEPH: Do those roots include people?

BARRY: I guess so.

STEPH: *(unenthused)* That's really deep.

BARRY: But do you understand what I am saying?

STEPH: I'm not a dumbhead, Barry!

BARRY: Good. It's nice to talk to someone who can relate to what I'm saying. *(They sit for some time in silence.)* The wind's really starting to blow.

STEPH: Barry? *(She glances at him, then stares off into the distance.)* Barry—

BARRY: What?

STEPH: Do you ever . . . *(She stops.)* Do—

BARRY: What!?

STEPH: What do you think about me?

BARRY: What do you mean?

STEPH: I mean, what do you think about me?

BARRY: I think you're great.

STEPH: *(upset)* You are such a creep sometimes. Please show some kind of emotions!

BARRY: *(He looks at her, then yells insanely.)* I think you're GREEEEAAAAT! *(He moans emotionally.)*

STEPH: Sometimes I really hate you.

BARRY: Well, what do you want me to say?

STEPH: Look—

BARRY: Yes.

STEPH: I have to tell you something.

BARRY: All right.

STEPH: I'm going away for the rest of the summer.

BARRY: What do you mean?

STEPH: I'm going to Europe with my grandparents.

BARRY: How long?

STEPH: Two months, maybe three.

BARRY: Well . . . when were you going to tell me this?

STEPH: I don't think I was.

BARRY: What do you mean?

STEPH: I'm leaving tomorrow.

BARRY: Well, why didn't you tell me?

STEPH: I guess I wanted to hurt you.

BARRY: Why did you want to hurt me?

STEPH: Because you have burned me off and on for the past four years.

BARRY: What do you mean?

STEPH: You have hurt me . . . really hurt me. I wanted to get you back.

BARRY: How have I hurt you?

STEPH: By not caring enough. By always being sort of there. I hate that detached air you have, like nothing can hurt you.

BARRY: Hey . . . I would go crazy if I didn't keep some sort of detached air. There is just too much to think about!

STEPH: Including me?

BARRY: Well, no . . . No! I think about you a lot.

STEPH: When?

BARRY: When I want—

STEPH: *(interrupting)* When you want someone to listen to your stupid plays, or—

BARRY: Stop it! I'm not some jerk who uses you for—

STEPH: *(Jumps up.)* I don't want to talk about this.

BARRY: You're the one who brought it up!

STEPH: I am leaving. I have decided something. You will never understand how I feel about you.

BARRY: I thought we were friends.

STEPH: Friends . . . FRIENDS! Barry, I am in love with you.

BARRY: What?

STEPH: Yes . . . and I have been for quite some time. And every time you forgot to call or went out with some stupid girl, it hurt . . . really hurt. And do you know what? I don't even want to love you anymore. I don't even think I like you!

BARRY: Don't say that. How can you say that? I never thought you—

STEPH: That's the problem, you idiot! You can never tell people how you really feel about them. I have tried so many times to get some sort of—*(pause)* some reaction. But I'm through. I'm leaving. *(She starts to leave, then stops.)* Someday you are going to care about someone as much as I do about you, and then you will understand how I feel.

BARRY: Wait!

STEPH: Good-bye. *(She exits.)*

BARRY: *(He stands for some time. He looks around, frowning and moving his mouth silently.)* What happened? *(Pause.)* Creep? *(Beat.)* EUROPE!

(Blackout. Music—strings.)

Scene Three

A café in France. A café table sits downstage right with two chairs. STEPHA-
NIE *is at the table reading a book. She is wearing a summer dress. Behind the
scrim is a cutout of a French cathedral. Lights up. A* WAITER *comes onstage
and walks up to the table. He is the same waiter from the Zim Zam Café
scene, although now his dress and demeanor are completely European.*

WAITER: *(speaking incredibly fast)* Bonjour, mademoiselle. . . . Ques-
quevousavezcematin?

STEPH: *(smiling)* Je besoin de café de crême.

WAITER: *(Snickers.)* Oh . . . you are A-merican. How lang have you
been in Fronce?

STEPH: J'arrive un mois à Lyons.

WAITER: *(grinning)* Please . . . spick English.

STEPH: Oh . . . great. Right. Uhhh. I've been here one month.

WAITER: Excellente! *(He stands for some time.)* Now, what would you
like?

STEPH: *(She stares at him.)* Café de crême.

WAITER: *(Cocks his head.)* What do you say?

STEPH: Café de crême.

WAITER: *(Stares at her, then gives a little laugh.)* Ahhhhh. *(He gestures for
her to follow his speech.)* Café de crrrême. *(He says the word, thick with
accent, making strange gurgling sounds in his throat.)* Écoutez. Café de
crrrême.

STEPH: Café de crrrrême.

WAITER: Wonderful. *(He bows slightly.)* Enjoy your stay in our beautiful
country. *(Exits.)*

*(*STEPH *goes back to reading. From stage left a* YOUNG MAN *enters. He is the
same person who played* AGENT 4-H *in the Zim Zam scene. Now he is dressed
like a college student, sunglasses around his neck, Stanford sweatshirt,
chinos.* CRAIG STRONGMAN *walks up to the table hesitantly.* STEPH *does not
look up.)*

CRAIG: Uhhh . . . excuse moy, mad-moysly. I uhhh . . . je avez—

STEPH: *(looking up)* What? I'm American.

CRAIG: *(sighing)* Oh . . . *great! (Big pause.)* Me too. It's nice to meet someone from the States.

STEPH: Yeah. My name is Stephanie Eckert.

CRAIG: *(Sits down.)* Mine's Craig . . . Craig Strongman.

STEPH: How long have you been in Lyons?

CRAIG: About two weeks.

STEPH: How do you like it?

CRAIG: It's great. Except every time I try to speak French, they say, "What? What are you saying? Speak English." It's their way of getting us back.

STEPH: I know what you mean.

CRAIG: How long have you been here?

STEPH: About two months. In Europe, that is. I'm here with my grandparents. What are you doing here?

CRAIG: *(Slinks down in his seat, puts on the sunglasses, and looks around nervously.)* Actually *(pause)* I'm a spy.

STEPH: *(startled)* What!?

CRAIG: *(Takes off glasses, laughs.)* I'm just kidding. Actually I'm heading down to Cannes *(says "cans")* for the film festival.

STEPH: Oh . . . *(Recovers herself from his joke.)* That's great. I always wanted to write screenplays and stuff. A friend *(beat)*, an ex-friend, that is, got me started on writing.

CRAIG: That's really cool. I want to be an actor, though. I guess I'm kind of a show-off.

STEPH: *(coldly)* My friend was like that.

CRAIG: Gee, you must not have liked this . . . friend.

STEPH: No. I don't. In fact, I hate his guts!

CRAIG: What did he do to you?

STEPH: He broke my heart. *(Silence, then the two start laughing.)*

WAITER: *(coming on with her coffee)* Enjoy your café. *(He gives* CRAIG *a patronizing stare, then walks off in a huff.)*

STEPH: So, where are you from, anyways?

CRAIG: I'm from Salinas, California. Where are you from?

STEPH: I'm from Ashland, Oregon.

CRAIG: *(slapping his forehead with the palm of his hand)* Oh, wow! I've been there!

STEPH: Really?

CRAIG: Yeah. We go to the Shakespeare Festival there every year. *(Pause.)* How bizarre!

STEPH: That is weird. Pretty chance meeting, eh?

CRAIG: Yes. You know what? I even know someone in Ashland.

STEPH: Really?

CRAIG: Yeah. It's a guy. You see, last summer, I was driving up to Portland and my car wiped out.

STEPH: Oh, no—

CRAIG: Yeah. It was pretty bad. I broke my arm and had a skull fracture. But I probably would have died if it hadn't been for this guy who came out of nowhere, pulled me from the burning wreck, and drove me to the hospital!

STEPH: My gosh. What an incredible story. What was this guy's name, anyway?

CRAIG: It was Barry. *(Beat, then turns and gives his line directly to the audience:)* Barry Daniels.

STEPH: *(Stands up and throws her chair back, then fumes.)* What? That heartless creep! I hate him. He is my worst enemy!

CRAIG: *(standing and facing her)* Hey, hey—I can't have you talking that way about the guy who saved my life.

STEPH: *(going crazy)* Shut up, you idiot! He is the biggest slob, jerk, dirtsucking, brainless—

CRAIG: Okay. That's it. *(He pulls out a revolver from his pants pocket.)* I'm going to have to shoot you. *(Points the gun at her.)*

STEPH: *(looking up to the heavens, screaming)* Baaaaaaarrrrrrry! I hate yoooooooouuuu!

(The shot goes off. Blackout. A special comes up on BARRY *as he jumps out of the wings onto the stage.)*

BARRY: *(writing furiously on a notepad)* Bye-bye, Stephy babe. Was nice knowing ya! *(Suddenly* STEPH *comes out of the darkness, grabs* BARRY's *arm, twists it behind his back, kicks his legs out from under him, presses his face into the floor.* BARRY *cries out in amazement.)* What in the—

STEPH: Your writing days are over, buddy. *(Pushes harder on his back.)* Say uncle!

BARRY: *(struggling)* Never—

STEPH: *(Gives him a knee in the side.)* UNCLE!

BARRY: *(screaming)* No . . . No! I am writing this!!* I am wri—

MOM: *(offstage)* BARRY! What in God's name are you doing!

BARRY: *(Looks up.)* Nothing, Mom. (STEPH *lets him go and exits silently.* BARRY *continues to struggle with his unseen nemesis.)*

MOM: *(offstage)* Where are you?

BARRY: *(Realizes the shadow figure is gone, jumps up.)* I'M IN MY ROOM!

(Lights come up. The set has been changed back to BARRY's *room.)*

MOM: *(offstage)* Barry. Don't you *ever* use that tone with me!

BARRY: *(downcast)* All right. Geez. I'm sorry.

MOM: What?

BARRY: All right. Okay. I'm sorry. *(Under his breath.)* Bite my head off.

(BEN *pokes his head into the room.)*

BEN: BEGAW! (BARRY *looks up at* BEN, *then sits at his desk and starts to type.* BEN *struts into the room.)* Hey, dude.

BARRY: *(not looking up)* Howzitgoin'?

BEN: Oh, I'm all right.

BARRY: Good. Good. *(Stops typing and stares at* BEN.) Well, Ben, I can tell you have something to say.

BEN: Huh?

BARRY: Well, what is it? Is it about Stephanie?

BEN: Uhhhh. Yeah. As a matter of fact, it is. *(Plops down on the futon couch.)* I got a letter from her the other day.

BARRY: *(Types again.)* Oh? How is the world traveler?

BEN: She's having a great time. In fact, she thinks she wants to live there someday.

BARRY: Whooaaa. Wouldn't we all.

BEN: She's still pissed off at you.

BARRY: *(startled)* What in the he— *(Beat.)* She's mad at me?

BEN: She told me all about the conversation before she left.

BARRY: Oh yeah?

BEN: Yeah. Gosh, Barry, you're one heckuva suave guy.

BARRY: Speak English.

BEN: Hey, I'm only telling you what she said.

BARRY: Well. What did she say?

BEN: No. Barry, I am not going to get in the middle of this.

BARRY: *(Crosses to futon couch.)* Just tell me! You little honis!

BEN: No.

BARRY: All right. *(Furious.)* Then get off my friggin' futon thing! *(He kicks it.)*

BEN: *(laughing)* You know what? You really are a jerk sometimes.

BARRY: Yes. I do know that. Because about every person in the world today has told me that about eight million times! *(Points to the dog photo on the bookshelf.)* My dog even hates me. *(Goes back to the desk, sits, and continues typing.)*

BEN: It's all those negative vibes you're putting out. Ya know? You just seethe anger.

BARRY: *(shaking his head)* I seethe, I seethe. *(Begins to seethe.)* I am the seething man.

(BEN walks around behind the desk, takes a pair of glasses off the shelf, and puts them on. Lights come on inside the lenses. BEN stands behind BARRY, leans over his shoulder.)

BEN: What are you writing?

BARRY: None of your stupid business.

BEN: Is it another play?

BARRY: Yes. Another moronic play. *(He rips the page from the typewriter, crosses to the futon couch, and sits.)*

BEN: *(taking off the glasses)* Whoooaaa. Where did you get all this anger?

BARRY: It's her.

BEN: Hey. I told you she was in love with you.

BARRY: No, you didn't.

BEN: Yes, I did, you bonehead. . . . I told you, and you said, "Naw, we're just good friends, that's all." Well, you blew it, pal, and now she hates your guts.

BARRY: Don't you think I feel bad?

BEN: Wait. The human wall has some emotions. This is unreal.

BARRY: I feel like a dirtball.

BEN: *(Crosses to the futon, kneels down.)* Do you love her?

BARRY: I . . . don't know.

BEN: Listen, Barry. I . . . the reason I came over here was because I just wanted to say . . . I'm here. If you wanted someone to talk to. I'm here. *(Stares at* BARRY, *puts his hand on* BARRY's *arm.)*

BARRY: *(Glares at him.)* What do you want me to do? *(Jerks his arm away.)* Butt-rub with you?

BEN: *(Nods his head, raises his hand as if to speak, stops himself.)* Here's her address. *(Tosses a piece of paper on the floor, exits.)*

BARRY: *(Sits for some time in silence. Starts to laugh.)* This is sooo boring. I hate plays. I really do. Plays are boring for the most part. Especially old Shakespeare. He could really drown you in dialogue. The only thing that kept Shakespeare from playwright oblivion was the fact that about fifty people got killed in every play. Some of the sword fights, though, are . . . *(He stops, smiles.)* Hey . . . that's an idea! A sword fight . . . a bloody sword fight!

(Adventure music erupts, the lights begin to dim.)

BARRY: Hey! *(Looking up.)* Don't I set the stage?

(The music stops, the lights come back up. BARRY *grabs his notebook and walks to center stage.)*

BARRY: Okay. The scene is in . . . *(pause)* France! Yeah . . . that's it.

(French music begins to play. As BARRY *gives his speech, the lights dim to blackness except for the special above his head.)*

BARRY: The evil duke of Normandy . . . Guy de Richmont . . . has seduced the beautiful girlfriend of the brave Englishman . . . Barry . . . Sebastien Barry of Gloucester and . . . the Lower

Dubervilles. Richmont has brought her to Normandy, promising her his kingdom and all the Brie she could imagine. But the girl *(pause),* Stephanie of Aragon, catches on to his plot and gets word to Barry with a cryptic message written on a slab of blue cheese. Barry takes off for France with his trustworthy, but extremely obnoxious manservant, Ben, and heads for Normandy in a rage of passion and fury, vowing to get Richmont really good.

(End music. BARRY exits. Lights up. As BARRY has been speaking, the stage has been cleared. BEN enters. He is dressed in Elizabethan regalia. He is carrying a backpack, several pots, a large sleeping roll, and a typewriter in carrying case. He stumbles to center stage, exhausted, stops, and sinks to his knees on the floor.)

BEN: My master, Sebastien Barry,
Comes sauntering hither thither—
From whence my pains of burden grow.
I feel weak with luggage carried 'cross the channel,
Everything from pots and swords to shirts of flannel.

My Master comes in a rage,
Ere this place of Frenchmen, a fight we'll wage.
To my heart dear Stephanie holds the key—
If it weren't for her, I'd surely flee.

BARRY: *(offstage)* Ben? Where scurry thee?

BEN: Oh . . . 'tis my suffering to be a rube—
For my master is such a boob.
He constantly threatens and jibes and commands,
Methinks he has some problem with his glands.

(BARRY enters the stage riding a long stick as if it were a horse. He makes whinnying noises, gallops to center stage, stops, and pretends to sit atop his steed.)

BARRY: How now, Ben?
Why dost thou lie so low,
Likest a dog bestricken with the plague?
All panting and scraggly,
Bedraggled and loathsome.

BEN: Master, 'tis only for my burdens that I feel this way.

BARRY: Oh, do be gay,
'Tis a bright and cheery day.
I could make it worse you know.
Hit you, bruise you, give you a blow.

BEN: Oh, master, hit me not—
For my tender skin could scarce take a striking
From one as mighty as thou.

BARRY: Your praises do thou service to me,
But forget about that, there's Castle Normandy.

(BARRY *starts to trot away.*)

BEN: My master is a cruel and heartless fellow.

BARRY: What was that, dear Ben?

BEN: *(getting up to leave)* Nothing, master. I follow.

(*Exeunt* BARRY *and* BEN *stage right. Enter* GUY *and* STEPHANIE. *They are dressed appropriately.* GUY *is running a knife over a whetstone.*)

STEPH: Guy?

GUY: Oui.
Stephanie?

STEPH: Dost thou lovest me likest thou hast sayed?
I must know, for my heart grows discontented.

GUY: But how, my tiny snail,
Could you doubt my heart's bewail?
I have given you the moon and sea—
Not to mention all that Brie.

STEPH: Guy, you are wicked and cruel,
And I thinkest you think of me a fool.

GUY: *(Stops whetting the knife, puts his hands on his hips.)*
Why sayest thou?

STEPH: I sayest I thinkest your intentions
Are not the greatest.

GUY: You hurt me with foolery.
You know how I feel,
With this kiss I doth seal— *(He kisses her.)*
For I have dear business to attend.
Ahh! Here is my servant, good man, and friend.

(BART, *dressed as a servant, peeks his head around the corner and gives* GUY *the "psssst" sign.*)

GUY: How now, good Bartholomew,
What hast thou to do?

BART: *(smiling evilly)* Good master, I needest speak wif you.

GUY: *(to* STEPH*)* Kind temptress, you must leave us to chat *(Glances up and down her body.)*
Please go and . . .
Play with your cat.

*(*STEPH *leaves, but stops by the door and listens to them speak.)*

GUY: Be quick, good Bart.

BART: Calm for the moment, master,
Listen to what's in store.
After you hear what I sayeth,
In haste you'll be more.

GUY: Do tell.

BART: Master, your enemy Barry comes sneaking.

(Pause, then GUY *and* BART *laugh together, maniacally.)*

GUY: *(bellowing)*
Ohhhh! Glorious day at last.
I will crush him and kill him—
Bring him to his knees.
And when I am done—

BART: *(Beat.)* Turn him to cheese.

(There is another long pause as GUY *takes in a deep breath, then explodes with laughter.* BART *holds out his hand—*GUY *takes his knife, puts the point on* BART*'s palm, and gives the blade a sadistic twist.* BART *cries gleefully.* STEPH *lets out a little gasp.* BART *and* GUY *exit right, followed by* STEPH. BEN *and* BARRY *enter left.)*

BARRY: Hither ho, meek Ben.
You slow us down, 'twill take all day.

BEN: *(staggering behind)*
Forgive me of my weaker traits,
But when death approaches, sometimes—
'Tis better to be late.

BARRY: What! You think I shall fail?

BEN: Well. To me a two-man siege does not sound like fun.
If it were up to me, we'd have brought a big gun.

BARRY: Silly Ben, so naive and meek.
Do you want me to slap at your cheek?

Assaulting and scaling is not our way.
We'll sneak in like shadows and steal my love away.

BEN: What if she doesn't like you anymore?

BARRY: Don't be daft and silly, man.

BEN: 'Tis only a thought.

BARRY: And one best left as one.

BEN: Master, a question—
As long as I'm thinking.

BARRY: Pray thee, get it over with.

BEN: Since stealth is the matter and essence of surprise,
Wouldn't it be better if I stayed outside?

BARRY: Dear God, have I heard you correct?
I am deeply hurt, my friend.
We are pals, you and I, to the end.

(BARRY takes BEN's hands in his. They do a silly handshake.)

I will hear no more, not a word.
Besides *(hands him the sword)*,
Who will carry my sword?

(They depart. Lights dim. We are now in a church. Gregorian chant music comes up. A special shines in the shape of a cross on the floor. BART and GUY, dressed in robes, their faces covered with hoods, walk slowly from either side and meet in the middle. BART giggles and whispers, "Master." GUY slaps him in the head and gives the "shhh" sound. They walk upstage and stand silently. STEPHANIE enters. She walks up to the light, kneels, and begins to pray. From stage left BARRY enters, dressed in a priest's robe. His face is covered. Behind him BEN stands at the entrance, nervously glancing about. BARRY walks up behind STEPH and puts his hand on her shoulder.)

STEPH: *(without turning around)* Oh, Father. I have confessions to make.

BARRY: *(imitating the voice of an old priest)*
Yes, child. Do tell.

STEPH: I have wronged my true love in Britain.
Now my heart is broken and smitten.

BARRY: *(overcome)* Oh, no, my dear child,
All is not lost,
For one's heart is wild—

With pain at no cost.
For one stands behind you, his throat all in lumps.
(His voice cracks and changes to his own.)
Turn around, Stephanie. I'm the one that you dumped.
(He throws back his hood.)

STEPH: *(Turns and looks at him.)* Oh, dear God. How many times have I prayed.
Your face is like an angel. Am I in dreams?

BARRY: No, my sweet, I have traveled the miles—
And all for your kindly kisses and smiles.

(They embrace.)

BEN: *(to the audience)* I'm the one doth deserve such reward.
Whilst he's off at parties,
I'm home alone, bored.

GUY: *(taking a step forward)* Now's my chance to slice up this looser.
Turn around, Barry. *(Throws back his hood.)*
Fight, you meek pooser.

(GUY throws off his robe and tosses it to BART. BARRY turns around and gasps as GUY takes out his sword.)

BEN: *(Tosses BARRY his sword.)* Barry! Watch out!

(BARRY and GUY fight a heated battle. They are both excellent swordsmen. At one point BART grabs STEPHANIE from behind and holds a knife to her throat. Then GUY envelopes BARRY's sword, spinning it around in a circle. GUY flings BARRY's sword away. BARRY, out of control, lunges the blade into BEN's chest.)

BEN: *(crying out)* Begaw!

BARRY: *(pulling the sword from BEN's body)* Ben! My friend. *(BEN falls to the floor, dead. GUY walks over and gives BART a "high five." BARRY becomes furious.)* Bloody French fiend!

GUY: *(sneering)* Stupid *(pause)* writer!

(They continue to fight. Near the end GUY backs BARRY into the wall, where BART is waiting with his knife. STEPHANIE screams BARRY's name. BARRY dodges the knife and slices BART across the stomach.)

BART: *(falling to the ground)* Master!

(GUY walks over to STEPH, grabs her by the hair, and drags her to the other side of the stage. BARRY is frozen with horror. GUY pulls back STEPH's head and kisses her unmercifully.)

BARRY: *(screaming)* DARRNNIT! *(BARRY lunges forward, off balance, and GUY grabs his sword by the blade and plucks it away. Then GUY brings his sword down as if to cleave BARRY in two. BARRY escapes the blow, grabs his sword from GUY's hand, and strips it cruelly from GUY's fingers. BARRY brings his sword across GUY's Achilles tendon, and the evil duke falls to his knees. He grabs GUY's head and places the blade to his neck. He turns to STEPH.)* Run! *(BARRY jerks back GUY's head.)* Now, Richmont . . . the victory is mine. *(He pulls the blade across GUY's throat. GUY crashes to the floor. BARRY runs to center stage, takes STEPH's hand and turns to go.)* Come, Stephanie. Let's away. *(Suddenly GUY lets out a low moan, "Aaaauuuuggghhhh!" He sits up, looks at the audience, takes out a knife, points the hilt at STEPHANIE's chest, and flings back his arm. BARRY watches helplessly as the knife travels across the stage. STEPHANIE clutches her breast, a knife stuck in her chest. She lets out a little gasp, pulls out the knife, lets it drop to the floor, then faints backward. BARRY catches her in his arms. He lets her fall gently to the floor. Carefully, he folds her little hands across her stomach and leans over her dead body. Forlornly:)* Oh, God! Why couldn't I . . . Why couldn't I tell you . . . touch your face . . . kiss your lips . . . your hair. *(Touches her hand.)* Your hands are so small. The first time I saw you— *(Stops, looks up with anguish, doing his best King Lear.)*

Oh, that a parrot, a squirrel, a giraffe should have life—
And not my Stephanie.
I would give—

MOM: *(offstage)* Barry! Come outside and help me move these planters. Hurry up!

BARRY: *(breaking character)* Okay. In a minute. *(Looks back up.)* That a man such as I could ever feel—

MOM: *(offstage)* Barry, where are you?

BARRY: *(Moans.)* All right! Ahhhh . . . bloody . . . crap! I can never finish anything. *(Gets up to leave.)* I am slave to the world. *(Exit BARRY.)*

(After several seconds, BEN stirs, then gets up. He looks around for a moment, then nudges STEPH.)

BEN: Pssst! Hey . . . he's gone.

STEPH: *(Jumps up.)* Oh, good. Now we can have some fun.

(Elizabethan music erupts. GUY and BART jump up. The FOUR do a zany parody of an Elizabethan dance. All of them laugh and smile as they sing.)

BEN: Barry's gone, Barry's gone—
Now we'll have some fun, fun, fun!

ALL: He's a bore, such a bore
Start the party, Barry's gone.

BEN: Barry is a hopeless geek.

ALL: Nonny, nonny, nonny, no.

BEN: Ugly, daft, and weak.

ALL: Nonny, nonny, nonny, no.

STEPH: Heartless—

GUY: Insensitive—

BART: Stupid—

BEN: And lame—

ALL: If he were someone else,
He would say the same!

(They dance together as the lights go out.)

Scene Four

A month later at the park. A park bench has been brought out. Lights come up. BEN *is sitting on the bench.* STEPH *comes onto the stage. He pretends not to see her. She kicks his foot. He laughs, grabs her, and they hug.*

BEN: God. It's good to see you.

STEPH: I know. It's good to be home.

BEN: *(Lets go of her. Stands back a little and looks at her.)* Did you get my message?

STEPH: Yes, but I couldn't get away from everyone. How long have you been waiting?

BEN: A couple of minutes. *(Pause.)* Okay. An hour . . . maybe two.

STEPH: I'm sorry.

BEN: It's all right. September is nice. I like being outside.

STEPH: *(They both sit down.)* I really missed you. *(Takes a deep breath.)*

It's so nice to be sitting in one spot. Grandpa and Grandma are on speed or something. They wore me out.

BEN: Well—

STEPH: Well—

BEN: Tell me about it.

STEPH: *(She starts to take off her shoes, peels down her socks.)* It was incredible. I've never felt so free. We would just go someplace, and if we didn't like it, we'd hop on a train and leave. *(She pulls a brown paper cutout in the shape of her foot out of her sock.)*

BEN: What's that? *(Takes the cutout from her hand, holds it up.)*

STEPH: That was Grandpa's idea. He saw it on *Merv Griffin*. He said that if you cut out grocery bags in the shape of your feet and wear them under your socks, you won't get jet lag.

BEN: Did it work?

STEPH: *(Lets out a little laugh.)* I did it for Grandpa. He did pay for the trip.

BEN: So, what was the most interesting thing that happened to you?

STEPH: Oh . . . I think it was how, wherever I went, I kind of wanted to melt into that culture . . . sort of disappear. You know, start dressing and acting like those people.

BEN: Like pretend you weren't with your grandpa and grandma.

STEPH: No. They were fun. Fun and fast. They wanted their money's worth out of everything. *(Pause.)* So, what did you do this summer?

BEN: I've been working a lot. It has been incredibly boring. I'm not trying to make you feel guilty or anything.

STEPH: It's all right. I'm through feeling guilty about anything.

BEN: Good.

STEPH: So, how's what's his name?

BEN: I haven't talked to him in about a month. *(Silence.)*

STEPH: Did you give him that one address?

BEN: Yes. *(Pause.)* Did you ever write him?

STEPH: No.

BEN: Stephanie?

STEPH: What?

BEN: You two are so stupid.

STEPH: How so?

BEN: I mean . . . both of you. You're going to regret not keeping in touch with each other. Just listen to me for a minute. You . . . you two are so stubborn. You know, it wasn't his fault alone that you . . . whatever. I mean—

STEPH: Listen, Ben. I know what you are trying to do. It's all right. Both of us will live.

BEN: I know . . . but . . . when you have friends, you shouldn't just drop them.

STEPH: Ben, I'm only eighteen. I'm young. I don't feel anything for him anymore.

BEN: I'm not talking about love. I'm talking about— *(Stops.)* When certain people get together and they talk, just being around each other . . . it's like . . . sparks. You can see that energy . . . you know . . . they just sort of—

STEPH: And Barry and I spark when we're together?

BEN: Yes. Sort of. You kind of fuel each other. But what I'm saying is that you should just remember, because twenty years from now . . .

(He stops as BARRY comes onstage. STEPH doesn't look at BARRY.)

BEN: I've got to go. *(He kisses her on the cheek.)* It was great talking to you.

BARRY: *(before BEN exits)* Ben? I'm sorry—

BEN: It's okay. *(He leaves.)*

BARRY: *(Walks up to the bench.)* Hi. I wanted to talk to you before you left for school.

STEPH: That's good.

BARRY: I missed . . . *(pause)* I miss—

STEPH: *(Cuts him off.)* So. How was your summer?

BARRY: It was all right.

STEPH: Good.

BARRY: How was the trip?

STEPH: Good.

BARRY: So. When do you go to school?

STEPH: Next weekend. How about you?

BARRY: Week after.

STEPH: Oh. *(Pauses.)* Did you finish your play?

BARRY: Sent it off today.

STEPH: Great. That's really great. Do you think you'll win?

BARRY: No. But I'm glad I tried. At least I won't regret it someday.

STEPH: Barry, I'm sorry for slamming you before I left.

BARRY: No. It was my fault. I deserved it. *(Pause.)* Steph. I don't want to regret anything . . . ever—

STEPH: Me neither.

BARRY: I have to say something.

STEPH: No. Barry . . . please, I have to go.

BARRY: I have to, Steph. After you left, I realized what a jerk I was. I have been afraid my entire life of ever telling anyone how I felt about them. No. Not just telling someone, but giving them a part of myself. I know it sounds cheesy, but—

STEPH: Barry . . . don't.

BARRY: Just listen. *(She gets up.)* I love you. Maybe not in the way you would have wanted me to . . . but I don't know. *(She starts to go.)* Wait! I have to know how you feel.

STEPH: I'm sorry. I don't think I feel for you the way I did before. Because . . . you have to understand . . . it hurts too much. I think I would rather hate you than fall in love with you again.

BARRY: Why?

STEPH: *(Looks at him.)* Because it's too much.

BARRY: I've figured out a lot of things this summer. The people you know . . . they are the most important thing in your life. You can either hide from them or be willing to— *(Stops.)* I'm not afraid of being hurt!

(She runs offstage. He watches her, then walks over to the bench and sits. Sad music comes up softly. BARRY *looks at the audience.)*

BARRY: In school they told me a play was a plot, characters, and action. But I have discovered that it is far more. I think that if someone goes through the trouble to write a play, even if everyone hates it, if one person is touched by something said, it's worth the trouble. Because the most important things a writer can write about are those which happen to him . . . really happen. *(Holds up his arms.)* I wrote a play! *(Looks down.)* But what happened to the happy ending?

(As the music rises to its ending, STEPH walks onto the stage. She goes up to the bench and sits down next to BARRY. He stares at her as if seeing a dream . . . an image . . . a character in his imagination. Behind them, a curtain rises, unveiling the scrim. We see a field . . . a house on a hill . . . trees . . . and the sun going down. Blackout.)

NOBLE MASON SMITH

(1987) Then . . .

When I was a very young boy, a psychic prophesied to my parents that in my life I would be speaking to a great number of people. My dad assumed this meant I was to be a door-to-door vacuum salesman. Fortunately this has not come to pass. The Indian mystics warn, "Whatever you desire will come to you." Well, I wished to be a writer. It was a yearning realized with the winning of the Young Playwrights Festival. The experience, however fantastic, was painful. I hated New York. If I could do it again, I would probably still hate New York, but certainly then I was too young to enjoy being on my own in such a monumental place. It was, though, one of the most thrilling events of my life to actually see real, live people live my words. Everyone at Playwrights Horizons was thoroughly professional, maybe a little too professional. The script went through numerous changes—albeit good ones. But the pressure I sometimes felt to succeed was so great, it made me wish I had never written the ridiculous thing after all. For me, working with professional actors and a talented director was fantastic. Several of the funniest lines in the play were made up by the actors. This is something most writers will never admit. They will say, and I agree, that the play is a vehicle, and without the initial work, none of the additional things would ever have been invented. But I must say, actors are imaginative people, and I was enthusiastic to let them develop their characters, to grow and make them into something personal and creative.

The day after opening night I was bombarded with opportunities. On the same afternoon, I met and signed with an agent, pitched story ideas to a cheesy TV executive, and met with an editor at Samuel French to have my play published. On the way back to my apartment I was grinning like a fool. And why shouldn't I be happy? I thought. I had seen my name in *The New York Times*—a good review at that! I was going to be a published author. I was going to have an agent . . . MORE PLAYS! SCREENPLAYS! MONEY! NO MORE COLLEGE! I'LL TRAVEL THE WORLD! Suddenly, an odd-looking man stepped out of the awning of a building. He had scraggly hair, a bloated face, and distant eyes. He staggered in front of me. I stopped for a moment. He looked at me and grinned, held out his hand. "I'm just a playwright down on his luck," he muttered. I felt a rush of adrenaline in my chest. I walked away quickly. How about that? I thought. That was so profound, I couldn't even have written anything profounder! I shuddered at this strange meeting and took it as a voice of wisdom from on high.

I have written several screenplays, two plays, and lots of garbage since my New York days. I am a senior at the University of Michigan. I'm still waiting to score again.

. . . And Now

In September of 1991 I went back to New York for the tenth anniversary of the Young Playwrights Festival. I got to see a great production of an excerpt of my play done at a Broadway theater. I also got to hold Alfred Uhry's Oscar for *Driving Miss Daisy*. He gave me some good advice too:

> ME: *(whining)* I want to be a writer but I can't sell anything!
>
> ALFRED: *(scoffing)* You little #$%¢! *(Exasperated.)* You're only twenty-three! What do you expect? *(Shakes his head.)* You little . . . *(Continues good-natured verbal beating.)*

I'm writing constantly and looking forward to the day when I can pay my rent with money I made doing something I love.

FIXED UP
A Play in Two Acts

by
TISH DURKIN
(age sixteen when play was written)
Essex Falls, New Jersey

∎

Fixed Up was performed at the Public Theater in New York City, May 9 through 20, 1984. It was directed by Shelly Raffle, and the dramaturge was Wendy Wasserstein. Loren Sherman designed the sets, costumes were by Patricia McGourty, Mal Sturchio was the lighting designer, and Bill Dreisbach the sound designer. The production stage manager was Esther Cohen.

The cast:

LAURA . . . . *Ellen Mareneck*
JEFFREY . . . . *Marc Epstein*

ACT ONE

The prom.

   LAURA *and* JEFFREY, *two adolescents of reasonably good looks, enter to-gether. She is wearing a typical pastel-colored prom dress; he a black tuxedo. As they arrive at the formally laid table for two, he pulls out her chair. No other tables are evident to the audience.*

LAURA: *(tucking her skirt under the chair)* Thank you.

JEFFREY: *(seating himself)* Uh—no problem.

LAURA: *(slight pause)* They picked a nice place for the prom, didn't they?

JEFFREY: Yes, yes. I like the, uh, walls. The walls are a nice color of . . .

LAURA: Gray.

JEFFREY: Right. *(Slight pause.)* They're—distinctive.

LAURA: I heard the band was good too. *(Craning her neck.)* It's hard to tell from here.

JEFFREY: They did give us one of the more—private—tables.

(Silence.)

JEFFREY: Uh—you look very nice tonight.

LAURA: Thank you.

JEFFREY: That's a nice dress. I like it.

LAURA: Do you *really*?

JEFFREY: Sure . . .

LAURA: My mother picked it out. I wasn't allowed to have my first choice.

JEFFREY: You weren't?

LAURA: No, and I loved it too. It was black, floor-length; this terrific satin . . . no straps and a slit. You should've seen it.

JEFFREY: *(with feeling)* Yeah . . . but that's a nice dress too.

(Silence.)

LAURA: I hear you're going to the Massachusetts Institute of Technology.

JEFFREY: Yeah. They, uh, call it MIT . . . for short.

LAURA: Oh, I *know*. That's so great.

JEFFREY: Thanks.

LAURA: Where else?

JEFFREY: Excuse me?

LAURA: Where else did you apply? I mean, you must've tried some-place besides MIT, unless your uncle owns it or something.

JEFFREY: *(uncomfortably)* Oh . . . Yale, Harvard, Tufts, Notre Dame, and Brown.

LAURA: What a laundry list!

JEFFREY: Do you know where you'd like to go?

LAURA: Anyplace that'll take me.

JEFFREY: That narrows it right down.

LAURA: Oh, it *does*. I'm not very academic.

JEFFREY: Well, what's your lowest grade?

LAURA: A-minus.

JEFFREY: Oh, you should be *petrified*.

LAURA: That's a regular school A-minus. If I ever went to a prep school like yours, I'd be lucky to pull C's! *(Eager to change the subject.)* Listen, I meant to tell you before. I'm *really sorry* about the scene at my house.

JEFFREY: Scene? That wasn't really a . . . scene.

LAURA: My mother always says things like that when dates come to the house.

JEFFREY: She does?

LAURA: I mean, the first *time* dates come to the house. She wouldn't do that to *you* again, if you were to— God, I'm sorry about my father.

JEFFREY: No problem.

LAURA: He just likes to be firm about things. I'm sure he didn't mean to get so . . . graphic.

JEFFREY: Hey, don't worry about it. I didn't mind at all. Your little brother's got strong fists, though. In a few years I wouldn't want to meet him in a dark alley!

LAURA: Her.

JEFFREY: What?

LAURA: Her; that's my sister Margaret.

JEFFREY: You're kidding, right? . . . Oh, boy. . . .

LAURA: It's a perfectly natural mistake; she's very masculine.

(Silence.)

LAURA: Do you think people look like their names?

JEFFREY: I guess so.

LAURA: *(thoughtfully)* You don't look like a Jeffrey.

JEFFREY: No?

LAURA: No, you look like a—a James, or Timothy. *(Exuberantly.)* That's it! You look like a Timothy!

JEFFREY: A Timothy?

LAURA: Yeah.

JEFFREY: *(uneasily)* What does a Timothy look like?

LAURA: Oh, tall, thin, clean-cut, kind of awkward, and— Do I look like a Laura?

JEFFREY: I couldn't say.

LAURA: Do I look like what you *thought* I was going to?

JEFFREY: Well, no.

LAURA: Really?

JEFFREY: No.

LAURA: Why? What did you think I was going to look like?

JEFFREY: Well . . .

LAURA: What did Ellis say?

JEFFREY: He said you had a nice personality.

LAURA: Yeah?

JEFFREY: He said you were fun to be with.

LAURA: What else?

JEFFREY: He said you were one of the nicest girls he knew.

LAURA: So . . .

JEFFREY: *(matter-of-factly)* I thought you were a dog.

LAURA: *(coughs)* Did he tell you I play tennis?

JEFFREY: No.

LAURA: Do you play tennis?

JEFFREY: No.

LAURA: *(hopefully)* Soccer? I play soccer.

JEFFREY: I think I saw you on the field once.

LAURA: I knew you played soccer! I was captain this year!

JEFFREY: I was walking the dog.

LAURA: Well . . . I didn't like it that much, anyway. Do you . . . like . . . movies?

JEFFREY: Sure.

LAURA: I'm mad about them. Especially the old ones, with Bergman and Bacall. The old stars had something about them. Bette Davis could say more inhaling tobacco than most could say in years of dialogue!

JEFFREY: I go for Raquel Welch myself.

LAURA: I guess there's something about her too.

JEFFREY: Yeah, and it's got nothing to do with tobacco.

LAURA: I *love* Paul Newman.

JEFFREY: He's okay.

LAURA: And Dustin Hoffman. And— *(At this point she begins to laugh hysterically.)* —and ROBERT REDFORD!

JEFFREY: Is something funny here?

LAURA: No; it's just . . . ROBERT REDFORD . . .

JEFFREY: What?

LAURA: ELLIS SAID YOU LOOKED LIKE HIM! *(She bursts out laughing and then shuts up abruptly.)* Well, you sort of do. *(Pause.)* I'm so glad you wore basic black.

JEFFREY: Well, I figured it was a good tux color and everything—

LAURA: Oh, it's the *only* tux color! Ellis told me you were okay, but I was terrified you might show up in something technicolor . . . banana yellow, or crushed velvet. I would've *dropped dead.*

JEFFREY: *(with a nervous chuckle)* I'm glad I wore it, too, then— I mean, who wants to slab out at the prom, right?

(Silence. JEFFREY, *with some effort, pulls a small flask out from his cummerbund and tips it toward her glass. He speaks now somewhat hesitantly.)*

I brought something along to make the conversation sparkle?

LAURA: Is that a question or did you really?

JEFFREY: I did really.

LAURA: *(having taken a sip)* My GOD, what *is* that?

JEFFREY: Dewar's.

LAURA: What's in it?

JEFFREY: Dewar's.

LAURA: Oh, well—I guess it is dangerous to mix drinks!

(She laughs at herself, and he returns the flask from whence it came.)

JEFFREY: So you play soccer.

LAURA: Well, yeah.

JEFFREY: You're *good* too.

LAURA: Not really.

JEFFREY: Two goals, two assists—AVERAGE—for every game? That's *good.*

LAURA: Well, it's okay. I mean, there are people a lot better than me. *(Pause.)* Hey, how did you know?

JEFFREY: Know what?

LAURA: Two goals, two assists.

JEFFREY: Oh, the newspaper. I saw your picture on the sports page.

LAURA: Oh, God—I was sweating and my shorts were too tight—

JEFFREY: And your nostrils were intimidating! *(Flares his.)*

LAURA: Oh, I just hated that coming out.

JEFFREY: Come on, it was great. . . . Is your hair different since then?

LAURA: Yeah, it's been washed.

JEFFREY: No, no, it's—I don't know . . . fluffy.

LAURA: Fluffy?

JEFFREY: Yeah—sort of like you could land something in it.

(Silence.)

LAURA: I do wish we were sitting with some other people. Not that this is *bad* or anything, but . . .

JEFFREY: I was wondering why we were alone.

LAURA: Well, to get seated with your friends you had to bring in your bid money on time; and since I didn't have a date till the last minute . . .

JEFFREY: Ellis told me you were going with your boyfriend till—

LAURA: That's right, but I hadn't brought in the money yet because I wasn't sure John would go.

JEFFREY: You weren't sure your boyfriend would take you to your *prom?*

LAURA: Well, he—he hates proms. John would've taken me, but he hates proms.

JEFFREY: *(dryly)* I can't imagine why.

LAURA: He's very outdoorsy . . . and very casual, and tuxes make him itch. Not that it matters now anyway, because he's sick as a dog.

JEFFREY: What's the matter with him?

LAURA: Typhoid.

JEFFREY: Your boyfriend has TYPHOID?

LAURA: *(coolly)* A mild case, yes.

JEFFREY: And you came here?

LAURA: Well, my mother made me. I'm ready to go to pieces, really, but my mother made me.

JEFFREY: Didn't she *understand?*

LAURA: She . . . doesn't like John. She doesn't like my boyfriend being so much older than me.

JEFFREY: How old is he?

LAURA: Twenty-two.

JEFFREY: Twenty-two?

LAURA: Well, he's immature.

JEFFREY: Did he go to college?

LAURA: Of course.

JEFFREY: Where?

LAURA: The—University of—Madrid.

JEFFREY: In SPAIN, Madrid?

LAURA: Yes. He has family there.

JEFFREY: How did you meet him?

LAURA: I met him—I met him at church.

JEFFREY: Church?

LAURA: Yes. He . . . had no money for the collection, and I gave him a quarter.

JEFFREY: And you've been going out ever since?

LAURA: Yes.

JEFFREY: And I'm here with you.

LAURA: You got it.

JEFFREY: Ellis told me his name was Matt.

LAURA: Who?

JEFFREY: The baseball player. He ripped his calf sliding into third. So then of course he couldn't come to the prom, and of course you needed a date, because of course you had paid all this money.

LAURA: You must admit, Ellis is creative. . . . May I have some more of that?

JEFFREY: *(pulling out flask and pouring)* Be my guest.

LAURA: So, what are you majoring in?

JEFFREY: Major in chemistry, minor in German.

LAURA: *(having taken a sip, smacks her lips)* German. I never liked German.

JEFFREY: You took it?

LAURA: No; I mean the way it sounds. Angry, or something.

JEFFREY: Oh, I find Germans friendly.

LAURA: How can you tell when they spit constantly? *(Exaggerated imitation.)* Ach and *ich*. Look at the way they say hello. *GUTEN TAG.* If you didn't know any better, you'd think it was "Shove it, buddy."

(Silence.)

JEFFREY: Well, you're quiet all of a sudden.

LAURA: Shock of the month.

JEFFREY: No, no . . .

LAURA: Gets on your nerves, doesn't it?

JEFFREY: No, no, not at all . . .

LAURA: Come on, Jeffrey, I *know*. I spoke my first sentence, for God's sake, and kept going. When I was three, my foot took up permanent residence in my mouth. *(Slower now.)* Yeah, I say too much. *(Beginning to babble.)* I mean, I know I do, even as I'm doing it, but I can't help it—and then after I've been blabbering on about nothing, which is what I usually do blabber on about, I feel so stupid. *(Sheepishly.)* Like now.

JEFFREY: There's really no need to feel stupid—

LAURA: *(ignoring this, as if just realizing something)* Funny, isn't it? I mean, I *hate* small talk. And it's what I do best. *(Flippant again.)* If I thought half as much as I talked—

JEFFREY: You'd need years of therapy. So quit apologizing for nothing.

(Silence.)

JEFFREY: So, do you have your license yet?

LAURA: No.

JEFFREY: Do you drive?

LAURA: *(morosely)* No.

JEFFREY: *(after a pause)* Oh, well. It's not as great as you think it is. Having your license, I mean.

LAURA: No?

JEFFREY: You always get nailed for rides and things.

LAURA: I guess you would.

JEFFREY: You can come and go when you want, though.

LAURA: THAT would be heaven.

JEFFREY: IF you can get the car. Usually I can get my dad's old Chrysler. I think Truman was in when they got it.

LAURA: They don't make 'em like they used to.

JEFFREY: If you had my car, you'd know why. I'm not complaining, though. It's a disaster, but it gets me where I want to go. *(Pause.)* Sometimes I just take that old thing, and drive.

LAURA: By *yourself*?

JEFFREY: By myself. I just turn up the radio, turn down the windows, and *drive*.

LAURA: Why do you do that?

JEFFREY: To be alone, I guess.

LAURA: Can't you be alone without one-twenty to the gallon?

JEFFREY: Well, if I'm home I've got to be doing something. Help my dad, hit the books—anything. Get something accomplished. When you're standing still, see, there's no excuse for wasting time. But in the *car*—in the car, you can't *do* anything else. You've got your two hands on the wheel, your eyes on the road, and your head wherever you feel like putting it.

LAURA: Your head wherever you feel like putting it. I'll drink to that!

JEFFREY: *(pouring)* I'm glad to see I brought your favorite.

LAURA: *(solemnly)* Actually, I *don't drink*.

JEFFREY: Really.

LAURA: Oh, I sip every so often . . . but I *don't drink.*

JEFFREY: Yeah, well, some people sip more than others.

LAURA: And I only sip certain things. Champagne! Wine!

JEFFREY: Scotch straight up!

LAURA: That's this, right? Yeah, this is okay. *(Pause.)* You aren't drinking any.

JEFFREY: No, I'm not.

LAURA: Why not?

JEFFREY: It—uh—makes me stupid.

LAURA: *(sadly)* Oh.

(Silence. She sinks into a sort of lull of depression.)

JEFFREY: So . . . do you have any brothers or sisters? Besides the one that attack—I, uh, met?

LAURA: One other sister.

JEFFREY: Really?

LAURA: Wendy. She's two.

JEFFREY: Oh?

LAURA: She drools a lot.

JEFFREY: Hmmm.

LAURA: She only knows two words. *Mommy* and *Fruit Loop. (Ponderously.)* I guess that counts as three words, doesn't it?

JEFFREY: I guess.

LAURA: *(after a pause)* You know what bothers me about little kids?

JEFFREY: They eat with their mouths open and smell bad.

LAURA: No.

JEFFREY: *No?* They can get downright revolting. My sister Ellen—she's five now—she went through this whole thing about sticking stuff up her nose. If it could fit, in it went.

LAURA: But you know what really gets me about little kids?

JEFFREY: What?

LAURA: They're so goddamned . . . happy.

JEFFREY: They've got one hell of a nerve, the little snots.

LAURA: I'm serious. It's not even *that* they're happy; it's *why.* Take Wendy. Saturday morning, it's not even light yet—and she's busting out of her Batman jammies over Josie and the Pussycats. Give her a crayon and she'll spend the whole day, singing and drawing on herself.

JEFFREY: Ellen sings in the bath. . . .

LAURA: *(with much more contempt than appropriate)* You should see her eat an Oreo . . .

JEFFREY: She, uh, likes to run around in the buff . . .

LAURA: . . . can't do it without that goddamned song. I won't give her cookies and milk at the same time. It's *suicide.*

JEFFREY: Well . . .

LAURA: Doesn't it bother you? I mean, they're short and loud and hang up the phone on people . . . swallow nickels and put peanut butter on the dog . . . can't tell a totalitarian from a Twinkie—

JEFFREY: They're not supposed to!

LAURA: It isn't fair. It just isn't fair.

JEFFREY: What are you talking about, fair?

LAURA: Nothing, I guess— Listen, Jeffrey, would you mind if I left you alone for a minute?

JEFFREY: *(smiling)* Not at all.

LAURA: *(tightly)* Then I think I'll go . . . freshen up a bit.

JEFFREY: You go ahead.

LAURA: *(rising)* Don't go away.

JEFFREY: Don't worry. *(Turning his head.)* I can't.

(Exit LAURA.*)*

ACT TWO

LAURA *is returning.*
    JEFFREY *has remained at the table.*

JEFFREY: Dinner was pretty good.

LAURA: I'm sorry I missed it. It wasn't my fault, though. I was held up by Mrs. Straussingheissen.

JEFFREY: Who?

LAURA: Mrs. Straussingheissen. My health teacher. Disgusting woman.

JEFFREY: Really.

LAURA: *(with tipsy indignation)* She wasn't going to let me back into the prom! She said I had been drinking!

JEFFREY: *(with mock astonishment)* No!

LAURA: I don't know why they had her at the door anyway, the old liver-spotted earthworm!

(Silence during which LAURA *huffs in anger and* JEFFREY *becomes nervous.)*

JEFFREY: So . . . do you want to dance?

LAURA: *(dreamily)* Oh, Jeffrey, do you *dance*?

JEFFREY: Not a step, but it's got to be easier than this.

LAURA: I've been waiting for you to ask me all night.

JEFFREY: It probably wasn't worth the wait, but why not?

LAURA: Oh, I'd *love* to dance, Jeffrey, but I'm too sleepy.

JEFFREY: You're sleepy?

LAURA: No . . . but if I get up, the room might take off.

JEFFREY: You didn't drink *that* much.

LAURA: Oh, yes, I did.

JEFFREY: *(almost hissing)* You drank in the *bathroom*?

LAURA: No!

JEFFREY: Thank God.

LAURA: However, on the way back . . .

JEFFREY: I don't believe it.

LAURA: I'm not that far gone, but I don't want to take any chances. I mean, you probably have to take that tux back tomorrow, and I wouldn't want to . . . get anything on it.

JEFFREY: *(muttering)* I should've known . . . you smell like eighty proof Chanel. Here, have some ice cream. It'll coat your stomach.

LAURA: Is it good?

JEFFREY: It's not exactly Mom's homemade, but I don't think you'll notice.

LAURA: Does your mother make ice cream?

JEFFREY: Yeah, she does. Sometimes.

LAURA: That's so American.

JEFFREY: Just call me Davy Crockett.

LAURA: What's your favorite flavor?

JEFFREY: Vanilla.

LAURA: Vanilla! You must be a conservative.

JEFFREY: I mean, *great* vanilla. All I have to do is think of summer and I can smell great vanilla.

LAURA: I smell salt.

JEFFREY: The air at the beach?

LAURA: The stuff on my french fries . . .

JEFFREY: Just think: two more weeks till high school is mere memory.

LAURA: Until September, anyway. We're going to the shore.

JEFFREY: So are we.

LAURA: Hey, have you ever heard of Bostwick's-on-the-Boardwalk? Now, *that's* great vanilla.

JEFFREY: Heard of it? I just about live there.

LAURA: Did you ever have the Holy Moses?

JEFFREY: I tried it once, but halfway through I almost died. All that pineapple sauce.

LAURA: I polished off two in one sitting.

JEFFREY: How'd you manage that?

LAURA: Lotsa practice. . . . One of these days we ought to get together and pig out.

JEFFREY: God, I can't wait for that vacation.

LAURA: It's kind of a headache, though. I mean, have you ever been to the beach with a little kid? They're *vicious* with water and sand.

JEFFREY: Here we go again.

LAURA: *(maliciously)* You know what's the worst thing you can do to a little kid at the beach?

JEFFREY: What?

LAURA: Knock down their sandcastle! I mean, they'll fry themselves alive, get eight pounds of sand in their pants, and still they sit there

—piling it and molding it and patting it together. Making a moat. Thinking. And then you come along and jump in it, tear it to absolute bits. All that work, all that tender imagination—reduced to a zillion grains of plain, ordinary sand. *(Pause.)* It's a great feeling.

JEFFREY: You really do hate them, don't you?

LAURA: *(wearily)* Oh, I'm just jealous.

JEFFREY: *(exasperated)* WHY?

LAURA: *(carelessly)* Oh, I don't know . . . *(Grandly.)* Their perpetual oblivion. That's as good a reason as any, isn't it? Per-pet-u-al oblivion. They like everything, believe everything—then they get to grammar school, and that's the end of that.

JEFFREY: Okay, so you find out Walt Disney isn't God. You can't find the Answer to Life in a box of Coco Puffs. It's not exactly the end of the world.

LAURA: *(pointedly)* I'm just not that eager to get out of school this year, okay, Jeffrey?

JEFFREY: The idea of summer does not excite you at *all*?

LAURA: Oh, I'm shaking all over. How about you?

JEFFREY: Yes!

LAURA: Why?

JEFFREY: Because the commencement of summer conversely entails the conclusion of academic pursuits during an interval commonly referred to as vacation. You know, "no more pencils, no more books"? Laura, the last day of school is like having been in a cage all year and then watching the wires snap.

LAURA: *(sarcastically)* What do you do once they free you, Jeffrey? Climb on cars at Jungle Habitat?

JEFFREY: Nothing, Laura; I just do *nothing*.

LAURA: Really? No cancer research for the next couple of weeks?

JEFFREY: Oh, boy.

LAURA: What?

JEFFREY: It's about to happen. I can smell it.

LAURA: What?

JEFFREY: Just say what you were going to say.

LAURA: I simply thought, Jeffrey, that with your brains—

JEFFREY: THERE IT IS!

LAURA: *(jumps in her seat)* What?

JEFFREY: The dreaded skeleton in my closet: brains!

LAURA: Are you telling me you're ashamed of your intelligence?

JEFFREY: No, just not proud of it.

LAURA: Don't be ridiculous.

JEFFREY: Are you proud of having ten toes?

LAURA: Of course not.

JEFFREY: Why not?

LAURA: I was *born* with—

JEFFREY: There it is. Why be proud of something I had nothing to do with?

LAURA: Be real. You talk about an IQ as if it's a disease.

JEFFREY: Some guys have athlete's foot; I have—

LAURA: Brains?

JEFFREY: Of course, brains. What are we talking about here?

LAURA: Jeffrey, I don't think it's right to compare your intelligence with—with the fungus on the bottom of some jock's foot. Don't tell me it's no advantage to be smart.

JEFFREY: An advantage, sure. But it's not *righteous*! Think about it. I could be the worst sleaze on the face of the earth, and it'd be okay because of my almighty SAT's.

LAURA: I don't want to sound nosy or anything, but—how good are your grades? I mean, are they *obscenely* high?

JEFFREY: You know how you get good grades, Laura? You tell 'em what they want to hear, and you tell 'em in a vocabulary they don't understand. *That's* the big secret.

LAURA: I'm sorry. I just assumed—

JEFFREY: Don't be sorry. Everybody assumes everything about everybody else, and they're always wrong. It's how we get through life.

(Silence.)

LAURA: *(getting up)* Oh, they're crowning the prom queen. I wonder who it is?

JEFFREY: I can't see either. I think she's blond, though.

LAURA: *(after a pause)* It was really nice of you to come, Jeffrey.

JEFFREY: Oh, it's my pleasure.

LAURA: I know it was very last minute, and you're great for doing it.

JEFFREY: Well, I'm having a good time.

LAURA: Oh, you don't have to say that.

JEFFREY: I'm not just saying that. I'm having a good time—not great, but good.

LAURA: I'm glad. A little surprised, but glad.

JEFFREY: Why are you surprised? Aren't you enjoying yourself?

LAURA: *(eagerly)* Oh, I am! I just didn't think you were.

JEFFREY: What gave you that idea?

LAURA: Well, you know, I'm not the kind of girl that— *(Breathes in, then gives a small smile as she speaks.)* I'm not exactly Raquel Welch.

JEFFREY: True.

LAURA: *(ignoring this)* I'm sure you know a lot of people who are more together; like, more sophisticated than I am. Everybody says I'm young for my age.

JEFFREY: Please don't do this to yourself.

LAURA: *(casually, but conveying her insecurity)* One of these days I'm going to be so gorgeous and so successful nobody in this room will recognize me. *(Chuckling, but with a slight bite to it.)* Dream on, Laura—

JEFFREY: WOULD YOU QUIT PUTTING YOURSELF THROUGH THE BLENDER? You're annoying me!

LAURA: I'm sorry.

JEFFREY: And stop it with the apologies, would you please? I'm surprised you haven't choked on them yet!

LAURA: Okay, okay! *(Slight pause.)* I know what you're thinking.

JEFFREY: This I've got to hear.

LAURA: You're thinking, "I can't believe Ellis put me up to this." You're thinking you can't wait to get this thing over with, and get the tux off, and . . . watch *David Letterman*. And tell your friends about this tomorrow night. I am no fool, Jeffrey. I know what reality is.

JEFFREY: You have no CONTACT with reality!

LAURA: Tell me about it. You know what reality is? Reality is knowing that just to find an ESCORT—not even a date, just someone to be *seen* with you—you have to dig somebody out from under a rock. And when that didn't work, you had to find a *friend* to dig *for* you. You know how that feels?

JEFFREY: Would you calm down?

LAURA: It feels *lousy*, Jeffrey. REALLY LOUSY.

JEFFREY: It's a high-school prom, for cryin' out loud! What's the worst thing that could have happened? You'd have spent tonight attacking your little sister! I'd feel sorry for her, not you!

LAURA: *(breathing hard, almost shuddering)* No, Jeffrey. The worst thing that could have happened already did. The worst thing is the questions—questions I ask myself, day in and day out. "Am I fat?" "Am I ugly?" "Do I have any acne I didn't know about?" OR—try this one on for size—is it ME? And there's no diet, and no astringent, and no mouthwash that can help me. I'm too far gone for that! What I need is a new personality. Where do I find the catalog for that? Try it sometime, Jeff. It tickles.

JEFFREY: *(slowly)* You are really, honest-to-God, certifiably nuts!

LAURA: SO THAT'S WHAT SCARES 'EM OFF!

JEFFREY: You know what you are, Laura? You are greedy.

LAURA: That's a new one.

JEFFREY: Yeah, it's a new one. You want everything. You want cover-girl bone structure, and thighs you could wrap a pinky around twice, and one of those perky party personalities so you can be popularity queen of the world! And then you want to get into every school with ivy crawling up it, and you want to kick the soccer ball from here to Helsinki. You don't just *want* perfection, Laura, you feel CHEATED without it!

LAURA: *(swallowing hard)* YOU—

JEFFREY: FACE IT. You're not Cheryl Tiegs and Helen Keller rolled into one. Well, you're not a martyr, either, so stop acting so goddamned put-upon.

LAURA: Shut up, Jeffrey.

JEFFREY: Fine.

LAURA: Let me tell you a thing or two. You don't know what it's like. You don't have to sit around waiting for somebody—

JEFFREY: Neither do you!

LAURA: What are you talking about?

JEFFREY: I'm talking about Dating. *The Dating Game.* It's a canceled game show, not your *life,* for God's sake! What goes through your head? A guy is a guy. He's human. He breathes. He's probably got a few disgusting habits. But you act as if you haven't got a right arm until you find some schmuck to take you out—and then you feel lucky he'd give you the time of day, because you don't think you deserve any better. No wonder you come on like a cold salami on rye. You set yourself up for your own misery. *(Resigned.)* Well, drown in it.

LAURA: *(meekly)* Can we leave now?

JEFFREY: And you know why little kids are so goddamned happy, as you so poetically put it?

LAURA: I don't care—

JEFFREY: Because they haven't got a checklist for what they're supposed to be. How *can* you be happy with a mirror to your face twenty-four hours a day? How can you look at anything when you're so busy looking at yourself and taking potshots at what you see?

(Her head is trembling visibly.)

JEFFREY: *(panicked)* Oh, God, don't cry . . . don't! . . . You're crying. I made her cry. *(Pause. Then softly pleading.)* Listen, I didn't mean it. I—I was only making conversation. Here, wipe your nose.

(She does not take the napkin he offers her.)

LAURA: They'll charge me for the linen.

JEFFREY: Come on, stop crying. People are going to pass us on the way out; they'll think I hit you. *(Desperately.)* Have some ice cream. You never finished your ice cream. . . . Please? *(Raises spoon, as if to feed a baby.)* Comin' down and it's headin' for the tunnel . . .

chug-a-chug-a-chug-a CHOO! CHOO! *(Glob of ice cream slides off spoon as it stops short in front of her tightly closed mouth.)*

LAURA: *(reacting spontaneously)* ACH—

JEFFREY: Oh, God. Now all I have to do is make you walk home.

(LAURA begins to laugh hysterically.)

JEFFREY: You're laughing? No, you're crying . . . no, I was right. You're laughing. Does the word *schizo* mean anything to you?

LAURA: This is the worst night of my life!

JEFFREY: You make a lot of sense.

LAURA: Vanilla ice cream is trickling down my abdomen. I cannot talk sense, Jeffrey.

JEFFREY: I'll have it cleaned.

LAURA: You are a piece of work . . . the only person I know who'll tear someone to shreds and then come out with "I'll have it cleaned."

JEFFREY: Okay, clean it yourself.

(They laugh.)

LAURA: Well, this has been interesting.

JEFFREY: That's safe to say.

LAURA: *(after a thoughtful pause)* Jeffrey? Are you scared?

JEFFREY: What is that supposed to—

LAURA: Are you?

JEFFREY: *(surprised by his own answer)* Yeah.

LAURA: I'm scared of the future.

JEFFREY: So is the rest of the world.

LAURA: *(carefully)* I'm scared of getting to the future and finding out that none of it is ever real.

JEFFREY: None of what?

LAURA: None of this—preparation. You're young, you spend your whole life looking *forward* to something. What if it's nothing? It really could be nothing, Jeffrey—like reading a brochure that says you're going to Paradise, and you wind up in the Holiday Inn. THE FUTURE, the great, perfect future. It's probably a lot of days, exactly like the ones we have now. And I'll spend all this time, running and rushing and cramming and making a good impression . . . and then one morning I'll wake up and see how dumb it was —how dumb *I* was—and I'll be the butt of this very obvious joke.

JEFFREY: Sometimes, when I'm stuck in the books—I mean, really crazy memorizing all those laws of chemistry and physiology—I get to thinking, This could all collapse. Some guy could come along and *disprove* the stuff to pieces. Make an idiot of Einstein and me both. And then what's all that agony going to be worth?

LAURA: Not a hill of beans, Jeffrey.

JEFFREY: But you know what the one great thing is?

LAURA: What?

JEFFREY: I don't care.

LAURA: What?

JEFFREY: I don't give a damn. I can't. *You* can't. Nobody can. Who'd spend sixty bucks for chicken croquettes and a table in Siberia? Who'd stick a shrub on her wrist and try to be Lauren Bacall? Who'd get anything done if they had to make sure it had *meaning* all the time?

LAURA: You know, you're right.

JEFFREY: Listen, I really feel bad about . . .

LAURA: What?

JEFFREY: Attacking you.

LAURA: Jeffrey, you haven't touched me all night.

JEFFREY: Verbally, I mean.

LAURA: Don't give it another thought.

JEFFREY: I only said it because—well, you've got a lot going for you, and you shouldn't swallow it so much.

LAURA: I got the message.

JEFFREY: I guess you did.

LAURA: Loud and clear.

JEFFREY: *(after a pause)* Sounds like they're doing the last dance . . . ? *(There is a hesitant invitation in his voice, to which they both wag their heads no.)* Well, then, I guess I'd better go find our coats.

LAURA: *(slightly disappointed)* Okay—have you got the tickets?

JEFFREY: I think so. *(Rises.)* I'll be right back. *(Starts to leave, then turns around.)* Hey—maybe we could find a Holy Moses someplace . . . without the pineapple sauce.

LAURA: I think I'd wear that well.

(Exit JEFFREY. LAURA, visibly brightened, picks up her still half-filled glass and looks at it for a second. Deciding to drink it, she gives an oh-why-not facial expression.)

Here's to you, Ellis.

CURTAIN

TISH DURKIN

(1985) Then . . .

At this point my "biography" is a lot of empty space waiting to be filled. The youngest of seven, I have lived in the same New Jersey house my whole life. I am interested in most things (except mathematics) and find that inquiry of any kind can turn itself back into writing of whatever form it wants to take—an essay, short story, or dialogue. Work in each of these areas only solidifies work in the others.

Since the staging of *Fixed Up* I have spent a summer in Strasbourg, France, and then a fall, winter, and spring at Yale, where I have done more reading than writing. Exposure to characters both between book covers and on the street has proven a real outing for my imagination but has left me at a loss on the question of the future. I hope it includes a pen in some essential spot, but my life changes faces more often than I change my sheets, so I am unqualified to comment.

About the Play

The Young Playwrights Festival always struck me as being fictional. I kept waiting for the odd quality of winning to rub off, but it never did. Instead, it expanded into the equally strange and lovely sensation of entering a world at once unknown and hospitable: Theater. It was real, I knew, but it never became quite plausible.

As a title, *Festival* is apt, for it hints at unreality. Like all pleasant exceptions—surprises and holidays—it is giddy and fantastic and filled with its own sense of being temporary. Even before it begins, there is regret for the moment when it will end. Like the best ride in the park, it is a taut wait, a decadent spin, an abrupt halt. A touch of vertigo. The giddiness fools itself, for a while, that it is still in motion, and lingers a little before it goes away.

A year of hindsight yields the glorious postscript: It is not missed. There is no time to pine after old graces. There is too much work. At the Festival *work* is freed from being a dishpan word, constantly begging to be interrupted. In theater, work is an interaction from which a fool would want to be distracted. It is concentration and energy and creation. It is the greatest fun, the grittiest satisfaction, the finest memory. It is the one rule less predictable than any exception. And unlike any piece of luck, work never runs out. The Festival offers a fine foreshadowing of what is real in theater. The variables change, but the process continues. Work provides the constant to which I can return, the temptation to try it again.

. . . *And Now*

Ballerinas know. If you fix your eyes on an unmoving object, you can spin very fast and never get dizzy.

Even before *Fixed Up* I had my unmoving object: writing. And since *Fixed Up* I have done a lot of spinning. I've started and finished college; traveled three times to Australia to explore an aboriginal story; sunned myself in the south of France. I've also temped and typed and waitressed. For magazine money, I've churned out blurbs, captions, capsules. I've gotten many rejections! And acceptances, and breaks, and gifts of encouragement.

I still write every single day. So every day I get frustrated. But I am always grateful to have my unmoving object. I can spin forever and never get dizzy.

TWICE SHY

by
DEBRA NEFF
(age eighteen when play was written)
Jamaica Estates, New York

■

Twice Shy was performed at Playwrights Horizons in New York City, September 12 through October 8, 1989. The director was Mark Brokaw, and Morgan Jenness was the playwright adviser. Sets were by Allen Moyer and costumes by Jess Goldstein. The lighting designer was Karl E. Haas, the sound designer was Janet Kalas. Mimi Apfel was the production stage manager.

The cast:

JONATHAN . . . . *Ray Cochran*
LOUISE . . . . *Katherine Hiler*
DESMOND . . . . *David Lansbury*
STEVEN . . . . *Mark W. Conklin*
COOKIE . . . . *Lauren Klein*

Prologue

The play begins in darkness, when LOUISE *enters, slams her fist on something, and shouts,*

LOUISE: I am tired of being a woman!

The lights come up suddenly on LOUISE *wincing and rubbing her hand. Blackout.*

Scene One

The apartment JONATHAN SEXTON *and* LOUISE COCO *share isn't too large but has good light. To the left is the living room. It's a typical college students' living room with details such as an old couch, a trunk used as a coffee table, a telephone, a couple of weird posters, some dirty dishes, some chairs that might have been bought at Azuma. There should be some doors off to the left: Jonathan's bedroom, Louise's bedroom, and the bathroom. Jonathan's bedroom might have an ACT UP poster on it. To the right is the kitchen. It's a small kitchen with limited cooking facilities but spotlessly clean. It might have a toaster and maybe a couple of boxes of herbal tea; definitely a coffee maker. It should also have a large table with bridge chairs that don't match set up around it. On this table there is a beautiful and elaborate flower arrangement.*

JONATHAN SEXTON *should be sitting at this table as the play begins. He has a huge pile of books in front of him and a mug of coffee.* JONATHAN *is twenty, and handsome in a very sweet sort of way. He is sweet, and very mellow. He never feels the need to please everyone. He is wearing oldish jeans, a T-shirt, Dr. Martens shoes. He should generally dress about this way.*

LOUISE COCO *enters fresh from the shower, but dressed. Louise is also twenty, kind of manic but very appealing. She laughs a lot, even at inappropriate moments. She is wearing black jeans, a T-shirt tucked in, black riding boots with her jeans tucked in, and a black motorcycle jacket that she never takes off as long as she's dressed. This is her uniform, and if she looks a little tough, it is only in order to feel more empowered. She looks at the flower arrangement.*

LOUISE: Is that your latest arrangement? It's really beautiful. Oh, good, you made coffee.

(JONATHAN *grunts at her. She pours herself a cup of coffee, then takes his mug and refills it as well. She takes out a carton of milk, sniffs it, makes a horrible face, and pours it down the sink. She takes both cups of coffee and puts them on the table.)*

LOUISE: I hope you didn't want milk in your coffee. It's sour.

JONATHAN: Coffee's stronger black.

LOUISE: Is that true?

JONATHAN: Well, it tastes viler, eviler black.

LOUISE: You want a bagel?

JONATHAN: We don't have any more.

LOUISE: Oh, dear. That means my mother's going to come visit, doesn't it?

JONATHAN: I don't understand why she won't tell us where in Boston she gets such good bagels.

LOUISE: How was your class? What's that class called again?

JONATHAN: "The Gentle Science of Floral Juxtaposition." It was good. We talked about color. Then I met Desmond downtown, and we went to a movie. Where were you? We wanted you to come.

LOUISE: You did? That's sweet. I had group and then I was in the library. Do you want pancakes?

JONATHAN: No, thanks, I really have to study. I have this engineering midterm tomorrow and . . .

LOUISE: You can study and eat, can't you?

JONATHAN: You sound like your mother.

LOUISE: If you don't want to be disturbed, why don't you just go lock yourself in your room?

JONATHAN: Desmond is still sleeping.

LOUISE: *(laughing)* Wait a minute. You're trying to throw me out of my own kitchen in my own apartment while Desy-wesy gets to sleep in?

JONATHAN: Um . . .

LOUISE: And you didn't ask me about group last night, or anything.

JONATHAN: How was group?

LOUISE: Group was fine.

JONATHAN: You always ask me to ask you about group, and then when I ask, all you say is, "Group was fine."

LOUISE: I just need to assure myself you're still interested. Well, at group we were talking about, you know, how we're all so angry at men. You know how I always say, "I hate men."

JONATHAN: Thanks.

LOUISE: Not you.

JONATHAN: It's always I hate men. Except you, Jonathan.

LOUISE: *Anyway,* what we were saying is that we should take the energy we put into being angry and use it to, um, change the world. So we all agreed to look into volunteer work.

JONATHAN: Is that going to be . . .

(DESMOND HARRIS, JONATHAN's lover, enters. He is older than JONATHAN and LOUISE, maybe twenty-six. He is a medical doctor, which he uses in combination with his extensive study of Asian medicine. He's very sincere. He is dressed in the softest, most comfortable-looking clothes you've ever seen. He kisses JONATHAN on the cheek.)

DESMOND: Good morning. . . . Did I just interrupt?

JONATHAN: No, of course not.

DESMOND: Oh, Jonathan. This flower arrangement is really beautiful. I think it's your best yet. You really captured the aesthetic best of the flowers, arranging them so that they complement each other yet never lose their own identity. The whole piece has a real feeling of . . . unity.

JONATHAN: Thank you, Des.

LOUISE: We always knew there was more to you than a future electrical engineer, Jonathan.

DESMOND: Oh, you're right, Louise. You're so right! I'm going to take a shower. Ugh, are you drinking coffee? Disgusting. And bad for you too.

(He leaves. JONATHAN gathers his books.)

LOUISE: I don't believe it. Your boyfriend just critiqued the centerpiece.

JONATHAN: And an excellent critique it was too.

LOUISE: You're not leaving.

JONATHAN: Yes, I am.

LOUISE: But I was talking to you.

JONATHAN: But, um, can it wait until tomorrow night? Because I am really stressed about this exam. . . .

LOUISE: No, it really can't wait, Jonathan, I was thinking . . .

(The doorbell rings. JONATHAN *goes into his bedroom, and* LOUISE *answers the door.* STEVEN LESTER, *an extremely attractive man, is standing outside.* STEVEN *is the sort of man one's mother would want one to date. He's about twenty-three or twenty-four, clean-cut.)*

STEVEN: Um, hi. Um, is Louise Coco here?

LOUISE: I am she, may I help you?

STEVEN: Is there another Louise Coco here?

LOUISE: What?

STEVEN: Well, a woman who said her name was Louise Coco hit me with her car this morning. She said I should stop by here and she'd give me money to fix my car.

LOUISE: Oh, wait a minute. Was she wearing red? Driving a red Saab?

STEVEN: . . . I think so.

LOUISE: That would be my mother. You'd better come in and I'll call her.

*(*STEVEN *comes inside, and just as* LOUISE *is about to close the door,* LOUISE*'s mother,* COOKIE COCO, *rushes in, grabs* LOUISE, *and starts walking across the room holding her hands. She does not see* STEVEN. *She is in her mid to late forties and is unfortunate living proof that you* CAN *have it all. She is dressed in a power-red Chanel suit, possibly real, and if she is a little overbearing, you'll have to excuse her. She didn't get where she is today by sitting on her bottom and letting life come to her.)*

COOKIE: Loula, you won't believe what happened to me this morning, I hit the nicest young man in my car. So I told him to come over here. I figured that was the best way for you to meet him. His name is Steven, so why don't you just go put on a pretty scarf, maybe a little lipstick?

LOUISE: *(laughing)* Is this the man, Mommy?

COOKIE: *(She turns around and sees Steven.)* Oh.

STEVEN: Hi again.

COOKIE: Oh, I see you've met.

LOUISE: *(with one eyebrow raised)* Yes, we have.

COOKIE: Oh, well then, I know I won't need to introduce my beautiful daughter, then. And I'm Cookie. Listen, I'm sorry I lied to you, but you seemed like such a nice young man. I figured you could use a friend in the city.

STEVEN: That was very thoughtful of you.

COOKIE: Thank you. But I'm sure my daughter is going to yell at me for this later on. Here, take off your coat and sit down. I'm sure if Louise were more used to having visitors, she'd have asked you in already, right, Louise? Oh, I read an article I saved for you: it was about how some women choose gay men for friends because they provide them with male companionship but aren't threatening in a sexual—

LOUISE: Mommy!

COOKIE: *(Laughs, shrugging her shoulders as if to say, "Teenagers are so silly.")* I brought you some more bagels.

LOUISE: We're going to find out where you get them, Mommy. I swear we are.

COOKIE: That's nice, dear. Is Jonathan here?

STEVEN: Who's Jonathan?

LOUISE: My roommate.

COOKIE: They're just friends. Is he here? I want to see him.

LOUISE: He's cramming for an electrical engineering test.

COOKIE: Now, how many times have I told him that's no way to study? If he'd been studying a little every day, this never would have—

(DESMOND comes out of the bathroom. He comes up behind COOKIE and says "Boo!" She jumps.)

COOKIE: Ow! Oh, it's you, Desmond. You scared me.

DESMOND: That's because you were tense!

LOUISE: You don't have to be tense to get startled when someone comes up behind you and says "Boo!"

(STEVEN laughs.)

COOKIE: No, Louise, he's right. You're right. I am tense. We have an appointment Wednesday, I think, it's on my calendar.

DESMOND: Well, I'll look forward to that.

(He goes into JONATHAN *'s bedroom.)*

STEVEN: Who is that?

LOUISE: That's Desmond.

COOKIE: Jonathan's lover.

LOUISE: He's my mother's acupressurist.

STEVEN: Does Desmond live here too?

LOUISE: Not officially . . .

STEVEN: *(Laughs.)* Well, listen, uh, Cookie, I got an estimate on the car, and they said—

COOKIE: Are you in a hurry? Because I brought breakfast. And I figured, after what I did to you, I could at least give you breakfast.

STEVEN: Well, thank you but . . .

COOKIE: Louise, set the table. Steven, help her. Well, go on, she'll show you where things are.

LOUISE: I want to talk to you, Mommy.

COOKIE: That's nice, Louise. We'll talk later, after breakfast.

LOUISE: I'm not hungry.

COOKIE: Who said anything about you? I'm talking about me. I was going to get breakfast when I hit poor Steven, I never had breakfast, and now I'm hungry. So set the table. *(Pause, nobody moves.)* Well, all right, I'll do it. *(She does, speaking the entire time.)* I always have to be the one to do everything, Louise, and I do not appreciate it. In order to make it in this world, you have to always be willing to give one hundred fifty percent and this applies to even the smallest details such as . . . setting the table. I can tell you it was especially difficult for a woman of my generation to become vice president of an advertising agency . . . that's what I do, Steven. Impressed? You should be. It's the take-charge attitude I am talking about, Louise. I wake up in the morning and I say, "I am confident today! I am energetic today! I am positive today!"

LOUISE: Do you say, "I will not hit anyone with my car today?" (STEVEN *laughs.*)

COOKIE: Yes, she's pretty funny, isn't she, Steven. Where are you from?

STEVEN: Philadelphia.

COOKIE: Oh. Where did you go to college? Or do you go to the university with Jonathan and Louise?

STEVEN: No, I went to Bowdoin.

COOKIE: So? Now what are you doing?

LOUISE: Mommy! Leave the poor man alone.

COOKIE: I'm curious. He doesn't mind, do you?

STEVEN: No. I'm an assistant editor at a place in Boston that publishes those little pamphlets you can get at the doctor's office.

LOUISE: You mean the ones on suicide prevention and breast cancer examinations?

STEVEN: Right.

LOUISE: Oh, I love those things.

COOKIE: That's a good job, Louise. What was your major, Steven?

STEVEN: Psychology.

COOKIE: Why don't you major in psychology, Louise?

LOUISE: Ugh, examining white male neuroses? No thanks. I'm going to major in women's studies.

COOKIE: Louise just decided to major in women's studies. I always thought of women's studies as one of those weird majors women who don't shave their legs take.

LOUISE: Mommy . . .

COOKIE: I brought that cream cheese you like, Louise, the kind with all the vegetables. You must think I have food on my mind all the time, Steven, and I'll tell you: I do. Once I went to an Overeaters Anonymous meeting. I told them my name, and they said, we're not allowed to talk about food by its name, so would you be willing to use a different name. What did they want to call me, Carbohydrate? Well, my real name is . . . Cordelia. And for that entire meeting everyone called me Cordelia. I decided I'd rather be fat Cookie than a skinny Cordelia, and that was that. Well, here it is. Louise, go call Jonathan and Desmond. (LOUISE *leaves.*) Do you have a girlfriend, Steven?

STEVEN: Um, no.

COOKIE: Really? What do you think of Louise? You should date her, I like you.

STEVEN: Thanks.

(LOUISE reenters with JONATHAN and DESMOND. STEVEN looks at her. COOKIE nods encouragingly.)

COOKIE: Jonathan, Desmond, this is Steven. *(Hi's all around.)* Sit down, Desmond. You, too, Jonathan; you're too skinny.

LOUISE: Mommy!

JONATHAN: I am not, am I?

COOKIE: Oh, we should all be lucky enough to have such problems.

DESMOND: I think Jonathan is great just the way he is. You know, in China it's an insult to refuse food as a guest. When I was traveling there, I ended up eating all sorts of things.

LOUISE: Like what?

DESMOND: Sea slugs.

JONATHAN: Were they gross?

DESMOND: No they were quite good actually. You would have liked them, Cookie, you're always looking to try new things. Anyway, my point was, you should move to China, Cookie, where it would be a real insult to refuse your food.

COOKIE: Well, I don't think I'd be too useful in China.

STEVEN: Excuse me, I really have to go.

LOUISE: Oh, no, don't go.

STEVEN: I wish I could stay, but I can't.

COOKIE: All right, here is Louise's telephone number, and you can get my number from her and I will mail you a check.

STEVEN: Actually it might be a lot easier if you gave me a check now.

COOKIE: Well, I hate to inconvenience you, but I don't have my checkbook with me.

STEVEN: What?

LOUISE: What?

COOKIE: So if you'll just call me, I'll send you a check, all right?

STEVEN: Well, all right. I'll be in touch. Have a nice day. Good-bye, Louise.

LOUISE: Good-bye. *(STEVEN leaves.)*

COOKIE: Oh, wasn't he nice? You know, he was just a dear when I asked him to take a check instead of reporting the accident. Because they'll raise my insurance if I report another accident, and it was just a little one.

LOUISE: *(laughing)* You're unbelievable.

COOKIE: And he was so nice.

LOUISE: Right. If you had done all that to me, you would be dead.

COOKIE: What did you think of him, Louise?

JONATHAN: She thought he was cuuuuuuuuute.

LOUISE: Shut up, Jonathan.

COOKIE: Jonathan is right, Louise, Steven is cute. And did you notice how polite he is? He has the nicest manners!

(Blackout.)

Scene Two

The next day. JONATHAN *sits at the table again, eating a bagel. There is the sound of running water in the distance.* LOUISE *enters in a towel, looks at her watch, and looks at the bathroom door. She knocks loudly. There is no answer. She knocks again. Still no answer. Now she pounds on the door.*

JONATHAN: What's all the noise?

LOUISE: Desmond has been in the bathroom for two hours.

JONATHAN: Oh, yeah, he's doing T'ai Chi.

LOUISE: *(laughing)* In the bathroom?

JONATHAN: He learned T'ai Chi by a river in China, and the sound of running water relaxes him.

LOUISE: Oh. Well, um, why doesn't he do it in the kitchen?

JONATHAN: All the people running in and out would disturb him.

LOUISE: Jonathan, I'm late for economics again, and I need the bathroom.

JONATHAN: Well, he shouldn't be too much longer.

LOUISE: Too much *longer*!

JONATHAN: Why don't you use the kitchen?

LOUISE: I pay rent for an apartment with a bathroom so that I do not have to pee in the *sink*.

JONATHAN: Will you relax?

LOUISE: Relax??? I have a mother who hits men with her car and brings them to meet me, and a best friend who wants me to pee in the sink!

JONATHAN: You liked Steven.

LOUISE: *(A door slams in her head.)* I did not.

JONATHAN: Yes, you did! I saw you flirting.

LOUISE: Flirting?

JONATHAN: Sure. You were making faces at each other.

LOUISE: That wasn't flirting.

JONATHAN: Listen. Steven is a very attractive man. There is nothing wrong with flirting with him.

LOUISE: But I wasn't flirting with him!

JONATHAN: Yes, you were.

LOUISE: Why would I do that?

JONATHAN: Maybe you liked him.

LOUISE: You know I don't want to get involved.

JONATHAN: Who said anything about getting involved? I was talking about flirting.

LOUISE: Flirting is the first step to involvement.

JONATHAN: You're too much. You barely say three words to a man, and you're already planning what you'll wear to divorce court.

LOUISE: That's utter nonsense. Um, I don't plan the divorce because I don't even consider the wedding.

JONATHAN: Well, I have some good news for you: Nobody is asking you to marry Steven. Just to date him.

LOUISE: Date him . . . Now, I'm not going to date him, I'm never even going to see him again.

JONATHAN: But what if you did?

LOUISE: Well, I'm not, okay?

JONATHAN: Oh, I don't know.

LOUISE: What?

JONATHAN: Maybe you will see him again.

LOUISE: What are you talking about?

JONATHAN: This was on the machine when we got home last night.

(JONATHAN *goes to the answering machine and presses Play.*)

STEVEN'S VOICE: Hi, Louise, it's Steven, you remember, we met the other day. Um, I'm calling because I still need your mother's telephone number, and I think I left my raincoat there. So give me a call, maybe we'll go out one night this week or something. My number is 555-9727.

JONATHAN: So? What do you think?

LOUISE: Well, go out one night this week—that's ambiguous.

JONATHAN: No, it's not.

LOUISE: Oh, well, no, it's not.

JONATHAN: So are you going to call him back?

LOUISE: Um. *(She means "Absolutely not.")*

JONATHAN: I wrote down his number for you.

LOUISE: *(sarcastically, smiling and laughing in a high-pitched voice)* Oh!

JONATHAN: Well?

LOUISE: *(brightly, as though nothing has happened)* Well, what?

JONATHAN: Call him back.

LOUISE: I'll do it later.

JONATHAN: You're not going to do it, are you?

LOUISE: Um, I don't want to talk about it. Can you get Dr. Aculove out of the bathroom, please?

JONATHAN: Don't you realize that it's time for you to think about having a "Dr. Aculove" of your own?

LOUISE: Oh, well . . . no.

JONATHAN: Well, I do.

LOUISE: You're bugging me.

JONATHAN: I want you to be happy.

LOUISE: You want me to fall in love and buy a futon, just like you.

JONATHAN: *Sex.*

LOUISE: What?

JONATHAN: When did you last have it? Christmas?

LOUISE: My birthday, excuse me.

JONATHAN: Your birthday! Your birthday was three months ago.

LOUISE: You never got me a present either.

JONATHAN: If you call Steven, I'll get you a present: anything you want.

LOUISE: *I want* your *boyfriend* to get out of the *bathroom. I want* to *pass* economics. And I want you to leave me alone.

JONATHAN: All right, let's just say the phone rings right now, and it's Steven and he wants to see you. What would you say?

LOUISE: I don't know.

JONATHAN: Well, you would say yes, right?

LOUISE: No! Okay, I wouldn't. I mean, I don't know what I would say. Jonathan, come on, now, I don't even *know* the man.

JONATHAN: Well, how are you going to get to know him?

LOUISE: Oh, um, we could astral-project onto a higher plane and have our souls commune as one? Or, we could have past-life therapy and discover how in a past life we were Romeo and Juliet, and have had to meet again in this life to realize our star-crossed love. Or we could become pen pals . . .

JONATHAN: Love is beautiful. Sex is very beautiful.

LOUISE: No, not really, to look at it isn't beautiful, all that hair and—

JONATHAN: I want to see you pick up that phone and call Steven.

LOUISE: Oh, all right.

JONATHAN: What?

LOUISE: I'll call him tonight. All right?

JONATHAN: You promise?

LOUISE: *(laughing) No,* I don't promise. But I'll do it, and that should be enough.

JONATHAN: *(Sings.)* Louise has a boyfriend, Louise has a . . .

(DESMOND comes out of the bathroom. LOUISE gives him a horrible look and goes in past him.)

DESMOND: What did I do?

JONATHAN: Desmond, will you give Louise a ride over to campus? She's late for class.

DESMOND: Oh, sure.

JONATHAN: Louise, Desmond will drop you off so you won't be late.

LOUISE: I'll walk.

DESMOND: No, really, Louise. I'll drive you.

LOUISE: *(coming out of the bathroom and looking at DESMOND in his T'ai Chi uniform)* It's all right, Desmond, I wouldn't want to put you to any trouble, or otherwise be in your way.

(She leaves. Blackout.)

Scene Three

The apartment is dark. LOUISE *and* STEVEN *enter.*
   LOUISE *turns on many, many lights and calls out.*

LOUISE: Jonathan! Desmond! . . . Nobody's home. I wonder where they are?

STEVEN: I don't know.

LOUISE: I mean, they're usually here, I don't know where they could've gone. What time is it?

STEVEN: Ten thirty.

LOUISE: Well, it was very nice of you to walk me home, I know you must be very busy.

STEVEN: It was no trouble at all.

LOUISE: Well, I do appreciate it and all.

STEVEN: Good.

LOUISE: Yes, well . . .

STEVEN: Here, I brought you something. It's one of the booklets, you know, from my job.

LOUISE: "A Bedside Guide to Contraception." Well, thank you, Steven, I'll be sure to read this. Um, would you like some coffee or something? I mean, I'm really sorry there isn't anything to eat here, but if you want, I'm sure I could—

STEVEN: Louise.

LOUISE: What?

STEVEN: Why are you being so polite?

LOUISE: *(Laughs.)* What?

STEVEN: Come here and sit down.

LOUISE: *(serious)* I'm sorry, Steven, I'm very tired.

STEVEN: You want me to leave.

LOUISE: *(nervous, but not sure if she wants him to go)* Well, you know, it's a funny thing, what I want. I mean, people are always asking me what I want. . . .

STEVEN: Do you want to know what I want?

LOUISE: *(Laughs.)* No.

(STEVEN laughs, and tries to kiss her. She avoids him.)

LOUISE: Steven, I think we should just be friends.

STEVEN: I don't think you want that.

LOUISE: *(Laughs.)* Oh, well: want. You know.

STEVEN: What's wrong?

LOUISE: Steven, I want to tell you something.

STEVEN: Of course.

LOUISE: Um, it's very hard for me to tell people, but I think that's part of dealing with it. Telling people, because it's admitting it. I had never told anyone until last year, when I told Jonathan. Well, I mean my mother knew, of course. But now I'm with a support group. Well, I don't know if that's really helping, but I mean it certainly is making me very open about it. We were talking about relationships, and we agreed to have to tell the other person, and part of the dynamics of the group is that agreements are binding, so . . .

STEVEN: What?

LOUISE: I was raped, Steven.

STEVEN: . . . When?

LOUISE: Two years ago. Senior year. In high school. My senior year in high school.

STEVEN: What happened?

LOUISE: *(wrong question)* Oh. Um, it happened at a fraternity party.

STEVEN: Did they catch him?

LOUISE: Well, um, actually they never looked. I mean, I never reported it. I mean, I was going to, but then my mother said I shouldn't because these stories get twisted and they would try to say it was my fault. It could end up worse for me. So, you know, I didn't press charges. Well, maybe she was right. No, she wasn't right. At least the group says she wasn't right. Oh, so, well, um, that's my life story. And then I came to the university, heh heh, and I lived at home until last year. So that's really my life story.

STEVEN: Well, thank you for telling me. I don't know what to say.

LOUISE: Yeah, well, I just wanted you to know.

STEVEN: I understand.

LOUISE: Thank you. Um . . .

STEVEN: Has there been anyone since?

LOUISE: Oh, well, no, not really. I mean, um . . . No, not really. Oh, well, you know. It hasn't been that long.

STEVEN: Two years, right?

LOUISE: That isn't that long.

STEVEN: No, it isn't. I think it might be good for you to try, though. You know, we could go very slowly. God, I sound like a fool. *(LOUISE laughs.)*

LOUISE: I'm sorry to have to dump all this on you, it's just that—

STEVEN: No, no! I don't mind, really.

LOUISE: Oh.

STEVEN: Dump on me anytime.

LOUISE: Oh! *(Laughs.)*

STEVEN: You know, it might be good for you to try.

LOUISE: Jonathan says that too.

STEVEN: Oh, really?

LOUISE: Yes. He says . . . that's what he says.

STEVEN: What do you think?

LOUISE: I don't want to talk about it anymore.

STEVEN: I like you, Louise. Do you like me?

LOUISE: Well, yes, but . . .

STEVEN: I'll tell you what, I'll leave now.

LOUISE: Okay . . .

STEVEN: Because I think you need time to think about things. You do, right?

LOUISE: I . . .

(STEVEN gets up and goes to the door. LOUISE follows him.)

STEVEN: And I want you to call me when you're ready, all right?

LOUISE: Um, all right.

STEVEN: Good. Well, um, 'bye.

LOUISE: Oh, 'bye.

(Suddenly they kiss. And then they kiss again. And then she pushes the door shut, and they're leaning on it and kissing.)

(Blackout.)

Scene Four

There is the sound of running water again. LOUISE *runs frantically out of her room, wearing a bathrobe and carrying a bag of Cheez Doodles. She looks at the bathroom door, then knocks. No answer.*

LOUISE: Jonathan? Desmond? *(No answer.)* Darn. *(She pounds violently on the door.)* DESMOND, ARE YOU IN THERE????? *(No answer.)* DESMOND, ARE YOU DOING T'AI CHI????? *(Still no answer. She looks at her watch.)* DESMOND, I HAVE A CLASS AND I'M LATE AND YOU HAVE TO GET OUT OF THE BATHROOM! *(Nothing.)* DESMOND!!!!!!!!

(DESMOND opens the bathroom door and sticks his head out.)

DESMOND: Did you call me?

LOUISE: Yes, I need the bathroom.

DESMOND: Okay, I'll be done in a few minutes.

(DESMOND goes back in the bathroom and shuts the door. LOUISE *pounds on it again.)*

LOUISE: Desmond, I don't have a few minutes! *(No answer.)* DESMOND!!

(DESMOND comes out again.)

DESMOND: All right, all right. Calm down.

LOUISE: Don't you have your own bathroom to do T'ai Chi in?

DESMOND: I was here and I'm used to doing it in the morning. How was I supposed to know you needed the bathroom?

LOUISE: I was pounding on the door and screaming.

DESMOND: I couldn't hear you. The water was running, and I was concentrating.

LOUISE: Why don't you go concentrate in your own apartment?

DESMOND: I told you, I was already here.

LOUISE: You're here all the time.

DESMOND: I didn't know I was in the way.

LOUISE: Good. I'm telling you.

DESMOND: Surly, surly, surly!

LOUISE: Sorry.

DESMOND: Well, I'm not surprised, look at what you're eating!

(He takes her bag of Cheez Doodles. She snatches it back.)

LOUISE: I'm late for class again, and you're in my way.

DESMOND: I'm not in your way. *(Indicates the bathroom.)* It's all yours.

LOUISE: For once.

DESMOND: Why do you hate me so much? When have I ever been anything but nice to you?

LOUISE: You're always underfoot.

DESMOND: I don't think that's it at all. I think you're jealous of Jonathan and I.

LOUISE: Jonathan and *me.*

DESMOND: So you admit it.

LOUISE: No, I was correcting your grammar. The direct object is *Jonathan and me,* and so you need to use the direct object pronoun, which is *me.* For example, you wouldn't say "He hates I," you would say "He hates *me.*"

DESMOND: Louise, you are an emotionally dishonest person.

LOUISE: Thanks.

DESMOND: Maybe you should try some relaxation techniques.

LOUISE: What, like a hot bath?

DESMOND: How about T'ai Chi?

LOUISE: Get out of my way! It's too late. I'm already going to miss my class. You're an idiot, Desmond.

(She pushes past him into the bathroom. He stares after her. JONATHAN *enters.)*

JONATHAN: Hi, Desmond.

DESMOND: Louise just called me an idiot, Jonathan. When are you going to tell her?

JONATHAN: I'll tell her today.

*(*LOUISE *comes out of the bathroom.)*

LOUISE: Oh, good, you're here. I need to talk to you.

JONATHAN: What's up?

DESMOND: Oh, Louise just needs to release some of her negative energy.

JONATHAN: If Louise releases her negative energy, there won't be anything left.

DESMOND: That's the wonder of T'ai Chi, because . . .

LOUISE: Jonathan, I need to talk to you alone.

JONATHAN: That's good, because, um, I have to tell you something.

DESMOND: Well, I had to leave anyway . . . work and all.

LOUISE: Oh, you mean you haven't been taking appointments here?

DESMOND: Grrrrrrrrr!

(DESMOND leaves.)

JONATHAN: That was unnecessarily nasty, Louise.

LOUISE: Jonathan, I understand that Desmond may be a very nice person, but it is very difficult for me to be nice to people who do T'ai Chi in the bathroom, especially when I need it.

JONATHAN: And Desmond has difficulty understanding people who eat Cheez Doodles for breakfast. But at least he tries.

LOUISE: My Cheez Doodles have never made him late for work.

JONATHAN: He's very sweet, Louise. He said he worries about the way you show disrespect to the temple that is your body.

LOUISE: Did he say that? Showing disrespect to the temple?

JONATHAN: No, I did.

LOUISE: Oh, that's *good.*

JONATHAN: He said he likes you, but it bothers him because you seem to be such a fundamentally unhappy person and—

LOUISE: So he offered a solution. I should eat better and take up T'ai Chi.

JONATHAN: Louise, please stop it! You need to stop.

(Pause.)

LOUISE: Aren't you going to ask me how group was?

JONATHAN: How was group?

LOUISE: Group was fine.

JONATHAN: Louise, I . . . don't you have a class right now?

LOUISE: I'm not going. It was only economics, and I hate economics.

JONATHAN: You're going to flunk. You never go.

LOUISE: I won't flunk.

JONATHAN: How's that man? Steven?

LOUISE: He's fine. He's okay.

JONATHAN: Are you going to see him again?

LOUISE: I guess. I mean, I guess he likes me. I mean, we had a small disagreement last night, but that's over now, you know. He knows about my, um . . . and all. So probably I will see him again.

JONATHAN: What happened last night?

LOUISE: Um, we had sex last night. And then I made him leave, even though he wanted to sleep over. I guess he was tired.

JONATHAN: You had sex?

LOUISE: Yes.

JONATHAN: Wow! Louise, that's wonderful. I'm really proud of you.

LOUISE: Why? It was just sex.

JONATHAN: No, but I mean, you know, sex with someone you care about.

LOUISE: It was just sex, really. I don't know why people always say it's better if you care about the person. To me it's just some man huffing and puffing a lot, and later he expects you to be impressed.

JONATHAN: Is Steven a bad lover?

LOUISE: No, no. Steven is a good lover. Well, not *good*. I mean he's okay. Adequate. No, I mean he's nice. He's really nice. Um, what did you want to talk to me about?

JONATHAN: Oh. That. Um, Louise, I have to tell you something.

LOUISE: Is it something bad?

JONATHAN: Sit down.

LOUISE: Tell me standing, I might need to kill you suddenly.

JONATHAN: Oh, well, um, it's not that bad, just that I'm moving out.

LOUISE: What?

JONATHAN: Desmond and I are going to get an apartment. Maybe in Cambridge—we were looking, in fact, we're signing the lease soon on this beautiful apartment . . . it's got a really big bathroom.

LOUISE: You went behind my back?

JONATHAN: I didn't know how to tell you.

LOUISE: That stinks.

JONATHAN: I know.

LOUISE: I mean, now I have to find another roommate. Where am I going to find another roommate?

JONATHAN: I'm sure you'll find someone, I mean, put an ad in the university paper, and I'm sure you'll find someone.

LOUISE: A stranger. You want me to live with a stranger.

JONATHAN: Well, maybe you have some friends who are looking. Someone from group.

LOUISE: Or I could move back home.

JONATHAN: Don't move back home.

LOUISE: Get out of here, all right?

JONATHAN: All right. Um, don't be angry at me.

LOUISE: So, I'm angry, so what? Big deal. You'll live, I'll live, it'll all blow over in a few days, you'll see.

JONATHAN: All right, I understand that you're angry at me. . . .

LOUISE: Your emotional honesty is really getting on my nerves. If I need you and you want to leave, then for God's sake, leave! Don't think for another minute about me, or my feelings, because I will live! But don't you dare ask me not to be mad.

JONATHAN: Louise . . .

LOUISE: Don't touch me. Get out of here, Jonathan. I'll, um, I'll talk to you tomorrow.

(LOUISE *walks into the coat closet and shuts the door. After a minute* JONA-THAN *walks into his bedroom. Blackout.*)

Scene Five

Now there is some evidence JONATHAN *has been packing to move out.* LOUISE *comes out of the bedroom wearing a robe. In a minute,* STEVEN *comes out of the bathroom, also wearing a robe.*

STEVEN: I'm really proud of you.

LOUISE: Why?

STEVEN: It was really thrilling to, uh . . . see you let go and enjoy yourself.

LOUISE: I was faking.

STEVEN: I know you're lying. I hate it when you lie.

LOUISE: Well.

STEVEN: It's just that I hated to see you just lie there the first time we made love, and I am really glad you were able to relax this time and enjoy it.

LOUISE: Steven, I don't go in for this postcoital-discussion stuff.

STEVEN: All right. As long as you know that I am very proud of you and it gives me a lot of pleasure to make you so—

LOUISE: Will you shut up already!

STEVEN: I'm sorry. *(Pause.)* It's just that I really—

LOUISE: That's Jonathan's.

STEVEN: What?

LOUISE: That robe. It's Jonathan's.

STEVEN: It was in the bathroom.

LOUISE: I know.

STEVEN: Well, is he going to mind?

LOUISE: I don't know.

STEVEN: I don't think he'll mind.

LOUISE: I'd mind.

STEVEN: What?

LOUISE: If you had just gone into the bathroom and worn my robe, I'd mind. I mean, if Desmond wore my robe, I'd mind.

STEVEN: Well, do you want me to put it back?

LOUISE: No.

STEVEN: Are you going to pick a fight with me every time we make love?

LOUISE: I hate that expression.

STEVEN: "Make love"? Some people hate it.

LOUISE: I hate it. Say "Have sex."

STEVEN: All right.

LOUISE: Well? Say it! "Are you going to pick a fight with me every time we have sex?"

STEVEN: I think I'll go home.

LOUISE: No! Steven. I'm sorry.

STEVEN: Do you want me to go?

LOUISE: No.

STEVEN: Good. I just want you to try, Louise. Tell me you'll try.

LOUISE: I'll try.

STEVEN: I brought you something. It's a pamphlet I'm editing from my job.

(He gets his coat, finds the rolled-up booklet in the pocket, and gives it to her. She examines it.)

LOUISE: "Getting Over Rape and Molestation: A Practical Guide." Thank you, Steven, that's sweet.

STEVEN: Oh, sure. Um, there was something I wanted to ask you.

LOUISE: Go ahead.

STEVEN: When is Jonathan moving out?

LOUISE: I don't know. Soon.

STEVEN: Well it's actually kind of good Jonathan is moving out. I mean, I know you're upset, but Desmond won't hog the bathroom anymore. Well, you know my sublet is going to run out, so I was thinking maybe I could move in here.

LOUISE: Oh. Well. I never thought of that, Steven.

STEVEN: Well, think of it.

LOUISE: Well, yes, I guess it would be okay. I mean, I told my mother I was going to move back home, and she got really excited and started making plans to redecorate my old bedroom. But I don't want to move back home.

STEVEN: So, it's ideal for both of us!

LOUISE: Would you take Jonathan's room, though? Or do you really need the bigger room? If you do, it's okay, we could switch, or . . .

STEVEN: Um, that wasn't quite what I meant.

LOUISE: Oh. I see. Well, Steven, I just don't know if I'm ready for that. I mean, how well do we really know each other?

STEVEN: With some relationships it's just like you understand the person. I understand you! And I feel really close to you. *(He kisses her.)* Things are moving fast, Louise. We have to keep up with them.

LOUISE: What are we, a bus?

STEVEN: Well, all I want you to do is think about it, all right?

LOUISE: I am thinking about it. I mean, you're hard enough to deal with just like sometimes, but if you moved in, you'd be here all the time.

STEVEN: Am I that hard to deal with? Besides, you have classes, and I have my job. So it wouldn't be all the time.

LOUISE: No, but like, for example: I'm on a meal plan. Would I stay on a meal plan, or would we eat together? And who would cook?

STEVEN: Well, I would like to eat together, but if you prefer dining hall food to my delicious cooking, I guess that's all right too.

LOUISE: What would we do with Jonathan's room?

STEVEN: Well, anything. We could make it into a study, or TV room.

LOUISE: Would we have to have sex every night?

STEVEN: I wish you would stop thinking of sex as an obligation!

LOUISE: And what if it didn't work?

STEVEN: What?

LOUISE: What if I asked you to leave?

STEVEN: But it would work. It would be wonderful.

LOUISE: Well, maybe.

STEVEN: All right, you think about it.

LOUISE: I will.

(He puts his arm around her and sort of pulls her in. She allows this.)

STEVEN: Um, Louise?

LOUISE: Yeah.

STEVEN: Do you ever want to talk about it?

LOUISE: About what?

STEVEN: About what happened. You never talk about it.

LOUISE: What's to say?

STEVEN: I don't know. I was just wondering why you never talk about it.

LOUISE: I don't want to talk about it.

STEVEN: All right, we'll talk when you're ready. All right?

LOUISE: All right.

(They sit that way on the couch.)

(Blackout.)

Scene Six

LOUISE, *wearing brown pants and a brown T-shirt with her usual leather jacket, stumbles into the apartment holding her head. She goes into the kitchen, takes two aspirin, and flicks on the answering machine.*

JONATHAN'S VOICE: Louise, do me a favor. Desmond was going to stop by at around eight. Tell him that I'm running late and I'll meet him at the restaurant. *(Beep.)*

COOKIE'S VOICE: Louise, I looked at paint samples and I found a really nice blue. You always looked beautiful in blue. Anyway I'll stop by one of these days and show you the colors, and you can choose for yourself, and we'll see if we chose the same one! *(Beep.)*

STEVEN'S VOICE: Louise, it's Steven. I'm going to come over at around eight and drop off some of my stuff, and then we'll go out like we planned. If you have a headache, I don't want to hear it. *(Beep.)*

(LOUISE *groans and lies down on the couch. There is a knock on the door. She looks at her watch.*)

LOUISE: Who is it?

DESMOND: *(outside)* Me. Desmond.

LOUISE: Come in, it's open.

(DESMOND *enters.* LOUISE *mumbles, "Hi," and keeps her head in her hands.*)

DESMOND: What's wrong?

LOUISE: Oh, nothing. I just feel a little sick. I think I'm coming down with something.

DESMOND: What hurts?

LOUISE: Everything.

DESMOND: Be specific.

LOUISE: I have a headache.

DESMOND: Where?

LOUISE: Here.

DESMOND: All right, let me see your hand.

(*He takes her hand and administers some shiatsu massage.*)

LOUISE: Oh, ow, stop it.

DESMOND: Just relax, this will help your headache.

LOUISE: No, ow, it hurts more than the headache.

DESMOND: Come on, Louise, relax. Take a deep breath. There, I'm done. How do you feel?

LOUISE: Okay . . .

DESMOND: Is your headache gone?

LOUISE: Can you cure my sore throat with this hand too?

DESMOND: What kind of sore throat? Scratchy or dull?

LOUISE: Scratchy.

DESMOND: Like when you swallow?

LOUISE: Yes.

DESMOND: Okay, that's in your foot.

(He starts to take off her shoe, to her feeble protests. Just then COOKIE *walks in carrying a large tote bag and a fish in a bowl. In this bag she has a hardcover book called* Once Bitten, Twice Shy, *and a few good groceries: sourdough rolls with raisins or something. She probably also has some fish supplies: food, and one of those little nets.)*

COOKIE: Louise? Oh, hi, Desmond.

DESMOND: Hi, Cookie.

COOKIE: Louise, why are you wearing all brown? You look like a roast beef.

*(*COOKIE *goes into the kitchen to unpack her tote bag.)*

DESMOND: Is Jonathan here?

LOUISE: No, he said to meet him, um, at the restaurant.

DESMOND: Oh, all right. Well, see you later.

LOUISE: Desmond?

DESMOND: What?

LOUISE: Thanks.

DESMOND: Sure, anytime.

*(*DESMOND *leaves.* COOKIE *comes out of the kitchen carrying the book.)*

COOKIE: Louise, I found a wonderful book for you today, called *Once Bitten, Twice Shy.*

LOUISE: *Once Bitten, Twice Shy?* That's pretty good. Oh, that should help me a lot. What is this? You don't call, you don't knock.

COOKIE: I didn't know you were hiding anything. Do you want a fish? I bought it; isn't it cute? But then I remembered I went to the aquarium with your father and it made him very hungry. If you don't want it, just flush it.

LOUISE: Oh, no, I love it. I adore fish.

COOKIE: I named it Derrick, after my old secretary. But you can change the name; he doesn't answer to it anyway.

LOUISE: Oh, no, Derrick is a beautiful name. I remember Derrick your secretary, he's the one you tried to get to take me to my senior prom.

COOKIE: Right. I brought over those paint samples for you to see.

LOUISE: Mommy, I have to be somewhere at eight. And I really don't feel like talking right now, I just want to sleep.

COOKIE: What's wrong?

LOUISE: I have a headache.

COOKIE: Didn't Desmond just look at that? Do you want me to see if he's still out there?

LOUISE: No, it's okay.

COOKIE: Well, he's really good with small ailments like headaches.

LOUISE: What makes you think my headache is a small ailment? I just need to get some sleep and then I'll be fine.

COOKIE: All right, just quickly look at these paint samples, because I have to order the paint, and then I have to arrange for the painters to come and then . . . Daddy and I are so happy you're moving home.

LOUISE: What did he say?

COOKIE: Oh, he was thrilled. He said, "What about her friend? The gay one?"

LOUISE: It always amazed me how he could remember my friends' sexual orientation but not their name.

COOKIE: Your father is very sweet, but he has that ditzy quality. I think you get it from him.

(STEVEN rings the doorbell. COOKIE answers it. They say "Hi," and he walks in carrying a huge load of books.)

STEVEN: Where do you want me to put this stuff?

LOUISE: Oh, um, I don't care. *(He looks at her strangely.)*

STEVEN: Are you feeling all right?

LOUISE: I'm *fine.*

STEVEN: I'm going to go home and get another load. You know, this would be a lot easier if you gave me a key, Louise, I wouldn't have to keep making you get up.

LOUISE: I'll be here.

(STEVEN leaves.)

COOKIE: What was that all about?

LOUISE: Mommy, I'm not coming home.

COOKIE: You're not?

LOUISE: No.

COOKIE: What are you doing, then?

LOUISE: *(brightly, as if she expects* COOKIE *to be really pleased even though she doesn't)* Um, Steven is going to move in.

COOKIE: Why?

LOUISE: *(keeping the cheery tone, not yet defensive)* His sublet is ending. He has nowhere else.

COOKIE: He told you that? He can find somewhere else.

LOUISE: He wants to live here. I thought you would be happy.

COOKIE: Happy. Well. How long have you known Steven?

LOUISE: I don't know.

COOKIE: Oh, yes, you do. Don't be a ditz.

LOUISE: Look, it's not that big a deal. He needs a place to live, I need a roommate.

COOKIE: You don't need a roommate! You can live at home. This whole relationship is like something you got dragged into.

LOUISE: You're right. You dragged me into it, you and Jonathan, and now I'm in it, and what? It's not going as you planned? Well, I'm a little sick of your plans and your stopping by here uninvited.

COOKIE: I think you're making a mistake. Look, you wouldn't date for years. You finally feel ready, you can't just commit yourself to the first man who comes along. Do you love Steven?

LOUISE: I guess so.

COOKIE: That's no good. If you really loved him, you would know.

LOUISE: He's very nice.

COOKIE: And your sex? How is that?

LOUISE: Mother!

COOKIE: Tell me.

LOUISE: Fine, not that it's any of *your* business.

COOKIE: You never were a good liar.

LOUISE: Well, he thinks it's fine.

COOKIE: And why isn't it? Does he do nice things for you?

LOUISE: You're embarrassing me.

COOKIE: Oh, I am not. Your generation doesn't get embarrassed. I know, I watch MTV.

LOUISE: Wait a minute. Why are you asking me questions about my sex life? And why did you bring me that book?

COOKIE: It's a present, Louise. When other mothers bring their daughters presents, they get thanked.

LOUISE: Thank you for the book, all right? And you can put it on the pile of self-help manuals there. Steven brings me them too. Obviously everyone thinks I even need help to help myself.

COOKIE: What's that supposed to mean?

LOUISE: I'm just really tired, that's all. I'm just really tired. Steven talks about things moving fast, you talk about redoing my bedroom, nobody asks me what I want!

COOKIE: All right. What do you want?

LOUISE: I want a cat.

COOKIE: This apartment is much too small for a cat. I mean, it would be almost cruel to confine it to such a small space. And Louise, the litter box would—

LOUISE: Stop it! I can't do anything right, can I? I mean, you asked me what I want.

COOKIE: You asked me to ask you.

LOUISE: Does this mean you don't really care what I want? Clearly it does.

COOKIE: All right, let me rephrase the question, all right? What do you want from me?

LOUISE: I just want some credit. You know. Just some credit. I mean, what is this what do you mean, ditzy quality. Because Daddy and I don't think like you, we're ditzy?

COOKIE: You don't have to think like me.

LOUISE: You have to stop making decisions for me, Mommy.

COOKIE: You have to start making them for yourself, then.

LOUISE: What do you think I'm trying to do?

COOKIE: Well, you're doing it wrong!

LOUISE: Listen to yourself!

COOKIE: I ask you what you want and you say you want a cat. I feel like we're stuck in this cycle, Louise, where I can't stop doing things for you because you can't get anything done yourself, and you won't do anything for yourself because I keep doing it for you.

LOUISE: Why do you do it, then?

COOKIE: Well, I don't think that's the issue at all. Louise, you wouldn't even leave the house until I made you.

LOUISE: Well, I'm leaving the house now, right? Yes, I am. And doing all the other things that other people do. So what does this mean, *Once Bitten, Twice Shy.* That is unacceptable. You show up here, you don't call me first, you criticize me, insult me . . . "Louise, you look like a lox. Louise, get a boyfriend. Louise, don't let your boyfriend move in. Louise, don't major in women's studies. . . ."

COOKIE: Well, maybe if you took my advice sometime . . . I worry about you. And I tell you these things because they're things I worry about. And they're for your own good.

LOUISE: Oh, that's really special. "Louise, you look like a lox" is for my own good.

COOKIE: I said you look like a roast beef, not a lox, and anyway it is for your own good. A fashion sense is very important in today's job marketplace. Women are forced to present an impeccable appearance, and clothing is—

LOUISE: Mother. I am tired of being a woman, Mother.

COOKIE: I don't know what you mean.

LOUISE: But I can't explain what I mean.

COOKIE: But Louise! You have to learn to articulate!

LOUISE: You're doing it again!

COOKIE: Will you stop overreacting! I can't say anything to you without getting attacked. You have to learn to handle people better, Louise, you—

(The doorbell rings. STEVEN again. He quickly goes into the bedroom and then back out to his car for another load.)

LOUISE: I'm not moving home.

COOKIE: So I gathered. Is Steven going to move in?

LOUISE: What will you do if I say yes? And what will you do if I say no? Mother, please go home. Go home and paint your own room blue. I don't want a blue room. You didn't even ask me if I wanted a blue room. My room is white.

(COOKIE *leaves.* LOUISE *sighs, looks around for something to do. She finds her book, picks it up, and starts reading it. After a moment* STEVEN *comes back from his car.*)

STEVEN: Wow. What was that all about?

LOUISE: Oh, the kitchen supplies are when they really get you. You know, when someone moves his kitchen supplies in, he's really here.

STEVEN: And hello to you, Steven, how are you? So nice of you to stop by and bring kitchen supplies, which we will need for our apartment! Look, you have a blender, a Cuisinart, even a cappuccino maker. I look forward to many happy meals with you, Steven.

LOUISE: Did you ever have this feeling, it wasn't like something you could really even explain, but everyone was acting like things are a lot simpler than they are?

STEVEN: What do you mean?

LOUISE: Well, like, say your house was robbed. They took everything! But worse than that, you kept reliving it in your mind. The way you came home and opened your door and first you noticed the mess, and then . . . or whatever else did happen, you keep reliving it. This goes on for a long time. But then one day you realized that you still had your cat. And you love your cat! But meanwhile everyone else keeps expecting you to still be upset about everything else you lost. Steven, you're never going to get back what was stolen, nor are you going to completely forget what you felt then. But you can stop thinking about it.

STEVEN: What are you trying to say, Louise?

LOUISE: I should have guessed you wouldn't get it.

STEVEN: Look, let's just get some sleep, all right? You're tired, I'm tired, I'll be more up to this kind of discussion tomorrow.

LOUISE: I don't want to talk about it tomorrow, I want to talk about it now. Before we squeeze another night into my tiny bed, you steal all the blankets—

STEVEN: Is that the problem? Well, we'll get a bigger bed.

LOUISE: For one of those sensitive men, you sure are an idiot. You want me to sleep with you now, when I'm so angry at you!

STEVEN: But what did I do wrong?

LOUISE: You treat me like I'm five years old. You treat me . . .

STEVEN: I treat you very well.

LOUISE: . . . You treat me like I'm fragile.

STEVEN: I don't—

LOUISE: And I let you because . . .

STEVEN: What are you talking about?

LOUISE: . . . I don't know, I mean, I guess in a way I expected you would treat me like I'm fragile. I know I shouldn't have told you you could move in, but really you left me no choice. I mean, it's always been very difficult to say no to the people I care about: my parents, Jonathan, you—

STEVEN: Louise, listen—

LOUISE: *Steven, will you stop interrupting me! (Silence.)* I mean, God, even now you aren't listening to me!

STEVEN: I'm listening.

LOUISE: I'm not sure we're suited for each other.

STEVEN: I don't believe I'm hearing this. Are you crazy? Have you completely lost your mind?

LOUISE: Steven! Don't yell at me!

STEVEN: *I'm not yelling!*

LOUISE: We made love that first night because I didn't want to seem like a tease.

STEVEN: Oh, thanks a lot! What is this, this all-men-are-rapists attitude. All you had to do was say you didn't want to.

LOUISE: All right, so now I'm saying it. I don't want you to move in here, Steven.

STEVEN: Right, and I'm not supposed to be angry?

LOUISE: Of course you're supposed to be angry.

STEVEN: I don't see why. . . . I haven't gotten angry in the past.

LOUISE: I wish you had.

STEVEN: I just didn't get mad at you, I figured you had enough problems. Louise, you say I behaved wrong, what was the right way, then? What was I supposed to do?

LOUISE: I don't know.

STEVEN: You don't know. Well, that's special, Louise. You don't know. I LOVE YOU! I want to help you, that's all.

LOUISE: For God's sake, "Dealing with Rape and Molestation, A Practical Guide" is going to help me as much as channeling and releasing my negative energy through T'ai Chi.

STEVEN: Don't I get any credit for my intentions?

LOUISE: Intentions!

STEVEN: I didn't do anything wrong. I was nice to you, and I tried to help you with your problems.

LOUISE: Well, thank you for your help, all right? Thank you for your stupid help. Steven, you can't move in here. I'd like to keep seeing you, but you have to understand that it just can't be a relationship that solves all my problems.

STEVEN: Why did you get involved with me in the first place?

LOUISE: I liked you.

STEVEN: Oh.

LOUISE: I still like you. But you bring me self-help books. And I don't want them. I only want you to be my friend, and my lover.

STEVEN: Well, maybe it's too late for that, for us.

LOUISE: And so . . . ?

STEVEN: And maybe it isn't.

LOUISE: And maybe it isn't. . . .

(Blackout.)

Scene Seven

LOUISE *sits at the kitchen table with a cup of coffee and a huge pile of papers.* JONATHAN *enters.*

JONATHAN: Um, hi.

LOUISE: Oh. Hi.

JONATHAN: I just came to pick up the rest of my stuff.

LOUISE: Oh, well, um, go ahead.

JONATHAN: Thanks. Um, how are you doing?

LOUISE: Oh, I'm all right. I think. Yes, I'm all right.

JONATHAN: You look pretty.

LOUISE: Oh, it's the morning light. Makes me look less like a witch. (JONATHAN *laughs.*)

JONATHAN: What are you reading?

LOUISE: I'm writing a paper on "The Freudianization of American Culture."

JONATHAN: Oh, really?

LOUISE: Yes.

JONATHAN: I'm making a new thing. You know, in design, it's kind of this portable food processor thing. I mean I didn't invent it or anything, but still it's kind of a neat thing. Desmond uses it to mush up all of his macrobiotic ingredients. You know how sometimes that stuff has to get mushed.

LOUISE: Yes. Um, do you want a cup of coffee?

JONATHAN: I'd love some.

LOUISE: All right, but I don't have any milk.

JONATHAN: Well, that's okay because actually you have some of that nondairy milk.

LOUISE: I do?

JONATHAN: Yes, you do. *(He gets it.)* Um, Desmond is teaching me T'ai Chi. He says I have too much negative energy built up. Are you . . . mad at me?

LOUISE: Oh, no. No, I'm not mad at you.

JONATHAN: It's okay if you are.

LOUISE: Well, of course it's okay if I am. But I'm not.

JONATHAN: Is Steven here?

LOUISE: No. He went home last night. I told him not to move in.

JONATHAN: You did?

LOUISE: Yes.

JONATHAN: Um, should I help you find someone to take the apartment?

LOUISE: Oh, I'm not leaving.

JONATHAN: You're not going home?

LOUISE: No, no. I'm going to stay here. By myself. For now. Unless I find someone better than me.

JONATHAN: You're going to be lonely.

LOUISE: Well, God, Jonathan, it isn't as though I don't have a life outside this apartment. I mean, you know, I live here. Do my work, sleep, and stuff.

JONATHAN: That's true.

LOUISE: It's funny.

JONATHAN: What?

LOUISE: I had a fight with my mother yesterday.

JONATHAN: You did?

LOUISE: Yes, I did. So, heh heh, that's all that's new with me.

JONATHAN: How is group?

LOUISE: Group is fine, Jonathan. Group is just fine. Except none of us wants to talk about it anymore. Last time we discussed baseball. You know, we're avoiding the subject, but then we decided that's okay. You know, we can avoid it if we want. Do you want to have a barbecue?

JONATHAN: A barbecue?

LOUISE: Well, originally I was thinking, over an open fire. Because there's all these self-help books over there we can use for kindling. But I guess that's impractical.

JONATHAN: Yes, it is.

LOUISE: Well, anyway, we could cook. I mean, you could come over here, and we could cook, have a few glasses of wine and stuff.

JONATHAN: What'll we cook?

LOUISE: Hmmmmm. Well, Desmond didn't make you into a vegetarian, did he?

JONATHAN: No.

LOUISE: Okay, well then, we'll cook this great pasta stuff, with meat in it all chopped up and this garlic sauce, I don't know what it's called, but my mother makes it a lot.

JONATHAN: And we won't invite anyone else.

LOUISE: Not a living soul. Not even a ghost!

JONATHAN: And then afterward?

LOUISE: We'll get *drunk*. And talk about sex.

JONATHAN: That's good, because we haven't gotten drunk and talked about sex in a long time.

LOUISE: I know. And actually I have some new observations on sex I think we should discuss.

JONATHAN: Oh, yeah? Like what?

LOUISE: Like is it normal to crack your knuckles during it?

JONATHAN: Oh, my God. That's the most disgusting thing I've ever heard in my entire life.

LOUISE: Well, he only did it once. You see, actually . . . forget it, because we'll talk about it later. It will give you something to look forward to.

JONATHAN: All right, I'll see you at seven.

LOUISE: Great.

(JONATHAN *picks up his boxes, they kiss on the cheek, and he leaves. After he is gone,* LOUISE *picks up the fish tank.*)

LOUISE: It's you and me.

BLACKOUT

DEBRA NEFF

(1990) Then . . .

I am from Queens, New York, and I attended P.S. 178Q where I began writing in first grade with two very important early pieces. One was entitled "I Climbed a Tree," and it went:

> I climbed a tree.
> I climbed so high, I touched the sky.
> Then I fell down and went to the Hospital.
> But now I am better.

The other one was entitled "Fish," and it went:

> Fish: blech.

Oh, so then after a while I went to Saint Ann's School in Brooklyn where I took my first playwriting course with Nancy Fales Garrett. I wrote two plays; one of them, *Children,* was done as a staged reading for the 1987 Young Playwrights Festival. Then I went to Tufts University for a while, and I wrote some other stuff, including this play. And I took some other courses and I went to England for a while and when I got back from England I called dessert "sweets," the bathroom "the loo," and the garbage pail "the dustbin."

I am a Sagittarius. My favorite colors are purple and green.

Let's Go Back in Time . . .

Somewhere in all of this *Twice Shy* was produced. I remember the summer/early autumn as hot and sparkly. It was pretty fun, if being really nervous all the time can be considered fun. (I guess it can.) Anyway, it was fun when I first met Morgan Jenness at auditions and she walked up to me and said, "Cool jewels."

It was fun bonding with the other playwrights, Janet Allard, Alex Membreno, and Bob Kerr.

Absolutely everyone was really nice and really helpful, even people who weren't working directly on *Twice Shy*. I remember one time during a technical rehearsal I got in the way, and someone at Playwrights Horizons, someone important, said to me, "Oh, you're a *playwright*. You're never in the way!" And I thought, "I'm really *in the way*!" But still it was nice that absolutely everyone behaved as though I weren't in the way and I weren't a pain in the ass changing the ending during the last previews.

Especially Mark Brokaw, who directed the thing. Mark Brokaw is the Deity of Directing.

The bad part was the press. Well, actually just one interviewer, whose premise for an article was "Young Playwrights Write About What They Know." But for me, that translated into "Debra Neff: Rape Survivor or Not?" Of course, I tried to dodge the question by giggling and giving answers like: "I think in every creative piece there are elements of both fact and fiction." So he printed that I was not raped, just because I didn't explicitly say that I *was*. Like, who cares anyway? I guess he was looking for a nice story. "Rape Survivor Author Spills All in Heartwarming Tale of Girl, Mother, and Fish." *Not*.

What I should have done is, I should have put my hand on my hip, wagged my finger, and said, "I am not going to answer that question, and I am very offended that you asked me. Understand this: Number one, I am not Louise, and number two, I have had reason to empathize with her feelings. Also, just to let you know, statistically, one out of three women has been or will be sexually assaulted; the statistics for men are unknown. It is safest to assume that *everyone* is a survivor of sexual violence, and to behave with appropriate respect and sensitivity."

And Now What Are You Going to Do, Honey?

I'm going to get a cat. That's the only thing I know for sure that I want.

Always Remember to Say Thank You

(This will be boring if you don't think I've mentioned you.)

Okay, so other than all the Young Playwrights people, thank you also to my family; to the original casts: Katherine Hiler, Laura Dubrule, Annabel Dimdore (Louise); Ray Cochran, Mark Libby, Jonathan Kornreich (Jonathan); Mark W. Conklin, Douglas Kiang, John Faria (Steven); Lauren Klein, Lisa Schwarz, Judy Bowman (Cookie); David Lansbury, Eric Schwartz, Jason Housecroft (Desmond); to Kristi Conkel, Angela Spann, and Lucia Gahlin; to Mark Brokaw, and Morgan

Jenness and Nancy Fales Garrett and D. B. Gilles and Wendy Lamb and Evelyn Catterson and Welly Pansing; to Tufts Pen Paint and Pretzels and University College London's Drama Society; to my oldest friend, Alex Tolk, for the title; to my friends Loulou, Nicotina, Vance Rancid, Electra Assassin, Patience Isa Virtue, Toto, and Muffy Sunshine St. Superstar.

. . . *And Now*

I graduated from Tufts in May 1991, and now I live still catless in New York City, where I've had jobs as a secretary and an editor of self-help pamphlets. Now I'm working as a fortune-teller on one of those 900 phone lines, and sometimes I am possessed by Donny from the New Kids on the Block who makes me sing "I'll Be Loving You Forever" and want to have a big huge Harley between my legs. I'm writing a new play called *The Mean Play* and a very long story called "Venus Probably Shaved Hers." I might apply to graduate school SOON.

REMEDIAL ENGLISH

by
EVAN SMITH
(age eighteen when play was written)
Savannah, Georgia

■

Remedial English was performed at Playwrights Horizons in New York City, September 16 through October 12, 1986. It was directed by Ron Lagomarsino, and the playwright adviser was Wendy Wasserstein. Sets were by Rick Dennis and costumes by Michael Krass. Ann G. Wrightson was the lighting designer. James M. Bay designed the sound. The production stage manager was Melissa Davis.

The cast:

VINCENT RYAN	*Greg Germann*
SISTER BEATRICE	*Anne Pitoniak*
ROB ANDREWS	*Nicholas Kallsen*
COACH	*Shawn Elliott*
CHRIS	*Jim Fyfe*
DAVID	*Adam Redfield*

Scene One

The setting: Cabrini Catholic Academy, a private high school for boys in a medium-size southern city; and VINCENT*'s home.*

The time: One day of school, and that evening.

The rising curtain reveals VINCENT *and* SISTER BEATRICE *alone onstage.* VINCENT *is seated right, and* SISTER BEATRICE *is seated behind a desk, left.*

VINCENT *is wearing the Cabrini Catholic Academy uniform of a blue knit sportshirt with the school crest over the left breast, khaki slacks, a black belt, and black penny loafers. He is in the waiting room of the office of* SISTER BEATRICE*, a teaching nun. She is, however, a post-Vatican II nun; she is wearing, not a flowing black habit and wimple, but a navy blue skirt, a white blouse buttoned to the neck, nurse's shoes, and a shapeless polyester blazer of white and light blue stripes. On the jacket lapel is a simple stainless-steel cross. At present, she is fully occupied grading test papers, and* VINCENT *is fully occupied waiting. In fact, the expression on his face as the curtain rises is enough to imply that he has been waiting for quite some time.*

VINCENT *leans forward in his chair as if to look through a half-open door into* SISTER BEATRICE*'s office. All he sees is* SISTER *gleefully wielding a red pen. He leans back, stretches, and then addresses her. She cannot hear what is essentially an interior monologue.*

VINCENT: Sister, I think it's very rude of you to keep me waiting like this. It's been fifteen minutes since you said, "I'll be finished in a minute," and unless I'm doing worse in algebra than I thought, you're off by fourteen minutes. Fourteen minutes may not seem like much to you—time moves pretty quickly after your hundredth birthday—but this is *supposed* to be my study hall. I have many important things to do during my study hall. I am developing a fascinating abstract pattern to fill the margins of my chemistry book; I'm right in the middle of *Lake Wobegon Days;* and I have almost finished my project of inserting the complete works of Judith Krantz into the library's card catalog. This is a school, after all, Sister. You of all people shouldn't want to see me wasting my time.

What did I do to merit such treatment? Is it because of that little tiff we had in English yesterday? Sister, we all say things in the heat of argument that we later regret. I'm sorry I called T. S. Eliot a "social-climbing Yankee papist." I don't even remember what I *meant* by that!

Have you forgotten all the good times we have had together? Don't you remember Dramatic Literature, when I was a sophomore? We read aloud to the class . . . I was Jean . . . you were Miss Julie . . .

Oh, good grief, *please* don't tell me you found the Sister Beatrice

Virgin Vote! God, how could I ever explain that? But if you *did* find it, you should at least be pleased with the results! Fifty-eight percent of my music class said that they thought you were a virgin. Sister, you've got to understand—such a large part of my life is spent in your company, and yet I hardly know anything about you! You've got to expect a certain amount of healthy curiosity and speculation. Do you ever wish you hadn't become a nun? What would you have done instead? Do you have any regrets? *Are* you a . . . Never any answers from this woman of mystery. Oh, well, you take your time, Sister, I don't mind waiting.

(VINCENT *returns to his seat.* SISTER *appears to be finishing up her work. She shuffles her paper into order, looks at her watch, and goes to the unseen door.*)

SISTER: There. I thought I'd never finish these. Thank you for waiting so patiently.

VINCENT: You know what a patient disposition I have, Sister. But I must admit, I am rather shocked to see you spending your mornings hurriedly finishing up work from the night before. I was always told to do my homework at home.

SISTER: I expect you to do as I say, not as I do. Besides, this is a Monday morning, my least favorite of the week, and these are from D-Group. You'll notice I used up three red pens.

VINCENT: Ah, D-Group. That's the class that laughs every time you mention a dangling participle.

SISTER: Perhaps, perhaps. But they have their good points, too. For example, they never contradict me, unlike certain young men. There is something very charming about a class that believes everything you say.

VINCENT: Now, that wouldn't be any fun. Your mind would rot.

SISTER: Speaking of mind-rot, I've been looking over your transcript.

VINCENT: Sister, it's a perfectly respectable transcript.

SISTER: Well, well, let's see. Shall we examine it more closely?

VINCENT: Do we have to?

SISTER: Now, your standardized test scores put you in the ninety-ninth percentile.

VINCENT: That's good.

SISTER: Yes, that's very good. It would lead one to believe that you were an intelligent young man.

VINCENT: *(Mr. Humility)* Well . . .

SISTER: But we know better.

VINCENT: We do?

SISTER: Of course. Because we come down here, and we see that your grade-point average is a C.

VINCENT: A very high C! Five one-hundredths from a B.

SISTER: It was enough to keep you out of the Honor Society.

VINCENT: I know.

SISTER: Vincent, there is no excuse for a student of your ability to be making such grades.

VINCENT: I have an A in your class, Sister.

SISTER: And what about algebra? And history? And Christian morality?

VINCENT: Now, sometimes I pay a lot of attention in that class.

SISTER: I'm not talking about waking up long enough to proclaim the death of God and then going back to sleep! Getting attention from you in class is like drawing blood from a stone. You're a million miles away every day. You have a mind! Why don't you use it?

VINCENT: I do! Remember all those "Beetle Baileys" I translated into Latin?

SISTER: That's very admirable.

VINCENT: Thank you.

SISTER: I am the last person to throw cold water on a young man's creativity. But the point I am trying to make is that you don't give everything equal access to that mind of yours. And so, Mr. Ryan, we come to the purpose of this little chat.

VINCENT: You mean there's more?

SISTER: Oh, yes! As you know, I have a class of D-Group students, all of whom are bright and eager to learn.

VINCENT: Despite the fact that they haven't quite gotten the knack of their opposable thumbs.

SISTER: *(after giving him a short, disapproving smile)* As it turns out, some of them want so desperately to learn that I have decided they should have personal tutors.

VINCENT: Are they failing that badly?

SISTER: Worse. But they need senior English to graduate, and the last thing I want is Mommy calling me up to ask why I am keeping her little Johnny from graduating with his friends.

VINCENT: What has this got to do with me? I'm not failing anything.

SISTER: It occurred to me that the best way to bring you down from your little cloud would be to give you a student of your own. You are going to be an English tutor.

VINCENT: You're going to make a problem student a tutor?

SISTER: I want you to know what it's like to talk yourself blue in the face to a blank wall. So for one hour every day, sometime after school, you will teach English to one of my D-Group students. Now, I was thinking of giving you Bubba Thompson. . . .

VINCENT: Uh, Bubba Thompson. Gee, I don't think so . . .

SISTER: What do you mean?

VINCENT: Well, we had cross words once, and I don't think we would get along very well.

SISTER: You had cross words with Bubba Thompson?

VINCENT: Well, I had cross words, and he just furrowed his brow and tried to understand what I was saying.

SISTER: I see. Well, who have we got?

VINCENT: *(hesitatingly)* What about, um, Rob Andrews?

(ROB enters from left and goes to his locker. A young man of VINCENT's age, ROB is drop-dead beautiful. He is wearing old shorts, shoes, and shirt for PE. He opens his locker, which contains his school uniform, and takes off his shirt.)

He's in that class, isn't he?

SISTER: *(checking her list)* Yes, he is. And he isn't doing any better than anyone else. Why? Would you rather tutor him?

VINCENT: *(thinking quickly)* Oh, well, it's just that I kind of know him from PE. Our lockers are across from each other.

(ROB *by now has taken off his shoes and socks, and he now takes off his shorts, revealing white cotton briefs. He stretches, and is apparently reluctant to put his uniform on.*)

We've become pretty good friends.

SISTER: Oh, well, that will never do. I can't have you tutoring your best friend; you wouldn't get anything done.

VINCENT: Oh, no, no, no! We're not *best* friends. We're more like nodding acquaintances. You know, we just sort of know each other. We only have one real class together, history, and so we kind of know who the other person is; that way, we wouldn't be going into this strangers. We could get right to work.

(ROB *has gotten his uniform out of his locker and put on his shirt.*)

SISTER: Well, then, that's fine with me. You will be paid five dollars an hour.

VINCENT: Great.

SISTER: And I'll tell Mr. Andrews.

VINCENT: Fine.

SISTER: Now, you've really got to make an effort to teach him.

VINCENT: Oh, I will.

SISTER: Because he needs to pass to graduate.

VINCENT: I understand.

(ROB *has got his pants on.*)

SISTER: So if that is all—

(SISTER *freezes for* VINCENT*'s next speech.*)

VINCENT: Uh, Sister, I do think I should tell you that the only reason I finagled my way into tutoring Rob Andrews is because he is the best-looking boy I have ever seen in my life, and I have been obsessed by him ever since we were freshmen. And the only way I know him from PE is I watch him change his clothes every chance I get. In actuality, I know him about as well as I know Mary Tyler Moore.

(ROB *has now got his school shoes on and his PE clothes put away.* SISTER *returns to normal.*)

SISTER: You've got a class shortly.

VINCENT: That's right.

SISTER: And this is your first day of tutoring.

VINCENT: Oh, really? I didn't realize.

SISTER: Yes, today. Don't forget.

VINCENT: I won't. 'Bye.

SISTER: Good-bye, now.

VINCENT: Uh, Sister, if you don't mind my asking, what did you do before you became a nun?

SISTER: I became a novice right after I graduated from high school. Why?

VINCENT: Just curious. Thank you. 'Bye.

SISTER: Good-bye.

(He leaves her office, then stops center stage.)

VINCENT: Virgin.

Scene Two

(The lights fade on SISTER *as* ROB *finishes dressing and moves center.* ROB *and* VINCENT *meet.)*

VINCENT: Looks like I'm going to be your tutor.

ROB: Yep.

VINCENT: So, like, when do you want to meet? After school?

ROB: Can't. Gotta work. How about eight?

VINCENT: Fine.

ROB: Where?

VINCENT: Uh—my house?

ROB: Okay. But I gotta leave by nine.

VINCENT: Perfect.

ROB: Yeah.

VINCENT: So I'll see you at eight, then. . . .

ROB: Sure.

VINCENT: Hey, have we got history next?

ROB: Uh, yeah, we do.

VINCENT: I guess I'd better get my book, then!

ROB: Yeah.

VINCENT: Well, I'll be seeing you. . . .

ROB: Sure.

(ROB *exits, and* VINCENT *watches him. After he is gone,* VINCENT *stands a moment, then collapses in a heap.*)

Scene Three

(*Lights come up on the history classroom. There are five desks. They contain* VINCENT, CHRIS, DAVID, *and* ROB. *There is one empty desk. Behind his desk sits the* COACH.)

COACH: (*disinterested and poorly informed*) And so, gentlemen, the uh, Greeks wound up going from pretty much Athens in the west, to uh, pretty much Persia and, uh, almost India in the east, which was pretty darned big in those days. And all this was pretty much the fault of Alexander the Great.

(CHRIS *raises his hand.*)

COACH: Uh, yes, Christopher, what may I do for you, sir?

CHRIS: Wasn't Alexander the Great a homosexual?

(*The class laughs, except* VINCENT *and* CHRIS, *who knows he can get away with this by playing it straight.*)

COACH: Well, Chris, are you looking for a role model or something?

CHRIS: No, no. I'm just trying to find out the whole story. I'm really into history, you know?

COACH: Yeah, I know. You're trying to be a jackass is what.

CHRIS: No, really, Coach, isn't that true? Wasn't Alexander the Great a little light in the loafers?

COACH: I'll be perfectly honest with you, I haven't got the slightest idea. But we are not here to discuss the, uh, questionable personal habits of historical figures. Now if you'll be so kind as to let me continue?

CHRIS: Oh, sure, Coach.

COACH: Thank you.

CHRIS: Anytime.

(COACH gives him a look that says "Shut up," and CHRIS laughs.)

COACH: As I was saying, the Greek Empire went from Athens to Persia, and the Greeks kind of spread their culture all over that area in between. It was called, I believe, Hellenic culture, and you might want to write that down, gentlemen. I don't think your memories are all that good, especially going by your last tests . . .

(The COACH's voice begins to fade, and the lights focus on VINCENT.)

VINCENT: Rob is really the most beautiful boy I have ever seen in real life. And when you think about it, being beautiful is as good as being smart, or athletic, or a really great singer. All of those things you're born with, so what makes being born smart better than being born beautiful? Everybody is born with a *most:* most beautiful, most talented, or, for that matter, most obnoxious. I hope my *most* is a good one.

(As soon as COACH speaks, the lights come back up, and VINCENT is taken by surprise.)

COACH: So, Mr. Ryan, what do you suppose the answer to that question might be?

VINCENT: Well, Coach, I've been giving that one some thought, and you know, I'm really stumped. That's a tough one.

COACH: Yeah, it is. The answer, gentlemen, is Sparta, the most militant of the Greek city-states. Now, if you guys think that this school is strict, you would've wet your pants in Sparta. . . .

CHRIS: Coach, if the Greeks were so tough, how did the Romans kick their ass?

COACH: That's a good question, Chris. . . .

(Once again, the COACH becomes silent as the lights focus on VINCENT.)

VINCENT: Chris is just bubbling over with *mosts.* I mean, he's just a great guy. He plays football and basketball both very well, and if his plays don't always make the team win, boy, do they make him look good. He's handsome, too. If you don't believe me, just ask him.

And he's so smart! Gets straight A's. He spends every night before a test studying his voluminous notes, and sometimes he changes those voluminous notes into little tiny notes. And sometimes he keeps on studying those little tiny notes right up to and during the test! What dedication!

DAVID: Coach, how could the Romans and the Greeks both have Asia Minor in their empires? I thought they were enemies.

CHRIS: Because they didn't have them at the same time! Look at the dates on the maps, you idiot!

(CHRIS leans far over in his desk to bop DAVID on the head with his book.)

DAVID: Ow!

CHRIS: Sorry about that, Coach. You've gotta discipline him, or he'll never learn.

VINCENT: David here is smart, but he tries too hard. If he would only calm down long enough to use his brain, he would have something to offer the world. He and Chris became friends in kindergarten over twelve years ago, and they've forgotten how not to be. They are best friends out of habit. In the same way, David is part of the group: out of habit. But if he were to walk into class today, not knowing a soul, I wouldn't give him one semester. On the other hand, he could surprise you. He has a very resilient ego.

(VINCENT goes over to ROB's desk and kneels beside it.)

VINCENT: And then there is Rob, who is . . . beautiful.

(VINCENT becomes lost in reverie.)

COACH: Mr. Ryan.

(Slowly VINCENT returns to his desk.)

COACH: Mr. Ryan.

(VINCENT sits.)

COACH: Vincent, are you there, sir?

(The lights return to normal. VINCENT looks up as the class laughs.)

COACH: Uh, would you like to tell us what was going on in there, Mr. Ryan? Or should I just mark you absent today?

VINCENT: Oh, you don't have to do that, Coach.

COACH: I don't. I feel like I should thank you or something. If you don't start paying more attention, I'll thank you with this stapler upside your head. Now, Chris, why don't you tell us what was so all-fired special about the way the Greeks ran their outer provinces.

CHRIS: Sure, Coach. Well, the Greeks didn't like to bring in a bunch of their own guys to run a conquered territory, so they just kept the local people and pretty much let them keep their own laws, too, not like the Romans who . . .

(As CHRIS*'s voice fades, so do the lights.* VINCENT *is still staring at* ROB.*)*

Scene Four

(Lights come up on VINCENT *alone, center stage.)*

VINCENT: The Cabrini Catholic Academy handbook is very clear on what is considered proper behavior in the halls. A student has exactly three minutes to get from class to class, during which time he is to conduct himself in a manner befitting an institution of learning; ergo, there is to be no running, no eating, no talking, and no roughhousing. However, if you want to talk, go ahead, that one is never enforced. Or better yet, sing. At the top of your lungs. Only one song, however, is considered proper for hall-singing:

*(*VINCENT *begins singing to an Army marching tune.)*

"Two old ladies lyin' in bed
One roll over and the other one said,
I wanna be an Airborne Ranger!''

Under no circumstances should you be caught singing "Over the Rainbow." As a general rule of thumb, any Judy Garland tune is out. If you find the official Cabrini bookbag too cumbersome, there is a world of variety in the way you can carry your books. There is this—

(in his right hand)

and there is this—

(in his left hand)

Never carry your books like this—

(across his chest)

All of these rules, of course, are widely disregarded. But you never know who is watching.

(VINCENT *looks carefully to the left, then to the right, then sings a few lines of a torch song in the style of a Forties crooner. He is transported to Carnegie Hall. He bows as the lights fade.*)

Scene Five

(*Lights up on the English room.* VINCENT, DAVID, *and* CHRIS *are sitting with expressions of mixed amusement, morbid curiosity, and disbelief;* SISTER BEATRICE *is reciting.*)

SISTER: "Hear the sledges with the bells—
Silver bells!
What a world of merriment their melody foretells!
How they tinkle, tinkle, tinkle
In the icy air of night!
While the stars that oversprinkle
All the heavens, seem to twinkle
With a crystalline delight!
Keeping time, time, time,
In a sort of Runic rhyme,
To the tintinnabulation that so musically wells,
From the bells, bells, bells, bells,
Bells, bells, bells—
From the jingling and the tinkling of the bells.

. . .
Hear the loud alarum bells—
Brazen bells!
What a tale of terror, now, their turbulency tells!
In the startled ear of night
How they scream out their affright!
Too much horrified to speak
They can only shriek! shriek!
Out of tune,
In a clamorous appealing to the mercy of the fire,
In a mad expostulation with the deaf and frantic fire,
. . .
By the sinking and the swelling in the anger of the bells—
. . .
Of the bells, bells, bells, bells,
Bells, bells, bells—
In the clamor and the clangor of the bells!
Hear the tolling of the bells,

Iron bells!
What a world of solemn thought their monody compels!
In the silence of the night
How we shiver with affright
At the melancholy menace of their tone!
For every sound that floats
From the rust within their throats
Is a groan!
. . .
To the tolling of the bells,
Of the bells, bells, bells, bells,
Bells, bells, bells!
To the moaning and the groaning of the bells!''

(She throws herself into a deep curtsy, then bounces up, very pleased with her performance.)

That was "The Bells" by Edgar Allan Poe. David, suppose you tell us what the chief poetic device of this poem is.

DAVID: Huh?! Well, uh . . .

(DAVID immediately becomes flustered and searches vainly through his book for the answer.)

I've got the answer right here. . . .

SISTER: Christopher, why don't you help him out?

CHRIS: Well—

DAVID: No, I know this one. I know it! *(His search continues fruitlessly.)*

SISTER: Christopher?

CHRIS: As I was saying, *personification* is . . .

DAVID: *(having finally found the answer)* Personification!

(DAVID gives up disgustedly.)

CHRIS: . . . the chief poetic device of this poem, "The Bells," by Edgar Allan Poe. A very fine poem, I might add.

SISTER: I'm glad you think so, Christopher. Why don't you tell us what it says to you?

(CHRIS does far better with one-word answers. He pauses. He has never, however, been one to let ignorance keep him from voicing an opinion, so he forges ahead.)

CHRIS: Well, this poem told me a lot about bells. I felt I really got to know the different kinds and their individual qualities—I especially enjoyed the part about the alarum bells, I could really feel the danger in the air.

SISTER: Very good, Christopher. Mr. Ryan, what did you think of "The Bells"?

VINCENT: Um, it had some interesting images. . . .

SISTER: Interesting images.

VINCENT: Some nice word-play . . .

SISTER: Word-play.

VINCENT: Very evocative descriptions . . .

SISTER: Good descriptions. What else?

VINCENT: To be perfectly honest—

SISTER: What?

VINCENT: It is the silliest poem I have ever read.

SISTER: Since you are so enthusiastic about "The Bells," class, why don't you write a simple thousand-word essay discussing the author's purpose in writing it?

CHRIS: But Sister! I *do* like it!

SISTER: Then you shouldn't mind writing about it.

CHRIS: *(more to* VINCENT *than to* SISTER*)* *I* didn't say it was silly.

SISTER: Right now we will go on to our next poem, since we're almost out of time. On page 232, you will find "A Noiseless, Patient Spider" by Walt Whitman.

DAVID: Wasn't he a homo?

SISTER: Be quiet, David.

(She takes a deep breath, opens her mouth, and is about to speak when the class-change bell rings. CHRIS *and* DAVID *fly out, leaving* VINCENT *and a disappointed* SISTER BEATRICE.*)*

VINCENT: Hear the lunch bell, joyful bell.

SISTER: Never make fun of a woman when she's down.

VINCENT: Are you down?

SISTER: Have you ever felt that you're spending your entire life trying to make a point that nobody gets?

VINCENT: You would be surprised, Sister.

SISTER: Your day is coming, young man. Have you spoken to Mr. Andrews?

VINCENT: Yes, this morning.

SISTER: You will soon know exactly what I'm talking about.

VINCENT: Oh, you are too smart for me, Sister.

SISTER: You have to get up pretty early, Mr. Ryan. Pretty early.

VINCENT: Sister knows best.

(SISTER *has her papers together and is about to leave the room.*)

SISTER: And by the way, when you are tutoring Mr. Andrews, keep your mind on English.

VINCENT: I beg your pardon?

SISTER: Your mind is so susceptible to wandering. Keep it on English, understand? 'Bye.

(SISTER *exits, and* VINCENT *looks after her thoughtfully.*)

Scene Six

(*Lights come up on the lunchroom. At a table sit* CHRIS, VINCENT, *and* DAVID. *They are eating their lunches.*)

CHRIS: Geez, David, sometimes you are such an idiot! The tangent wave begins at negative one-half pi, not zero; when you're drawing the phase shift, you start at negative one-half pi, not zero. When you draw the phase shift for sine or cosine, then you begin at zero! Jesus!

DAVID: But I thought Mrs. Allen said—

CHRIS: Will you forget what you thought Mrs. Allen said? You never think right anyway. For God's sake, you're usually fuckin' asleep in that class anyway. No wonder you're failing.

DAVID: I'm not failing.

CHRIS: Oh, Jesus, excuse me, you've got a fucking D minus, that's such a big difference!

DAVID: Well, it's not failing.

CHRIS: You will be failing after the test tomorrow; I can see you getting a twelve.

DAVID: The only reason you're passing is because you cheat all the time.

CHRIS: *You* cheat! But you still fail! You're the only person I know who can cheat on a test and still get a forty-four. *(to* VINCENT*)* You know what he did? He had all the answers to the multiple choice in code on his pencil, but this idiot starts at the wrong end of his pencil and fills them all in backward! You're just lucky Mrs. Allen didn't realize that if she had graded your paper backward, you would have had a hundred. Jesus, you're stupid!

DAVID: Vincent, what did you get?

VINCENT: What?

DAVID: In algebra and trig?

VINCENT: Oh, an eighty-two.

CHRIS: I got a ninety-eight.

VINCENT: Yeah, but I got an honest eighty-two. An eighty-two to be proud of. An eighty-two that says, "Hey, I learned eighty-two percent of this chapter." Your ninety-eight says, "Chris can cheat without getting caught."

CHRIS: That's an accomplishment, too.

VINCENT: I thought we were in school to learn.

CHRIS: Learn? Here? Ha! We're in high school to get practice in faking our way through life.

DAVID: And to party.

CHRIS: And to party! *Party!* I think I can safely say I have fully learned the art of partying. All you need is three kegs and a hundred people.

DAVID: And a good band.

CHRIS: Right. Aw, shit. You know what I heard? They're gonna get the same band for the prom this year that they had last year. That sucks.

DAVID: Yeah, well . . . Who are you taking?

CHRIS: Patricia. Who are you taking?

DAVID: You know who I'm taking.

CHRIS: Sharon?! You're actually taking Sharon?

DAVID: What's wrong with that? I like Sharon.

CHRIS: Why? Does she fetch? Can she play dead?

DAVID: Very funny.

CHRIS: Does she have a sister? Or should I say a litter? We could fix Vincent up—

VINCENT: Leave David alone. He should be able to attend the prom with the date of his choice, free from harassment.

CHRIS: Who are you taking?

VINCENT: Me?

CHRIS: Yeah, who?

VINCENT: *(after a pause)* I don't dance.

CHRIS: You can't get a date?

DAVID: You don't have to dance.

VINCENT: I can get a date.

CHRIS: Who are you gonna ask?

VINCENT: I don't know.

CHRIS: Yeah.

(The lights focus on VINCENT.*)*

CHRIS: Sharon. David, you are a jerk.

VINCENT: Actually, Chris, I was thinking of asking Rob Andrews.

DAVID: Would you just forget it?

VINCENT: I think we would look pretty sharp together, in evening wear.

CHRIS: How can I? I have to be seen with you.

VINCENT: I can't dance, though. Of course, he could lead. . . .

DAVID: You don't even know her!

VINCENT: I've never asked someone for a date before; I don't know how. . . .

CHRIS: I hope to keep it that way.

VINCENT: Rob in a tuxedo . . .

DAVID: There's more to a girl than just being pretty.

VINCENT: We'd go to dinner afterward. I guess I'd have to pay.

CHRIS: I've noticed. That's what makes them such bitches.

VINCENT: I'd say good-bye to him on his front porch. . . .

DAVID: You've got to have a better reason for wanting to spend time with a girl than just she's good-looking. Don't you agree, Vincent?

(Lights snap back to normal.)

VINCENT: Yeah! What?

DAVID: Shouldn't you have a better reason for going with a girl than just she's beautiful?

VINCENT: Absolutely.

CHRIS: What would you know?

VINCENT: What I lack in experience I make up in moral fortitude. A girl's physical attractions should be the last of her qualities put under consideration.

(As VINCENT *finishes that little pontification,* ROB *enters from the right and crosses to the left.* VINCENT *sees him, feels terribly hypocritical, puts his head on the table, and covers his face.)*

VINCENT: Oh, Jesus.

*(*CHRIS, *meanwhile, stops* ROB.*)*

CHRIS: Rob, what time is it?

ROB: Five after one.

CHRIS: Yo, wait up. The bell is about to ring; wake up, guy. You'll be late.

*(*VINCENT *sheepishly picks up his head.)*

VINCENT: *(to* ROB*) Hello.*

ROB: Hi.

VINCENT: Haven't forgotten about tonight?

ROB: Nope. Eight.

VINCENT: Eight.

(ROB *and* DAVID *exit.*)

CHRIS: What's at eight?

VINCENT: I'm going to tutor Rob in English.

CHRIS: You're going to tutor Rob Andrews?

VINCENT: Yeah.

CHRIS: Ha! Good luck!

VINCENT: Why, thank you, Chris. Maybe I will get lucky.

Scene Seven

(Lights come up in the locker room. VINCENT *has his PE clothes in a bag.)*

VINCENT: It is interesting to note, I believe, that fidelity is responsible for the making of more saints than the apparition of Mary and the Stigmata combined. Among favorite plot devices in opera, fidelity is second only to the intercepted letter and is way ahead of the babe kidnapped at birth. It is my belief, however, that both Bernadette and Butterfly would break under the weight of maintaining fidelity of thought in the Cabrini locker room; especially to a jock who had difficulty remembering their names. Nonetheless, I am the picture of nonchalance and self-control in the locker room. The jock of my dreams is wearing nothing more than a towel as he walks by me? I'd rather hear about David Gray's sister's braces; very complex orthodontal tools, those. The finest ass in the school is walking back from the shower stark naked? I wouldn't notice such a thing; I'm too busy trying to repair a badly frayed shoelace. *(He pulls out a tennis shoe.)* You can't let these things go on too long. You could wind up with serious sneaker damage.

*(*DAVID *enters and sits down on the bench in front of the locker next to* VINCENT. ROB *enters left and exits right, gym bag in hand.* DAVID *and* VINCENT *begin to change for PE, starting with their shoes and socks.)*

DAVID: I'm not failing, and he knows I'm not. I've got a seventy-four, and if I get anything higher than an eighty-nine on this next test, it will be seventy-five, and that's a C. Of course, if I get anything lower than a forty, I'll have a sixty-nine, which *is* failing, but I'm not worried about that. The only reason I got that forty-four was be-cause of the term paper in global perspectives—I didn't have any time to study. I'll probably wind up with a C, or if I really work, I could have a B. But I'm not failing. Chris is the one who had better watch out about failing. One of these days, he's gonna get caught cheating, and then see if he's president of the Math Club!

VINCENT: Why are you telling me all this? Tell Chris. You shouldn't let him talk to you the way he does.

DAVID: Nah, then I'd never hear the end of it.

(There is a pause.)

DAVID: You know, Miz Culbert caught him cheating once, but she didn't do anything. She just took his test. If I got caught cheating, I would be put on suspension so fast, it wouldn't even be funny.

VINCENT: No, you wouldn't, and neither would I. We're too well liked by the faculty.

DAVID: You know, Miz Culbert would be pretty, but her tits are too small.

VINCENT: What?

DAVID: Miz Culbert's tits are too small. She would be pretty, but she's got no chest.

VINCENT: Are you serious?

DAVID: Yeah, haven't you ever noticed?

VINCENT: No, I can't say that I have.

DAVID: Really? How could you help it?

VINCENT: I just don't notice that kind of thing.

DAVID: That's weird, man.

VINCENT: It's not weird. Why is that weird?

DAVID: I don't know. That's all I think about in music. What about Miss Sanders? Have you ever noticed her chest?

VINCENT: *(exasperated)* Christ, David, you've known me for three years, can't you—

(There is an awkward pause. VINCENT is afraid to finish what he has begun, and DAVID doesn't often see VINCENT upset. Then, from offstage, we hear CHRIS's voice, followed shortly by CHRIS.)

CHRIS: "Two old ladies lyin' in bed!

(He appears.)

"One roll over and the other one said,

(He hits DAVID on the head with a football.)

"I wanna be an Airborne Ranger!"

(To DAVID.) Come on, man, you're on my team today. Vincent, think fast! *(He throws the football at VINCENT and exits.)*

DAVID: Are you going to play today?

VINCENT: I don't think so.

(DAVID exits. Lights up on VINCENT, center, tossing the football in one hand.)

VINCENT: I've grown to like PE. I'm not much into sports, but then the coaches aren't much into getting me into sports. So I just pretend like I'm participating, and they pretend like they don't know I'm pretending. It works out very nicely; they can concentrate on coaching the guys who are actually interested in football, and I can concentrate on the guys. Well, really, one guy in particular. It's a purely academic interest, mind you—after all, I have only a scant five hours to prepare for an evening tutorial.

Scene Eight

(The lights come up on the living room of VINCENT's house. There is a sofa center. VINCENT tries on clothes to find the right look. Suddenly, he hears a silent doorbell ring. He goes to the door, and opens it, revealing ROB. They fall into a passionate kiss. Then VINCENT, still embraced by ROB, pulls his head back and looks at the other boy.)

VINCENT: Sure you're gonna do that.

(He pushes ROB out the door. He starts to pace, occasionally looking at his watch and the wall mirror. Then he sits down. The doorbell really rings. VINCENT opens the door, and ROB enters, dressed in a jacket, a tank-top T-shirt and jeans. He carries a textbook, a notebook, and a pen.)

Well, hello. Come in.

ROB: Hi.

VINCENT: Did you just get off work?

ROB: No, I had to go home and shower first.

VINCENT: Oh, I see.

ROB: Why, am I late?

VINCENT: Only about forty minutes. I hadn't really noticed until now.

ROB: I'm sorry.

VINCENT: Don't worry about it, but we don't have a whole lot of time left. Didn't you say you had to be somewhere at nine?

ROB: Yeah.

VINCENT: So . . . have a seat. (VINCENT *notices that* ROB *is already seated.*) How are you doing in English? Sister Beatrice made it sound like you were having some trouble.

ROB: I guess you could say that.

VINCENT: What are your grades like?

ROB: Mostly failing. But I did get a C the other day.

VINCENT: Well, that's . . . average, at least.

ROB: Yeah.

(*There is a pause.*)

VINCENT: What are y'all studying right now?

ROB: English.

VINCENT: Yes, but, uh, what aspect of English?

ROB: Oh, we're in poetry right now.

VINCENT: Yeah, she's got my class on the same thing. Does she read to y'all?

ROB: Yeah.

VINCENT: She's quite a character, sometimes.

ROB: Yeah.

(*Pause.*)

VINCENT: Is that your book?

ROB: Yeah, it is. Here.

(ROB *hands the book to* VINCENT.)

VINCENT: What page are y'all on?

ROB: 547.

(VINCENT *finds the page.*)

VINCENT: Ah, "There Is No Frigate Like a Book." Have you read this?

ROB: Maybe, I don't remember.

VINCENT: Oh. Okay. I'll read it.

"There is no frigate like a book
  To take us lands away,
Nor any coursers like a page
  Of prancing poetry.
This traverse may the poorest take
  Without oppress of toll;
How frugal is the chariot
  That bears the human soul!"

Um, did you notice how the words she chose enhanced the meaning of the poem?

ROB: What was the meaning?

VINCENT: Well, what do you think?

ROB: I don't know, we haven't gone over that one yet. Sometimes she gives us stuff to read and never does tell us what it means.

VINCENT: Yeah, she does that to us, too.

ROB: But she expects us to know it for a test.

VINCENT: Oh, well, that's her way. . . .

ROB: She's a bitch, that's all.

VINCENT: Well, be that as it may, when Emily Dickinson wrote "There Is No . . ."—

ROB: What was her name?

VINCENT: Emily Dickinson.

(ROB *gets out his pen and starts to write in his notebook.*)

ROB: Dick—in—son. . . . Wasn't she the bitch who lived locked away in her house all her life?

VINCENT: Uh, yes, but I wouldn't exactly call her a bitch.

ROB: You know what I mean. It doesn't sound like she was completely normal.

VINCENT: Nobody is.

ROB: Whatever. So what does it mean? *(He is poised to take notes.)*

VINCENT: She is just saying that books are a way of traveling around the world in your mind, that doesn't cost anything, and—

ROB: Wait!

(ROB is writing laboriously. VINCENT is amazed to find that he is taking down his every word.)

. . . doesn't . . . cost . . . anything . . . and. What now?

VINCENT: I guess that pretty much says it.

ROB: Great. What's next?

(ROB smiles; apparently poetry is going to be easier than he thought.)

VINCENT: Um, well, let's see. *(He looks at the next page.)* It's "On Going to the Wars" by Richard Lovelace.

ROB: Like in Linda?

VINCENT: I suppose so, yeah. It goes like this:

"Tell me not, Sweet, I am unkind
    That from the nunnery
Of thy chaste breast and quiet mind,
    To war and arms I fly.

"True, a new mistress now I chase,
    The first foe in the field;
And with a stronger faith embrace
    A sword, a horse, a shield.

"Yet this inconstancy is such
    As you, too, shall adore;
I could not love thee, Dear, so much,
    Loved I not honor more."

This poem always gets on my nerves.

(ROB starts to write this down.)

No, no, you don't have to write that. I'll tell you when you should write something down. I was just going to say that my personal opinion of the poem is that it is highly irritating, not to mention philosophically unsound.

ROB: Why's that?

VINCENT: Well, here's this guy telling his girlfriend he's going to risk his life for honor. That's stupid; he's probably fighting over hunting rights in some royal forest, and he'll probably come out without a scratch while a couple hundred of his serfs will be hacked to death—in the name of honor. Wars aren't fought for noble reasons; they're fought over money. I can't think of any war worth fighting.

ROB: Well, what if the Russians invaded us, what then?

VINCENT: If they want the country that badly, let them have it.

ROB: That's stupid.

VINCENT: No, think. Communism and dictatorship will never take hold in America. Russia's known nothing but tyranny for the past thousand years. We've had freedom since the sixteen hundreds. We'd never stand for it; it just wouldn't work.

ROB: So we would have to fight them.

VINCENT: No, we could use peaceful methods like civil disobedience or passive resistance. Haven't you ever heard of Gandhi?

ROB: The guy in the movie?

VINCENT: Yeah. He freed India from the English without fighting a war.

ROB: Oh.

VINCENT: Yeah!

ROB: Well, I still think we should nuke 'em off the face of the earth.

VINCENT: That is the most asinine statement I have ever heard in my life.

ROB: Oh? What does *asinine* mean? *(He takes off his jacket to reveal a tight tank-top T-shirt.)*

VINCENT: Asinine means . . . interesting; that is the most . . . interesting statement I have ever heard in my life. That brings us to "Oh, Who Is That Young Sinner" by A. E. Housman.

ROB: Hey, are we almost done? 'Cause I've got to meet my girlfriend soon.

(Pause.)

VINCENT: Girlfriend?

ROB: Yeah.

(Pause.)

VINCENT: Oh, who is it—she! Who is she?

ROB: Joan McNamara.

VINCENT: Oh, I know Joan! Does she still drive that pink Volkswagen?

ROB: No, she totaled it.

VINCENT: Wow, was she hurt?

ROB: No. But her father had to relay the foundation of their pool.

VINCENT: Oh . . . heh, that sounds like Joan. Y'all are supposed to go out tonight?

ROB: Yeah.

VINCENT: Gonna get something to eat?

ROB: Maybe. Might just hang out at her house. But, hey, don't think I won't have any time to study.

VINCENT: No, no. I wasn't even thinking about that. Just being nosy, I guess. I don't go out much.

(There is a pause.)

But anyway. Our next poem is "The Garden of Love" by William Blake.

ROB: Sounds like a porno flick.

VINCENT: "I went to the Garden of Love
And saw what I never had seen.
A chapel was built in the midst,
Where I used to play on the green.

"And the gates of the chapel were shut,
And 'Thou Shalt Not' writ over the door;
So I turned to the Garden of Love
That so many sweet flowers bore;

"And I saw it was filled with graves
And tombstones where flowers should be;
And priests in black gowns were walking their rounds
And binding with briars my joys and desires."

So you see that the Garden of Love is really a metaphor for organized religion. He is saying that the "Thou Shalt Not" approach to religion takes most of the innocent fun out of life. It's binding with briars his joys and desires. (VINCENT *takes a deep breath.*) And I really doubt he was thinking of this when he wrote the poem, but I can't help but associate that last line with—homosexuality.

ROB: You mean this poem is about fags?

VINCENT: No! I mean . . . it could be, if you wanted to see it that way. I mean, uh, it fits in with the general idea, in that homosexuals don't really hurt anyone, and yet most of organized religion is screaming at them that they are sinners, when all they are doing is having sex, and what's so awful about that?

ROB: When it's two guys? That's sick.

VINCENT: Maybe to you, but not to them, so why is it your business? Why is it the Church's business?

ROB: It's in the Bible.

VINCENT: A lot of things are in the Bible! In the Old Testament it says not to eat ham, do you follow that? In the New Testament it says to forgive your enemies, to turn the other cheek, an idea the Old Testament totally contradicts. Do you know that in grade school, the nuns told me it was all right to kill during a war? That God wouldn't mind?

ROB: That's true. It's okay when there's a war on.

VINCENT: Not if you follow the teachings of Christ. And I have yet to meet a Christian who does.

ROB: You're a Christian.

VINCENT: Not really. I'm an atheist.

ROB: You are not.

VINCENT: Yes, I am. Is that hard to believe?

ROB: You're really an atheist?

VINCENT: Sure. My belief about God is that there is none. Jews don't accept Christ. Well, I don't accept any of it.

ROB: You've got some strange ideas, man.

VINCENT: What, that I think that if two people love each other, they should be able to have sex, be it man-man, woman-woman, or even man-woman? That it's wrong to kill people wholesale over something stupid like oil lanes, or land, or worse still, politics? That Christ should be taken at His meaning, not at His word? Those ideas aren't strange at all. In fact, the poets have been screaming all of that at the pigheaded human race ever since time began! If you ask me, to believe anything else is not only strange but dangerous!

(There is a short pause as VINCENT *exults in self-righteousness.)*

ROB: Should I be takin' notes or something?

(That takes all the wind out of VINCENT. *He slumps down onto the sofa.)*

VINCENT: No.

ROB: Okay. *(He looks at his watch.)* Hey, I've gotta be going. *(He gathers his books.)* It's been real interesting.

VINCENT: Really interesting. It's been really interesting.

ROB: Oh. Sure. So, uh, will I see you tomorrow night, same time?

*(*ROB *freezes.)*

VINCENT: Tomorrow night, same time? You mean forty minutes late? What nerve! Sister Beatrice meant this to be a challenge, but I'm not up to it! He calls Emily Dickinson a bitch, can't figure out "There Is No Frigate Like a Book," and is a warmonger to boot! I don't care how beautiful he is, if he tries to walk through that door tomorrow night, I'll clobber him with the family Bible!

ROB: Will I see you tomorrow night, same time?

VINCENT: Sure.

ROB: Great. Well, I've gotta be going. See ya.

*(*ROB *is at the door.)*

VINCENT: Wait! *(Lightly.)* Do you feel like you've learned anything tonight?

ROB: *(enthusiastically)* Yeah! I've got that Dickinson bitch down cold.

VINCENT: Oh. Well, that's great.

ROB: See ya.

*(*ROB *exits.* VINCENT *stands a moment in thought. He then crosses to the mirror in which he looked at himself at the beginning of the scene, and looks again. He looks away, then crosses to the sofa, where he picks up* ROB's *English book and distractedly thumbs through the pages. Then he remembers something. He looks up a certain page in the book and reads aloud.)*

VINCENT: "I have heard of reasons manifold
Why love must needs be blind,

But this is the best of all I hold
His eyes are in his mind.''

(Lights fade to black.)

EVAN SMITH

(1986) Then . . .

"I've got to go home. I'm writing this play to enter in this contest, and it has to be in the mail tomorrow, and I haven't even begun to type it.''

"I'm going back to Savannah. Yeah, I know three weeks is a short time, but I'm sure that art school isn't for me. Maybe I'll be a writer. I'm waiting to hear from this contest. . . .''

"I'll know definitely by March, but I'm sure I won't win. The play is godawful.''

"What do you mean, someone from the Young Playwrights Festival called?! Where was I? Why didn't you get me?! My God, don't you realize what this means?!''

"Well, the guy who played Matthew Broderick's best friend in *Ferris Bueller's Day Off* was gonna do it, but he got offered this movie. Yeah, that's what I said.''

"I've been trying to think of something for the ending.''

"What do you think of this for the ending?''

"I have an idea for the ending.''

"Well, it's too late to worry about that now.''

"Oh, I've been a big fan of yours ever since I got the album of *Sweeney Todd.*''

"John Simon surprised me, too.''

"I've already missed a week of winter quarter, but anyway, good luck with next year's contest. 'Bye.''

"No, it wasn't done on Broadway. It was Off Broadway. It's kind of hard to explain, but I did meet some pretty important people. I met Stephen Sondheim. What? Oh, well, he writes musicals, you see. Have you ever heard that song, 'Send in the Clowns'?"

"Whadda they mean, *The Ground Zero Club and* Other *Plays*"?

. . . *And Now*

Evan Smith graduated from Vassar College and is a graduate student in the playwrighting program of the Yale School of Drama.

THE GROUND ZERO CLUB

by
CHARLIE SCHULMAN
(age eighteen when play was written)
New York, New York

■

The Ground Zero Club was performed at Playwrights Horizons in New York City, April 7 through April 28, 1985. It was directed by John Ferraro, and Wendy Wasserstein was the playwright adviser. The sets were by Loren Sherman, and the costumes were by Jennifer Von Mayrhauser. The lighting designer was Stephen Strawbridge, and the sound designer was Scott Lehrer. Kate Stewart was the stage manager.

The cast:

TOURIST	*Thomas Ikeda*
GUARD	*Tom Mardirosian*
VOICEOVER	*Bill Schoppert*
ANGELA	*Elizabeth Berridge*
SAL	*Larry Joshua*
FEONNA	*Polly Draper*
BOB	*Bill Schoppert*
TANYA	*Lucinda Jenney*

The set is on two levels that divide the stage in half. Downstage is the outside viewing area. Downstage right is a viewer telescope, which requires a quarter to operate. Four stairs lead up to the raised half upstage, which is inside the observation deck. Inside stage left a corner of the souvenir stand can be seen. Upstage left is a public telephone hanging on a side wall. In between the stand and the telephone is the only entrance/exit. A backdrop of New York City at night surrounds the stage. The backdrop may be a drawing, a photograph, or a cut-out, as long as a feeling of looking down on the city is conveyed. Hovering over the stage is a red, white, and blue glow that emanates from the top of the building.

Staring through the viewer telescope at individual members of the audience is the TOURIST. *The faint sounds of sirens, car horns, and general panic in the streets can be heard as searchlights scan the sky and stage. In the midst of this confusion, the disheveled figure of the* SECURITY GUARD *can be seen bursting through the door and down the steps. Loud static can be heard coming from the walkie-talkie that he holds in front of him. As he looks over the side and into the street below, the lights slowly come up.*

GUARD: *(screaming into the walkie-talkie)* What do you mean, nobody can do anything about it?

VOICEOVER: Sorry, Jack, it's a nuclear war. Yes, nuclear war!

GUARD: What?

VOICEOVER: Yes, nuclear war!

GUARD: What am I supposed to do now?

VOICEOVER: You can take the rest of the day off.

GUARD: I'd rather have the overtime.

VOICEOVER: Okay. *(Static is heard.)*

GUARD: So what do we do now? I've never seen so many people down there. Traffic is not moving at all. Who knows the emergency plan to get the hell out of this city? Did they say it on the radio? Jesus Christ, what's a guy supposed to do during a nuclear war, anyway? All I did was go to the bathroom, and when I got out, all this was going on, and everyone had left—even Marcie, who runs the souvenir stand. She probably wanted to be with her boyfriend. *(He takes a sip from his flask.)* So I'm the one who winds up feeling stupid for having no place to go. I wish I had someone I was close to. There's my mother, of course, but she lives down in Florida. *(Static is heard.)* Hello! *(More static. He turns off the walkie-talkie and returns it to his belt. He runs back inside to the public telephone and dials a number.)* Three dollars and fifty cents? *(He searches his pockets.)* Damn! *(He drops the receiver and climbs over the souvenir stand.)* Marcie, you cleared out the register. *(He climbs back over and picks up the receiver.)* Yeah, operator, I would like to make a collect call to Florida. My name is Jack. Hello, Mom, it's Jack. *(Bursting into tears.)* I can't believe this is happening but I love you, Ma, I love you. *(Suddenly he stops crying.)* What do you mean, you won't accept the charges? I don't have any money on me. How can I visit you? I live in New York! Ma!

(They have been disconnected. He hangs up the phone, walks over to the window that separates the inside from the outside, presses his face up against the glass, and begins to cry. SAL ID *and* ANGELA *enter.* SAL *is pulling* ANGELA, *who is resisting, by the wrist.* SAL *sports a sleeveless T-shirt with a picture of his dead hero, Sid Vicious.* ANGELA *is just a girl from Queens. She bites* SAL *on the arm.)*

SAL: Ahhhhh!

*(ANGELA *exits.* SAL *follows her, muttering under his breath. They reenter,* SAL *carrying* ANGELA *under his arm.)*

ANGELA: Let go of me, you bastard! Get your hands off of me!

*(SAL *puts his hand over her mouth.)*

SAL: We're the first ones here! *(Fiendishly.)* Lucky we were in the neighborhood.

ANGELA: Why did you bring me here? This place is for tourists!

SAL: Don't be stupid, Angela. You heard what they said on the radio, just like I did.

ANGELA: *(looking over the side)* You can't just leave the car like that in the middle of the street with the keys in the ignition.

SAL: We don't need it anymore.

ANGELA: Let's go home, Sal, please? Let's go back to Astoria.

SAL: Forget it. We'd never make it back past the Fifty-Ninth Street Bridge, and even if we did make it back, what good would it do us? Maybe something will go wrong, and they'll blow up New Jersey instead. Wouldn't that be great? No more bridge-and-tunnel traffic crowding up the bars!

*(The GUARD *selects a postcard from the souvenir stand and presses it up against the window.)*

ANGELA: If we went back, we could say good-bye to everyone. I want to see my mother. We should be with the people who care about us.

GUARD: *(writing on the postcard)* Dear Anybody.

SAL: What difference does it make? Look, Angela, we are with the people who care about us—we're with each other. I don't want to go back there. I've been spending my whole life trying to get out of that place.

ANGELA: In that case you haven't done very well.

SAL: I'm not there now, am I? That's the great thing about this country. You can blow up anywhere you like. They don't have that kind of freedom in Russia.

ANGELA: I once heard that if you were up here and dropped a penny over the side, it would make a three-inch hole in the pavement. I wonder if it's true? *(She drops a penny over the side.)*

SAL: Don't you know where you are, Angela? This is ground zero. This is the spot where all those missiles are aimed at. Maybe we'll get a good look at one. *(Looking around.)* The observation deck of the Empire State Building. Believe me, Angela, this is the best place to be at a time like this. We're lucky—we're going to see the last that anyone does of this town. So enjoy the view while it's still there. *(They both look out at the city.)* You know, I've never told you this before, but I'm a member of the Ground Zero Club.

ANGELA: What are you talking about? You never belonged to anything before.

SAL: Well, I belong to something now. All the members are supposed to meet here right before a nuclear war to join together for one last tremendous party. I'm sure the rest of the members will be getting here soon. I sure have waited a long time for this.

ANGELA: I don't believe this is happening. I never asked for this. It's not fair. I haven't had any fun yet. I haven't enjoyed anything at all yet. I was just about to become happy. It would probably have started tomorrow.

SAL: It's just like the seventh game of the World Series, when the announcer says, "There is no tomorrow." I get such a kick out of hearing them say that.

ANGELA: All I ever asked for was a dishwasher and a house to put it in, with children who would take turns loading it.

SAL: Yeah, I was really looking forward to that, but there's no point in dreaming.

ANGELA: We could have had so much together. Another ten years, and we would have been able to move out of my parents' home. Of course, you're fucked up now, but you would have straightened out.

SAL: We're better off this way. We would probably have gotten divorced in a few years anyhow. What if the kids turned out to be jerks who had terrible personalities and were addicted to drugs like I am? What would we have done then? One day we would have come home and found them with all these electrodes hooked up to their brains. I woulda hadda said, "Kids you don't need to get high with a computer. In our day we just smoked pot and ate Quaaludes."

ANGELA: You're wrong, Sal. Our children won't get high from computers. They'll take the same drugs that we did. We'll have plenty of liquor around the house, so there won't be any need for computers.

GUARD: *(writing)* I am up here on the observation deck. If you are as lonely as I am and have no one to be with during this nuclear war, then you should come up to the top so that we can spend our last moments together.

ANGELA: How much time do you think we have left?

SAL: Who knows? Maybe ten, fifteen minutes.

GUARD: Sincerely, a concerned citizen.

SAL: But a lot of things can still happen if we make every second count and fill our time with intensely profound revelations. I'm good at those when the pressure is on.

(The GUARD drops the postcard over the side.)

ANGELA: Oh, no! The seconds are just passing by, and I'm not having any revelations. What are we going to do? We can't just stand here. I mean, should we pray or what?

GUARD: What's the point in praying? The human race is committing suicide. Nobody goes to heaven.

ANGELA: I'm not committing suicide. I didn't put those missiles there. I never wanted a nuclear war.

SAL: Don't worry, baby. Hell might be a terrible place, but it's probably better than your parents' house. I'm sure we'll be able to find a nice neighborhood. Yeah, I'll get a job, we'll buy a mobile home, raise a family—it'll be just like life, only much more horrible. Burning for eternity couldn't be as bad as it sounds. I'm sure you just pass out after a few minutes, anyway.

ANGELA: Maybe the radio made a mistake! It doesn't feel like there isn't any time left. If we really only had twenty minutes to live, I'm certain I wouldn't be doing what I'm doing right now.

SAL: What would you be doing?

ANGELA: Something wild and exciting. I wouldn't still be planning for the future. I would never be here if this was really happening.

(The sound of the viewer telescope running out of time can be heard. The TOURIST *looks up for a moment, puts a quarter into the machine, and resumes looking at the audience.)*

SAL: *(to the* GUARD*)* Hi, mister, glad you could make it. It just seems right that we spend our last few minutes with a total stranger. *(To* ANGELA.*)* What is it that your mother always says?

ANGELA: *(reluctantly)* "The best friends you'll ever have are the people you were forced to be with."

SAL: Ain't that the truth? *(The* GUARD *takes a sip from his flask.)* I'm Sal Id. You might have heard of me or seen my band, Violent Apathy.

GUARD: I don't think so. Where have you played?

SAL: We had a few gigs down at the . . . *(Pauses to think for a moment.)* But they closed it down. We also gigged at the . . . *(He thinks for a moment.)* But now it's one of those fancy cheese and pasta shops. Actually, we don't play together anymore.

ANGELA: They had a vicious argument because nobody cared about the band.

(The GUARD *passes his flask to* SAL.*)*

SAL: This is my girlfriend, Angela.

GUARD: It certainly is a pleasure to die with you two.

ANGELA: You mean it's definite? Maybe they made a mistake.

GUARD: Not likely. At least, everybody down there doesn't seem to think so. They're all rushing to something or other. It's too bad it takes a nuclear war to make some of these people do what they've always wanted to do.

SAL: That's what's so terrific about it. Things that we've always wanted to do but couldn't for whatever reason, we can do right now.

(They all stand in silence for ten seconds, not doing anything.) Isn't it a great feeling?

ANGELA: It's kind of hard to think about my own death when I haven't even gotten over John Lennon's yet.

SAL: I'm sick and tired of hearing about how wonderful John Lennon was! It's easy to want everyone to love each other when you have three hundred million dollars. Sid Vicious, on the other hand *(pointing to his shirt)*—now, Sid was the real thing. He never placed himself above the scum that came to see him play. He was a real working-class hero. Didn't let being famous make him look like some kind of great guy. In fact, as he got more famous, he became more fucked up on purpose, just to prove that being a star was nothing but a bunch of bullshit.

GUARD: You've got a real good sense of humor, kid. How do you like that? Just when you think it's all over, you find a new friend.

(They shake hands and share the bottle. BOB *and* FEONNA *appear inside. They have been on an expensive night on the town.* BOB *is wearing a tuxedo, and* FEONNA *a silver lamé jumpsuit.)*

BOB: *(to* FEONNA*)* Are you certain you want to come here? I have pull at Windows on the World. I'm sure we could get a table there.

FEONNA: No, no, no, absolutely not. This is the more appropriate place to die.

BOB: I wonder how things will be after this is all over?

FEONNA: Exactly like that "after the nuclear holocaust" party we went to last Friday. Remember when we asked for ice to put in our drinks?

BOB: Wasn't that terrific? *(He laughs.)* "No ice," they said. "There will be no ice after the bomb." What a thing to think of. No ice. *(Laughing.)* Hard to imagine, really.

ANGELA: You know, maybe this isn't the safest place to be right now.

GUARD: *(to* SAL*)* If you ever need someone to talk to, you can come to me.

SAL: Thanks, that's real nice of you.

ANGELA: I know the view is great, but maybe we'd have a better chance if we were somewhere else.

BOB: We can still go to Windows.

FEONNA: Are you insane? Do you realize how difficult it will be to get a cab?

SAL: To tell the truth, I sort of do have a problem.

GUARD: Nothing too heavy, if you know what I mean? Nothing monumental. Little things, trivial things, if you can get at what I'm saying.

SAL: She's pregnant.

GUARD: I was just making a gesture, damn it! I don't want to hear your problems. I was just being a nice guy.

SAL: Yeah. You know, I'm feeling kind of guilty. I would have married her. I would have done the right thing. Lucky it didn't have to come to that, though.

ANGELA: Maybe we should go underground, Sal.

SAL: Why would you want to do that?

(SAL and ANGELA continue talking as the GUARD looks on. The door swings open, and FEONNA walks outside, followed by BOB.)

FEONNA: I see no reason why I shouldn't jump from here. This is as good a place as any—even better.

BOB: All I'm saying is that the Twin Towers are a bit higher, that's all, dear. And they have a bar.

FEONNA: Out of my way. I'm going to jump. Good-bye, Bob.

(She makes a move to jump over the side, but the GUARD stops her.)

GUARD: I'm sorry, ma'am, but I can't let you do that.

FEONNA: Why not?

BOB: Let go of my wife.

FEONNA: Give him some money, Bob.

(BOB gives him fifty dollars.)

BOB: What's the matter? Fifty isn't enough?

GUARD: You want to pay me so your wife can kill herself?

BOB: Of course I don't want to pay you, but it doesn't look as if I have a choice, does it?

(The sound of the viewer telescope running out of time can be heard. The TOURIST looks up, takes a quarter out of his pocket, puts it into the machine, and resumes looking through the viewer.)

GUARD: But she's your wife! Don't you want to spend these last moments together so you can comfort each other?

BOB: Look, we weren't born together, we didn't travel together, so I see no reason why we should ruin it all by dying together.

FEONNA: Why shouldn't I die the way I want to instead of the way somebody else wants me to? I find this whole nuclear issue so distasteful that, frankly, I don't wish to have any part of it. All people ever talk about is nuclear war, nuclear war, nuclear war. Even after they had that TV movie, people were still talking about it. It's just so passé.

SAL: That movie was great. I was hoping they would turn it into, like, a weekly series out of it.

FEONNA: But today was the final straw. There we were, celebrating Bob's new appointment, when this man came running into the restaurant with this vulgar news.

GUARD: *(to BOB)* What kind of appointment, Bob?

BOB: Oh, it's nothing, really.

FEONNA: Don't be silly, Bobby. A government position in Washington is not nothing at all.

SAL: What kind of position?

FEONNA: Bob is the new assistant secretary to the associate secretary of the secretary to the secretary of defense.

ANGELA: Secretary of defense? What are you doing here? You should be trying to do something to stop this.

BOB: I don't officially take office until Monday.

FEONNA: *(to the GUARD)* Why don't you be a nice man and let go of my arm before my husband sees to it that you never work in this town again?

(The GUARD backs off.)

SAL: *(embracing ANGELA)* Oh, Angie, this is turning out better than I ever thought it would. Everybody dies together, and nobody has to miss a thing. Finally some justice—everyone suffers equally. Can you believe it? *Me* and the assistant secretary to the associate secretary of the secretary to the secretary of defense at the same time in the same place? This is unbelievable. This could only happen in America.

(TANYA appears inside. She is holding a box of buttons in one hand and a postcard in the other. She peers out at the rest of the people, in search of someone.)

ANGELA: Maybe we shouldn't just give up and die, Sal.

TANYA: Get your buttons here! All antinuclear paraphernalia half off. Clearance sale—everything must go!

FEONNA: Oh, Bob, a sale!

TANYA: Better active today than radioactive tomorrow!

SAL: Oh, come off it. Some people never know when to give up and relax.

TANYA: At least I did my best. Now I'll try and raise consciousness until the end.

(The sound of the viewer telescope running down can be heard. The TOURIST looks up, puts another quarter in the machine, and resumes looking at the audience.)

BOB: *(to FEONNA)* What's the matter, dear? Why don't you jump?

FEONNA: Aren't you going to stop me?

BOB: Why would you do that if this is what you want? You know I always try to make you happy.

FEONNA: My analyst would have tried to stop me.

BOB: What could he do for you? The man broke down and cried when he saw Freud's couch on a visit to Vienna.

SAL: Wasn't that the guy who wanted to kill his father and sleep with his mother? I never wanted to do that.

TANYA: *(shouting over everybody)* It's time for everybody to face up to the fact that they saw this coming and didn't do anything about it.

SAL: I always wanted to kill my father and my mother and then sleep with both of them.

BOB: *(to TANYA)* The human race was out of control a long time ago. It's a good thing this is happening now, before we did something really terrible.

TANYA: Don't you see that you are all responsible for this?

ANGELA: What about him? He's a politician.

BOB: Don't look at me—I'm just a cog in the wheel.

ANGELA: *(to* TANYA*)* He was just appointed to something really big today.

TANYA: So you're the new secretary of the secretary to the secretary!

BOB: *(backing up)* I don't take office until Monday.

TANYA: Okay, everybody, we got this guy right where we want him.

BOB: I'm innocent, I tell you! (SAL, ANGELA, TANYA, *and the* GUARD *circle around* BOB.) I wouldn't worry if I were you. I'm sure our government knows what's going on and that they're doing everything in their power to avert a disaster. Why, we're probably speaking with the Russians right now.

FEONNA: *(taking out a cigarette)* Bob, I need a light.

BOB: All right! I tried, I really did. We thought we could prevent a confrontation, but I guess I was wrong. Everybody makes mistakes.

(He forces a smile.)

FEONNA: *(to the* TOURIST*)* I need a light.

BOB: Of course, somebody has to take responsibility for this and, well, it might as well be me. *(They nod their heads.)* I'm as much responsible for this as anyone. *(They nod again.)*

FEONNA *(throwing the cigarettes over the side):* In that case, I quit.

BOB: I should be punished for this! Really I should! *(All nod as they close in.)* I should be tortured! Someone torture me slowly and painfully. Please! I'll buy all these buttons. How many do you have?

TANYA: About three hundred. (BOB *hands her ten dollars and takes the box. As he picks up the first button, he begins to weep. Slowly he puts every button in the box on his clothing.)*

FEONNA: Bob, I changed my mind. I don't think I wanted to come here after all. Why don't we go home and watch the rest of this on the news?

BOB: *(crying and oblivious to* FEONNA *as he looks at the button that he is putting on his collar)* "What if they gave a war and nobody came?"

GUARD: *(finishing what is left in his flask)* It's empty. I guess I might as well quit also.

(He throws the flask over the side.)

ANGELA: Sal, I think we should break up.

SAL: What are you talking about? You're just upset, that's all.

ANGELA: No, Sal, I don't think you're very good for me.

SAL: You can't do this to me, Angela. We need each other right now. You can't leave me in the middle of a nuclear war!

ANGELA: It's always something with you. If it wasn't a nuclear war, it would be something else.

SAL: Look, we'll discuss this in hell. *(They continue arguing.)*

TANYA: Is there a concerned citizen here?

GUARD: Yes?

TANYA: I got your postcard. *(She holds it up.)*

GUARD: I was hoping you would.

ANGELA: When are you going to get off this rebel punk stuff, huh? You're twenty-five—you're too old to be a punk rocker. Look at yourself. You're growing facial hair.

SAL: What do you want for me to do, sell out? I would if someone was buying.

ANGELA: Look at the way you dress, Sal. You're out of date. Sid is dead, and all that shit is over.

SAL: So what? Who cares? So big deal—I'll never be a big star. So what? Who cares! But let me tell you one thing. It took me a long fucking time to hit rock bottom, and I'm not going to stop there. *(He takes out a pair of drumsticks from his back pocket and pretends to play the drums.)*

One, two, three, four!

> "Anarchy burger, hold the government!
> Anarchy burger, hold the government
> . . . Please!"

ANGELA: I've known a lot of losers in my life, but you are the most boring.

SAL: *(holding a bag of pills)* Yeah? Well, I guess there's no point in saving all these for the weekend. *(He eats them all.)*

BOB: *(still crying and looking at another button that he is putting on his clothes)* "War is not healthy for children and other living things!"

FEONNA: *(finally realizing that nobody cares whether she jumps or not)* I feel so out of place. I don't have anything in common with these people. This is just like all the parties I go to. I feel so lonely and bored.

GUARD: I know we hardly know each other, and I know it's hard to say "I love you" to a stranger, but I think I really do. You're special. I don't know you, and I never will. *(The* GUARD *and* TANYA *begin to kiss.)*

FEONNA: *(to* ANGELA*)* Maybe we have something in common. Do you play tennis?

ANGELA: No.

BOB: *(still crying and putting on buttons)* "Draft beer not boys!"

*(*TANYA *and the* GUARD *stop kissing.)*

GUARD: What's the matter?

FEONNA: *(to* ANGELA*)* Do you like to go horseback riding?

*(*ANGELA *shakes her head.)*

TANYA: I don't know. I just don't feel the same way I used to, that's all.

FEONNA: Wind surfing?

GUARD: Did I do something wrong?

FEONNA: *(to* ANGELA*)* Do you have any hobbies?

TANYA: It's just that I'm not quite ready for a relationship at this point of my life. It's not you, it's me. Of course I'm flattered about the way you feel toward me. I just have no time for this right now. It's my work. It's very important to me. I hope you're not taking this personally.

GUARD: Don't worry about me.

*(*ANGELA *starts to cry.)*

FEONNA: Don't cry, honey. Everything is going to be all right.

ANGELA: What do you mean, everything is going to be all right? We're all going to die.

FEONNA: That's what I mean.

ANGELA: I feel like I've wasted my whole life. I never did anything, I never went anywhere.

FEONNA: Don't feel too bad. I went everywhere, and I still didn't do anything.

ANGELA: If only we had some time left, I would get out of Astoria. I would either go to Wilfred Academy to become a beauty practitioner and do some real perming and bleaching, or even better, I would go to college and become a lawyer so I could have some real power and get elected and change everything.

SAL: I hope that everybody here is having a good time. That's what we're here for anyway, and I think it's a great thing that everyone could make it here today. I also think that at this time we should not forget our fellow members who could not be here, for they are here in spirit.

FEONNA: What fellow members?

SAL: The members of the club who couldn't be here for whatever reason. Coming up here was a great idea, and I just want to say that all things considered, this is the best thing that I have ever been a part of.

TANYA: What club?

SAL: The Ground Zero Club! This is the only time we ever met. That's why everybody is here! *(To the* GUARD.*)* Isn't that why you came?

GUARD: I'm sorry, but I don't think I've ever heard of the Ground Zero Club. I just work here.

SAL: *(to* BOB, *who is still down on his knees sobbing)* What about you? Aren't all you guys in Washington secret members?

BOB: *(almost completely covered with buttons)* "Bread not bombs!"

SAL: *(to* FEONNA*)* What about you?

FEONNA: Oh, I came here to kill myself, but I changed my mind.

SAL: *(pointing at* TANYA*)* You!

TANYA: Me?

SAL: Why did you come here?

TANYA: I came for two reasons. The first one was that I was invited.

(She waves her postcard.)

SAL: By a member of the club?

TANYA: No.

SAL: Oh. What's the other reason?

TANYA: Because I wanted to witness for myself the destruction of the greatest phallic symbol in America.

SAL: Sorry I asked.

ANGELA: How did you hear about this club, Sal?

SAL: I don't remember.

FEONNA: Are you sure that it exists?

SAL: Of course it exists! I don't believe this! Where are all the members?

(Everyone turns their head toward the TOURIST. *The sound of the viewer telescope running out of time can be heard. He looks up from the viewer, takes a quarter out of his pocket, inserts it into the machine, and resumes looking through it.)*

ANGELA: There aren't any. At least, none of them showed up.

SAL: *(turning on everybody, like a madman)* What do you mean, none of them showed up? What do you call all you people? You're all members of the club, whether you like it or not! Don't give me no bullshit reasons. I know why you all came here! Because you all want to see this happen! It turns you on, doesn't it? Huh? You get a kinky thrill out of watching everything be blown to smithereens, don't you? Everything has been leading up to this day. We have wanted this for a long, long time! Everybody here can't wait until it's all over.

(The TOURIST *motions to the* GUARD.*)*

GUARD: Huh? You want me to have a look? *(He looks through the viewer telescope as the* TOURIST *motions out toward the city.)* The Statue of Liberty. *(The* TOURIST *nods his head.)* There she is, the old lady herself. And here it comes! I can see a missile coming straight toward us! These machines are pretty powerful. I wonder who makes them. *(The* TOURIST *smiles.)* It's getting closer. This is really amazing!

SAL: *(in a drug-induced frenzy)* This is it!

TANYA: Remember, the revolution will be after the nuclear holocaust!

(The machine turns itself off.)

GUARD: Son of a bitch! Does anybody have a quarter?!

SAL, ANGELA, BOB, *and* FEONNA: Ten, nine, eight . . .

GUARD: *(to the* TOURIST, *complete with gestures)* Do you have a quarter for the machine?

(The TOURIST *shows his empty pockets.)*

SAL, ANGELA, BOB, *and* FEONNA: Seven, six, five . . .

GUARD: Well, this is it, fella. Good-bye.

(He shakes the TOURIST*'s hand and then hugs him. The* TOURIST *and the* GUARD *passionately kiss, while* SAL, ANGELA, BOB, *and* FEONNA *shout "Three, two, one!" The lights go out, and everyone screams as a loud crashing sound is heard. The lights come up. The noise from the street that has accompanied the play stops. Everyone is lying on the floor, along with half of a missile that has partially crashed through the ground, taking the* TOUR-IST *with it. Nothing remains of the* TOURIST *except his camera, which lies perfectly intact in front of the missile. There is a long silence.)*

ANGELA: What happened?

FEONNA: We must be dead.

GUARD: I don't think the missile detonated.

ANGELA: This is just like every New Year's Eve in Times Square. You spend hours in the cold getting mugged while waiting for this little ball to drop so everyone will know that it's New Year's. And then the little ball drops and everybody acts crazy, but soon you realize that nothing has really changed. It's still cold, and you're still getting mugged.

BOB: Are we still alive?

ANGELA: Yes.

BOB: This is really embarrassing.

GUARD: *(looking down through the hole that the missile made)* For one moment I found the love, meaning, and beauty that I had been searching for my whole life. *(*BOB *looks through the hole.)* Do you think he's dead? *(*BOB *nods his head.)*

FEONNA: So am I.

ANGELA: You're not dead. *(Looking for* SAL.*)* SAL! *(She rushes over to him.)*

BOB: I would like to make a donation to the cause to show my strong commitment to peace. *(He takes off his pants and shirt, which are covered with buttons, and hands them to* TANYA. *He then walks inside and makes a phone call.)*

ANGELA: *(taking* SAL*'s pulse)* He's still alive.

FEONNA: He is?

ANGELA: *(opening* SAL*'s eyelids)* It's just his brain that's dead. Drug overdose.

GUARD: *(crying)* I just can't . . . I don't understand . . . what's the matter with this country? We can't even pull off a successful nuclear war. What will happen to us now?

(BOB *opens the door and leans out.*)

BOB: Well, good-bye all. I have a meeting in Washington in the morning.

FEONNA: Good-bye, Bob. Oh, did you find out what happened?

BOB: It seems that we sabotaged their missiles and somehow they sabotaged ours. Apparently there was such a high level of infiltration that the KGB was actually the CIA and vice versa. Now I must go to Washington, expose everyone, and become a national hero. *(To* TANYA.*)* I said we would never let a nuclear war occur, and I was right.

ANGELA: What about all that stuff you said about making a mistake and taking responsibility?

BOB: I don't recall making any such statement. Now, enough of this. I must be going, but don't worry, friends, I won't let you down.

(He exits.)

ANGELA: *(looking down at* SAL*)* Well, I guess I'll just bring him back to Astoria, where his mother can take care of him for the rest of his life. *(Looking over the side.)* I hope the car is still there.

FEONNA: Don't go back to Astoria. Why, you can come and live with me. Together we can develop some interests.

TANYA: I guess I have some buttons to sell.

ANGELA: Do you need some help?

GUARD: I'll stay here. After tragedies like this, someone has to clean up.

(FEONNA *and* ANGELA *hold up the buttons and bumper stickers.*)

TANYA, FEONNA, *and* ANGELA: *(not in unison)* "Cruise people, not missiles!" Get your buttons and bumper stickers right here! All antinuclear paraphernalia full price!

(Blackout.)

END

CHARLIE SCHULMAN

(1986) Then . . .

I am currently a senior at the University of Michigan, where I am a creative writing and literature major and a two-time recipient of the Avery Hopwood Award for Drama. *The Ground Zero Club* is my second play to be produced at the Young Playwrights Festival and was part of the first International Young Playwrights Festival in Sydney, Australia. I am now twenty-one years old (almost twenty-two) and very much an aging Young Playwright. I wrote *The Ground Zero Club* a few years ago and at the age of eighteen enjoyed the unique experience of having my second play receive a professional production. Since then I have been writing plays and short stories while working a part-time job as a rock and roll roadie/stagehand.

. . . And Now

Both *The Birthday Present* and *The Ground Zero Club* have been performed by numerous high schools, colleges, and community groups throughout the United States, Canada, Australia, England, and Japan. Both plays appeared in previous anthologies published by Dell/Delacorte and are also published by the Dramatists Play Service.

HEY
LITTLE
WALTER

by
CARLA DEBBIE ALLEYNE
(age sixteen when play was written)
Brooklyn, New York

■

Hey Little Walter was performed at Playwrights Horizons in New York City, September 10 through October 6, 1990. Mark Brokaw was the director, and OyamO was the playwright adviser. The costumes were designed by Claudia Stephens. The sets were designed by Allen Moyer and lighted by Pat Dignan. Janet Kalas designed the sound. Cathy Diane Tomlin was the stage manager.

The cast:

WALTER	*Harold Perrineau*
RAKIM	*Seth Gilliam*
MAMA	*Cynthia Martells*
ALBERT	*Merlin Santana*
LATOYA	*Natalia Harris*
NICKY	*Lisa Carson*
TREYBAG	*Sean Nelson*

Scene One

SETTING: *Ghetto illusion.* WALTER *is standing with his back against a graffiti wall. A dim spotlight is on* WALTER. *He has an excessive amount of gold chains around his neck. The song "Little Walter" is heard.*

WALTER: *(stage right)* Listen, man, yo, can you hear me? Hey! Look, don't. Please, man. What are you doing? Why you selling out? *(Pause.)* Can you hear me? *(Louder.)* Can you hear me? *(Pause.)* Damn! *(To audience.)* Damn! *(Hears song.)* Yo, yo, yo not yet. I gotta put them down on my program. *(Public Enemy song plays.)* Yeah, that's more like it. *(Pause.)* Yeah, I got caught out there. It happens all the time. Nothing new, right? "Black Youth Shot," you know the daily headline. Nothing new, right? Wrong! Wrong, 'cause it's more than just guys like me going down. *(Thinks, pause.)* Damn! See my story needs to be told, and if you think it's just mine that's where you're wrong again. Yeah, it's 1990 and we're still wearing these. *(Points to chains.)* Yup, they come in all shapes, sizes, and colors. *(Points to audience.)* And I sold out and didn't even realize it. *(Looks at watch.)* Look, time is running short and I gotta get on with my story. *(Pause.)* Yeah, I messed up, but such is life. *(Fixes cap.)* Look, I didn't want it at first, it just happened.

(Music grows louder, blackout.)

Scene Two

SETTING: *Brooklyn, New York.* WALTER*'s kitchen, neatly furnished with all the necessities of a kitchen.* WALTER *is sitting on the table talking to* RAKIM. ALBERT, *his little brother, is under the table doing his homework unnoticed, but paying close attention.*

RAKIM: Man, dollars is my middle name. I'm not talking about pocket change, I'm not talking 'bout just a little money, but mucho duckettes.

WALTER: *(excited)* You're playing my tune, man, now sing the song.

RAKIM: Don't get too excited—let me explain the concept.

WALTER: Yo, Rakim, I'm all ears.

RAKIM: Good! Okay, remember when I told you my cousin Jeff and his friend Benny had a little business?

WALTER: *(reluctant)* Yeah, rings a bell.

RAKIM: Well, they need a little help.

WALTER: A little help for a little business.

RAKIM: That's it, except the business is far from little. *(Pause.)* How about it?

WALTER: *(thinking)* Wait a minute, isn't that your cous that got shot in the eye?

RAKIM: That's him, but he's wearing designer shades now.

WALTER: Nah, I ain't with it.

RAKIM: Why not, Walter?

WALTER: I'm not ready to die yet, and if I 'member right, your cous Jeff is a big-time drug dealer.

RAKIM: So what?

WALTER: So what? You think I'm buggin', man?

RAKIM: *(making fun)* You mean to tell me you petro,* Little Walter?

WALTER: No, I'm not scared, and don't call me Little Walter—that's only for my family.

RAKIM: Cool, so you down?

WALTER: Nah, man, I said I ain't with it.

RAKIM: Yo, it ain't that bad. Much people do it. *(Pause.)* Look at Darrell, he pumps and it's no big deal.

WALTER: Darrell sells?

RAKIM: Of course, where you think he get the money to buy his fresh gear?

WALTER: His moms? I don't know.

RAKIM: Walter, please, nobody's mother can afford to buy Gucci, Fendi, MCM, and leather gear at the same time.

WALTER: I know, but—

RAKIM: *(Cuts in.)* But he's just making a living, and he's getting paid.

WALTER: You call selling poison to people honest?

* petrified

RAKIM: If you don't give people what they want, then that's not honest!

WALTER: Rakim, man, sometimes I cram to understand you.

RAKIM: Wake up and smell the coffee—look what's going down around you.

WALTER: Yeah, man, but stupid brothers are dying over this drug business.

RAKIM: Listen, man, I understand where you are coming from, but think like me. If the brothers are dying, you might as well get yours before you go.

WALTER: *(Thinks.)* That's a way to look at it.

RAKIM: It's the only way to look at it and still come out sane.

(There is silence. You can see WALTER *is thinking.)*

RAKIM: *(Breaks his concentration.)* I heard Nicky is sweating Darrell.

WALTER: Please, I got Nicky under my wing—she's whipped.

RAKIM: *(giving him an unbelieving look)* Well, that's not what I heard.

WALTER: What did you hear?

RAKIM: I heard that Darrell gave her a ride home yesterday in his BMW.

WALTER: Yeah, right. *(*RAKIM *shrugs.)* I'll find out myself today when she comes over.

RAKIM: Well, I hope you can take bad news.

WALTER: Step off.*

*(*WALTER*'s mother enters with a bag of groceries in her hands.* WALTER*'s mother is wearing a nurse's uniform.)*

WALTER: *(noticing)* Hi, Mama.

RAKIM: Hi, Ms. Anderson.

MAMA: *(showing exhaustion)* Hi, boys. Hey, Little Walter, help me with these bags.

*(*WALTER *rushes to her rescue, grabs the bags, and starts unpacking.)*

MAMA: Thanks. *(Looks around.)* Where's your brother and sister?

* Back off

WALTER: *(unpacking)* Latoya's at her friend's on the sixth floor, and Albert's in his room doing his homework.

MAMA: Oh, okay. *(Tiredly rests her hands on her hips.)* Alexander love, how's your mother doing?

RAKIM: *(Blushes.)* Oh, she's fine.

MAMA: Tell her I said to stop by anytime.

RAKIM: Okay.

MAMA: I'll be right back. I want to get out of these sweaty clothes. *(She exits.)*

RAKIM: I wish your mother would start calling me by my real name.

WALTER: Alexander is your real name.

RAKIM: No, Alexander is a sucker name. I'm Rakim, a brother of knowledge and understanding.

WALTER: Oh, save that garbage, man. I thought you were through being a five-percenter.*

RAKIM: Yo, I put it to the side, but my belief in knowledge and understanding is still here.

WALTER: *(unbelieving)* Oh, brother . . .

RAKIM: Man, I told you I'm a God—omnipotent, my boy.

WALTER: Yo, save it, Rakim. Next you'll be trying to sell me the Brooklyn Bridge.

(RAKIM sighs. Enter MAMA.)

MAMA: Walter, your brother is not in his room like you said he was.

WALTER: Did you check Latoya's room?

MAMA: I checked everywhere. He's nowhere to be found. *(Pause.)* Walter, please, you know this city—

WALTER: *(Cuts in.)* Don't worry, Mama, he's got to be around here somewhere.

MAMA: But . . .

(ALBERT, who is hidden under the table, jumps out and yells.)

ALBERT: Fooled ya!

---

* A member of a branch of the Nation of Islam

MAMA: *(scolding)* Oh, Albert! *(Smiles.)* Come give your mama a hug.

(ALBERT runs and embraces her while RAKIM and WALTER, in confusion, stare at each other.)

WALTER: How long have you been down there, Albert?

ALBERT: *(Thinks.)* About a minute. *(RAKIM and WALTER sigh.)* No, actually an hour! *(ALBERT runs and exits left.)*

(RAKIM and WALTER stiffen as MAMA exits.)

RAKIM: *(Looks at watch.)* I'm outta here!

WALTER: Wait. *(Pause.)* What's up?

RAKIM: Chill, beep me later.

WALTER: You don't even have a beeper.

RAKIM: Soon. Peace! *(He exits right.)*

WALTER: 'Bye . . .

(WALTER paces the kitchen floor.)

WALTER: That little snot!

(Enter ALBERT. He goes into the grocery bag and grabs an apple.)

WALTER: *(Grabs his brother.)* Why were you listening to our conversation, you little weasel?

ALBERT: I was not listening to your conversation. I was just sitting under the table doing my homework, and your conversation just got in the way of my studying, so I listened.

WALTER: You could have left the room or told us you were under there.

ALBERT: What do I look like to you, a fool?

WALTER: *(Shrugs as if giving up. Serious.)* Albert, what you heard?

ALBERT: Everything—do you think I'm deaf or something?

WALTER: Oh, brother.

ALBERT: If you're worried about me telling, don't be.

WALTER: *(unbelieving)* And why shouldn't I?

ALBERT: Because as long as you make me a part of your little business, I'll keep my mouth shut.

WALTER: Oh, really.

ALBERT: Yeah, and you can start now by giving me fifty cents—no, make that a dollar, candy prices are high these days.

WALTER: There's no way I'm going to sit here and let you blackmail me.

ALBERT: Let me help you and Rakim out. Come on, Little Walter, I can do it.

WALTER: *(Can't believe what he's hearing.)* Are you crazy, kid?

ALBERT: I'll give you a day to accept my proposal.

WALTER: I don't need no day because the answer is *(spells)* N-O, no!

ALBERT: You're forcing me to do something that may damage you for the rest of your life.

WALTER: What?

ALBERT: *(Shouts it out.)* Tell!

WALTER: Shhh!

(Enter MAMA.)

MAMA: What's going on here?

WALTER: Ahh, nothing, Mama. Right, Albert? *(No answer, slaps ALBERT on the back of his head.)*

ALBERT: Nothing, Mama.

MAMA: Good, now you boys stop that fighting. *(Looks around.)* Walter, where did you put today's mail?

WALTER: On the dressing table in your room, Mama.

MAMA: Okay. *(MAMA begins to exit.)*

ALBERT: Mama. *(MAMA stops.)* Can I have that money now for my sneakers?

MAMA: Albert, I'll give you ten dollars tomorrow.

ALBERT: Ten dollars! Mama I can't even buy the laces with that.

MAMA: Albert, how much are these sneakers anyway?

ALBERT: Mama, they're good sneakers.

MAMA: How much?

ALBERT: Mama, these sneakers are fresh, they're the new Air Jordans. Everybody's got a pair.

MAMA: How much?

ALBERT: Mama, genuine leather. Soles that will make me fly.

MAMA: (Shouts.) Albert, how much?

ALBERT: One hundred and twenty dollars.

MAMA: What! Boy, you must be joking.

ALBERT: No, Mama, I'm serious.

MAMA: Albert, there's no way I can afford that.

ALBERT: But, Mama, please. Mama, all the kids at school make fun of these K mart sneakers you bought me, and I need good sneakers for practice.

MAMA: Albert, I'm sorry, but I just can't.

ALBERT: Oh, Mama, I promise I'll never ask you for anything for as long as I live. Mama pleeease.

WALTER: Albert, cut it out. You heard Mama.

ALBERT: No! Mind your business.

MAMA: I've heard enough from you, Albert. Take your little butt to your room.

ALBERT: Aww, Mama.

MAMA: (Grabs him by the collar.) Come on, Mr. Smart Mouth.

ALBERT: Oh, brother.

(They exit as the doorbell rings. WALTER gets the door. Enter NICKY, a slim, attractive young lady.)

WALTER: Nicky!

NICKY: Hi, Walter, what's up?

WALTER: Just chillin'. Where have you been hiding? You've never answered any of my calls.

NICKY: That's what I came to talk to you about.

WALTER: (a little worried) Come sit in the kitchen. (Leads her to a seat.) Okay, what's up?

NICKY: Well . . .

WALTER: (Stops her.) Wait!

(He checks underneath the table, twice.)

NICKY: What are you doing that for?

WALTER: Ahh . . . just checking to see if a little rat is listening.

NICKY: Rats mind their own business.

WALTER: Not the ones in this house, like Albert.

NICKY: What?

WALTER: Forget it.

NICKY: Can we get back to what I came here for?

WALTER: *(relief)* Yeah, okay.

NICKY: *(trying to find the words)* Walter . . . the reason I haven't been accepting your calls and seeing you for the last week is because . . . *(Pause.)* I needed time to myself.

WALTER: What? I don't understand.

NICKY: *(solemn)* Walter, let me finish.

WALTER: *(easily angered)* No, let me finish. Don't even try to put that ''time for myself'' shit past me! I heard you talking to Darrell. . . .

NICKY: *(wide-eyed)* Well . . . I . . . ahh . . .

WALTER: Well, what?

NICKY: *(Comes back.)* Look, I don't want to put up with this. I'm leaving. *(Gets up.)*

WALTER: Don't leave until you tell me how you feel about me.

NICKY: *(Sits.)* I . . . like you a lot.

WALTER: ''Like''? That's it?

NICKY: *(sarcastic, loud)* What do you want—a true love at seventeen?

WALTER: *(Hurt shows.)* Nah . . . but . . .

NICKY: *(seeing the hurt, softer)* I'm not ready to fall in love yet.

WALTER: Well, that's not what I heard about you and Darrell.

NICKY: *(offended)* I don't love Darrell. *(Pause.)* I don't think you know the meaning of love yet, Walter.

WALTER: Baby, please, I know what love is. *(Pause. They look at each other.)* Who do you want—him or me?

NICKY: I can't compare you to Darrell. . . . Darrell's different.

WALTER: How?

NICKY: He buys me clothes, he takes me out to fancy places. *(She thinks to herself happily.)* We drive to the beach in his BMW. He treats me real good, Walter.

WALTER: I treat you good. *(She shrugs.)* Yo, what about that time I took you to Coney Island. Didn't you have fun?

NICKY: *(frowning)* Yeah, I had a great time, except for when I sat in gum on the train and ruined my new leather shorts and when you spent all your money trying to win me a bear and I had to pay for our dinners.

WALTER: *(trying to make the best of things)* But you still had fun? *(Silence.)* Didn't you?

NICKY: Walter, that is how all our dates go. I mean, either you don't have any money and we stay home and look at TV or we go somewhere cheap and I spend money.

WALTER: Who do you think I am—Donald Trump?

NICKY: *(Thinks.)* It's just that you're no Darrell, Walter.

WALTER: Please, I know you ain't trying to diss.*

NICKY: Walter, you just don't give me the same security he does. *(Pause.)* I don't want to end up pregnant and penniless like my sister.

WALTER: Do you see security with Darrell?

NICKY: I don't feel like talking about Darrell.

WALTER: *(upset)* Why not?

NICKY: Because I don't want to hurt you. I know how much you care about me.

WALTER: Say what?

NICKY: This conversation isn't going anywhere. I'm leaving.

WALTER: Before you leave, answer this question.

NICKY: *(getting up)* What?

WALTER: If I had money, would you still be talking to me?

* disrespect

NICKY: *(Pause.)* Most likely. I like you, and all. Look, Walter, we go back a long way, but Darrell has what I want.

WALTER: Why is money everything to you?

NICKY: Walter, I come from a poor family. I want to better myself. I like the way girls look at me when I'm with Darrell. He makes me feel important. *(She begins to exit.)*

WALTER: Wait, what happened to me and you—us?

NICKY: What about us? *(She exits.)*

WALTER: *(Yells out.)* Nicky, wait!

(He exits right, and MAMA *enters from left. She has changed, now wears a robe.)*

MAMA: Now what? (MAMA *shrugs and begins to look at the mail in her hand.)*

(Enter WALTER *stage left. He looks piqued.)*

MAMA: *(Looks over the mail.)* Hey, Little Walter, what's going on? What was all that yelling for? *(She begins to open another letter.)*

WALTER: *(distant)* Nicky was here. *(Pause.)* I broke up with her.

MAMA: *(opening the letter)* People who care about each other always has breakups.

WALTER: *(Mumbles.)* I was the only one who cared.

*(MAMA *is too much into the letter to hear him.)*

MAMA: Oh Lord!

WALTER: What's wrong, Mama?

MAMA: They're going to cut off the light.

WALTER: Why?

MAMA: *(Sighs.)* I forgot to pay last month's and this month's.

WALTER: How much is it?

MAMA: Don't worry about that. Go to your room, Walter.

WALTER: No, Mama, maybe I can help.

MAMA: *(upset, but holding anger in)* I appreciate your gesture, Walter, but there is nothing you can do.

WALTER: But Mama, maybe I can help. I know I can get a job or something. . . .

MAMA: A job? Walter, who's going to take care of your brother and sister?

WALTER: Mama, there must be something I can do. How about a night job?

MAMA: Look, boy, please. The money you'll be making won't be able to feed the roaches in the apartment, much less pay my bills.

WALTER: But, Mama, maybe . . .

MAMA: Maybe what? Walter, there is no way you can afford to pay $186 for the lights or $633 for the rent, and boy, the list goes on and on.

WALTER: But, Mama . . .

MAMA: Mama what? You want to help me so much, do it by leaving me alone. *(WALTER exits.)* I work so hard for nothing, all my money gone to bills, no savings, nothing! If I die now, who's going to take care of you? I'm never gonna get that house. I'm just going to work my body to nothing for nothing! Damn! And where is the man who brought you all into the world? *(She walks over and yells it stage right.)* Where is good ole daddy, huh? Well, don't ask me. I don't know. The last time I saw him, he said he was going to buy a pack of cigarettes. *(She breaks down.)* "I'm going to get a pack of cigarettes," he said, and that was that.

(The doorbell rings.)

MAMA: *(Slowly rises.)* Who is it?

LATOYA: Latoya! *(Latoya enters, a little black girl about six.)*

MAMA: *(wiping away her tears)* Hi, baby!

LATOYA: Hi, Mama. *(Gives her mother a kiss.)*

MAMA: Did you have fun?

LATOYA: Yeah, look what I made for you. *(She gives her a piece of paper.)*

MAMA: Oooh, that's nice. *(Pause.)* What is it?

LATOYA: A family portrait *(Takes the picture.)* See, there's you, Albert, Little Walter, me, and *(pointing)* there's Daddy. *(MAMA's expression hardens.)* I'm thirsty. *(She runs into the kitchen.)*

MAMA: *(staring into the picture)* Latoya?

LATOYA: *(looking into the cupboard)* Yes, Mama.

MAMA: What's that in your father's hand?

LATOYA: A pack of cigarettes, Mama. *(She walks up and hugs her mama.)*

MAMA: How 'bout we go and get ready for bed.

LATOYA: Sounds good to me.

MAMA: Child, sometimes I think you're twenty-five years old.

(LATOYA laughs, they exit stage left. Blackout.)

Scene Three

SETTING: *Ghetto illusion.* ALBERT *enters, pretending to play basketball.* WAL-TER *is already there. He stands in the position of a basketball hoop. The song "Criminal Minded" by BDP is heard.*

ALBERT: S'up Boys? Here I am, ready to play. *(Pause.)* What you laughing at? Yo, man, gimme time. Mama's gonna hook me up with some fly sneakers soon. *(Pause.)* Yo, what? Look, K mart happens to be a very popular store. Dag, man, why you always trying to diss? Now, if I told everybody your mom is on welfare, you'd get mad, right? Oh, so now you want to challenge me? You know I can dunk better than you. Aight, aight, I'll go first. *(Dribbles.)* Magic, watch out! *(Heads for* WALTER*'s hoop and trips.)* Damn these sneakers. *(Looks up.)* Yo, why yawl laughing? Stop laughing at me. You just wait and see. *(Runs off.)* Just wait and see.

(The music grows louder, blackout.)

Scene Four

SETTING: *In an alley. The stage is bare except for trash cans.* WALTER *stands center stage.*

WALTER: *(Looks at his watch.)* Man, what's taking him so long? *(Pause.)* Yo, he better hurry up.

(Enter RAKIM.*)*

RAKIM: What's up?

WALTER: *(looks in his direction)* What took you so long?

RAKIM: I had to get the info.

WALTER: *(Closes his eyes in thought.)* What's the deal?

RAKIM: My cous Jeff and Benny ain't in business for themselves.

WALTER: Who they work for?

RAKIM: Yo, they pushing for the top.

WALTER: Say what?

RAKIM: The big guys. A white dude name Steve runs the show. He give them the merchandise and they get it out on the street.

WALTER: So what are we going to do?

RAKIM: Let me finish. I want to prove something to you.

WALTER: What?

RAKIM: I didn't tell you who Steve works for.

WALTER: Who does he work for?

RAKIM: He is the under man for public officials.

WALTER: What?

RAKIM: Public officials, man. I'm talking senators, judges, lawyers, maybe even the mayor, man. They are all in, man, all of them!

WALTER: Get out!

RAKIM: Word up, I'm dead serious.

WALTER: How do you know?

RAKIM: Steve told me himself.

WALTER: Yo, that's wacked. Word, though?

RAKIM: Word to Herb, and they consider us their family.

WALTER: Cool, so what do they want us to do?

RAKIM: Aight, this is the deal. *(Pause.* RAKIM *looks around.)* This, man, is our secret.

WALTER: Well, you could have done a little better than this dump you made me meet you at.

RAKIM: Man, this place has class. That's my garbage can over there. *(Points to trash cans.)*

WALTER: *(impatient)* Give me the info, info!

RAKIM: Aight, aight. First they want us to go pick up a shipment in D.C.

WALTER: Washington, D.C.! That's in another state!

RAKIM: No shit!

WALTER: So how can I get that past Mama?

RAKIM: Tell her you spending the weekend with me.

WALTER: She'll call.

RAKIM: Tell her we're going to New Jersey to spend the weekend with my pops.

WALTER: I'll try it. What about you?

RAKIM: Don't worry 'bout me. I got my mama in deep check.

WALTER: So how are we going to get all the way there?

RAKIM: Hop a plane there and then rent a car to drive back. Once we get there, we pick up the stuff, sight-see, and head back. That's all to it.

WALTER: Sounds simple.

RAKIM: It is! And the dollars are even better.

WALTER: How much?

RAKIM: Five grand apiece.

WALTER: *(Yells.)* Get out! (RAKIM *nods.*) We be in the money.

RAKIM: And now we're part of the family, the New York drug-dealing family.

WALTER: *(Yells in joy.)* Hooo! We hit the jackpot. (RAKIM *joins in.*) Well, what are you waiting for? Let's pack!

RAKIM: I'm down. Peace.

(They exit.)

Scene Five

SETTING: *Ghetto illusion.* MAMA *stands in front of graffiti wall.* WALTER *sits on a garbage can listening to her. There is a dim spotlight on her. The song "Papa Was a Rolling Stone" by the Temptations plays.*

MAMA: Walter baby, where are you going, son? Oh, okay. Don't forget to pack your toothbrush. Remember the last time you forgot it? Boy, don't worry about me. I have your brother and sister under control. *(Pause.)* Walter, I've done it before, I don't need you to take care of my children. I'll just come home from work early, that's all. Come home from work early. *(Pause, low tone.)* Walter boy, I know when you lie to me. I know when all my children lie to me. *(*WALTER *removes a gold chain and places it around her wrist.)* I know you're not going where you say you are. But, boy, I can't say no, I can't ask any questions. Remember when I used to say no and ask your father questions all the time? Your father used to say to me, "Woman, why you ask so many questions?" And then that man done gone and left me. But, boy, go on and have a good time with your friend Alexander. 'Cause as long as I don't ask any questions, you'll be with your mama. Yes, my child, the older you get, the better you deal with that funny feeling around your ankles and wrist. To the point where you can't even feel it anymore. *(Shows chains to audience.)* Like it's not even there. *(*MAMA *laughs lightly.)*

(The song grows louder. Blackout.)

Scene Six

SETTING: *Hotel room in D.C. It's nighttime now, and the room is dark. There is one bed and two suitcases on the floor. The room is empty. Enter* WALTER *and* RAKIM. *They rush in very fast as if running from someone.* RAKIM *falls to the ground,* WALTER *ducks. A spotlight goes around the room two times. There is a second of silence and darkness that quickly ends when* WALTER *cuts on the lights.*

RAKIM: *(Gets off the floor, looks stage left, smiles.)* Oh, shit. I can't believe it, man. We did it.

WALTER: Word, I still can't believe it. Man, I thought I was in a movie. When that D.T. bust in there, I thought it was over.

RAKIM: Yo, me too. Man, that was smart of you to say "Run."

WALTER: Black instincts, man! *(They laugh.)*

RAKIM: I thought we was caught.

WALTER: Me too. After the cops busted in and you yelled out *(Mocks him.)* "Hey, we're not buying drugs!" I thought it was over.

RAKIM: Man, I was scared as hell. *(They laugh.)* But tell me I didn't freak it when I lost the cops.

WALTER: *(searching in his backpack for a change of clothes)* Well, being you were driving a Jag and the D.T.'s was in a beat-up Buick, I wouldn't expect less.

RAKIM: *(pretending to be driving)* Just like an old Starsky and Hutch show. *(Brakes.)* Damn! Crime is exciting.

WALTER: Maybe a bit too exciting.

RAKIM: A bit too exciting? Man . . . that was slamming!

WALTER: Word, but I can't just help but wonder.

RAKIM: Wonder 'bout what? How you're gonna spend your money?

WALTER: Yo, Rakim, it's just that doing this *(pause)* . . . you know, worries me.

RAKIM: Nah, man, I don't know. All I do know is we're getting paid, and that's all that I care about.

WALTER: Man, but what about the kids, man? *(Pause.)* Look, if someone tried to sell Latoya and Albert drugs *(pause, anger)*, I don't know what I'd do.

RAKIM: Look, man, I know where you're coming from.

WALTER: No, you don't. I mean, I wouldn't be here now if it wasn't for my family, man. I'ma get my mama a house.

RAKIM: Yeah, you do that. Rakim is going to hook up Rakim.

WALTER: Dag, since we were kids, you were always for self. When are you gonna grow up and think about your family?

RAKIM: Man, growing up with thirteen brothers and sisters, I learned to live for self. Know what I'm saying?

WALTER: You never had a dollar without giving me fifty cents.

RAKIM: That's 'cause you're my boy. *(Puts his hands out.)* Yo, man, we be making dollars.

WALTER: Word, man, that case of coke they handed us looked like it was worth nuff.

RAKIM: Damn straight it is, and when they turn that into crack, they'll be pulling in a cool mil.

WALTER: Yo, and ten thousand of that is ours.

RAKIM: *(Laughs.)* Yeah, boy, gear, girlies, cars. *(Pause.)* Nuff respect. . . .

WALTER: *(Laughs.)* Word 'em up, Rock!

RAKIM: Yo, man. *(Puts his hand out.)* Welcome to money, man, the fast life.

WALTER: *(hesitant)* We're risking it all, man.

RAKIM: *(determined)* Big deal! For generations we were poor. The white man took everything we ever had from the beginning. But now we got something and they can't stop us. We're getting . . . paid . . . in . . . full!

WALTER: *(Slaps his hand.)* Then it's worth it.

RAKIM: The fast life, man. You won't regret it.

WALTER: Word, wait till Nicky sees me.

RAKIM: Man, get off her strap. Lemme put you down on what my cous told me. Once you become a dealer, a good dealer, you ain't never gonna find a woman you can trust. They all looking to use you. The trick is to use them before they use you.

WALTER: Yeah!

RAKIM: So when she comes, sex her and leave her. *(They laugh.)*

WALTER: *(Rises to turn off light switch.)* Let's get some z's, man.

(Blackout.)

Scene Seven

SETTING: *Ghetto illusion.* RAKIM *stands in front of graffiti wall.* WALTER *sits on the floor listening. The song "Dopeman" by N.W.A. is heard.* RAKIM *dances.*

RAKIM: *(elated)* Yeah! Sing it, boys. Pump it, boys. Uhhmm, more money, more money, more money, more. *(Pause.)* Yo, Moms. Yo,

Moms! *(Pause.)* Moms, yo, I'm trying to talk to you. *(Pause.)* Are you listening? *(Upset.)* Yo, look, I just want to let you know don't look out for me. I'm outta here this weekend. Okay? That's it? Don't you want to know where I'm going? *(Pause.)* Damn, Ma, defrost your heart, won't you. Nah, I ain't going to Trenton State Prison. I saw Pops last week. *(Pause.)* Huh? I don't have any money to give you. I'm broke. *(Pause, alarmed.)* Yo, who you called me? Look, Moms, I'm your seventh, Alexander, remember. Charlie is your fifth, and he ain't here. I am. *(Pause.)* Damn, Moms, I can't believe you sometimes. When will you get my name right? *(Pause.)* What? I told you I don't have any money. *(Digs into pocket, throws two dollars onto the ground.)* Here, that's all I got. I gotta go, I got things to do, places to go, and dollars to make. (WALTER *places a chain on his wrist.)* What? Oh, now you want to know where I'm going? Timbuktu! See you when I get back.

(Music grows louder. Blackout.)

Scene Eight

SETTING: WALTER*'s kitchen (same as Scene Two).* ALBERT *and his friend* TREY *are playing cards on the table.* LATOYA *is coloring on the floor. Enter* WALTER *from the bedroom. Looks as if he's been sleeping.*

WALTER: *(tired)* What's up?

LATOYA: *(Runs up and hugs him.)* Little Walter!

WALTER: Hi, Latoya.

ALBERT: How was New Jersey, Walter?

WALTER: New Jersey?

LATOYA: Didn't you . . .

WALTER: Ooooh, yeah, I had a great time.

ALBERT: Which part did you go to?

WALTER: New Jersey.

LATOYA: We know New Jersey, but what part, Trenton?

WALTER: Yeah, Trenton. Ahh, how did you know, Latoya?

LATOYA: I checked out a book in the library.

WALTER: Ooooh!

LATOYA: Did you go to Newark too? *(Pause.)* You come home last night?

WALTER: Ahh, yeah. *(Skips question.)* Where's Mama?

LATOYA: At work.

WALTER: *(entering the kitchen)* Who's that? *(Points to TREY.)*

LATOYA: This is homeboy Trey.

WALTER: What's up?

TREY: Wha' 'appening?

ALBERT: Trey is from Jamaica.

WALTER: Word!

LATOYA: *(loudmouth)* Trey sells drugs. His street name is Treybag.

WALTER: *(surprised)* Say what?

ALBERT: Latoya, you got a big mouth.

WALTER: *(serious)* How old are you, man?

TREY: Me go a be twelve in two months.

WALTER: Just twelve.

ALBERT: His parents don't care 'cause his father make him do it.

WALTER: Albert, I want to talk to you.

(Doorbell rings.)

WALTER: *(Gets the door.)* Rakim?

(RAKIM rushes in. He looks frightened.)

WALTER: What's wrong?

RAKIM: *(Blurts it out.)* Dead! My cousin, Steve, Benny. Their brains splattered all over the concrete.

(LATOYA, TREY, and ALBERT pay close attention.)

WALTER: *(Appears scared too.)* Slow, man, slow down. Take a seat. *(He takes him to a seat in the kitchen.)*

RAKIM: *(Catches his breath.)* Walter, they're dead—a professional hit, the cops said. They're dead, Walter, dead!

WALTER: When did you find out?

RAKIM: Last night after I dropped you home, I went by Steve to drop the stuff off. *(Pause.)* I saw a lot of people and cops standing in front of the house. I walked over there and saw my cousin laying on the floor with his face blown off. It was nasty.

WALTER: Where's the stuff?

RAKIM: Blood was all over the place, everywhere on the lawn. Oh, God! My cousin's dead! My cous is dead!

WALTER: Rakim! Where is the stuff?

RAKIM: What?

WALTER: The stuff! The coke!

RAKIM: I got the hell out of there as fast as I could.

WALTER: Where . . . ?

RAKIM: I took it in the alley and dropped it in a trash can.

WALTER: Rakim!

RAKIM: *(In a panic.)* They never take out the trash back there!

WALTER: Good! Did you take the car back to the rental place?

RAKIM: *(Falls apart.)* Car? My cousin's dead!

WALTER: *(Grabs him up.)* Rakim! Get your shit together. Harden up!

RAKIM: What? What are we going to do?

WALTER: We didn't get paid, but since we got the merchandise, we are going into business for self. You down?

RAKIM: *(teary)* But . . . but, what about my cousin Jeff?

WALTER: Big deal! For generations we were poor. They kept us down and took everything we ever possessed. But now we got something and ain't no way they could stop us. Rakim, we're getting paid in full. You said that, man! *(Shakes him.)* Remember!

(WALTER puts his hand out. Teary RAKIM grabs it. Stage left, ALBERT and TREY join hands too. LATOYA backs up and watches. She clutches her hands as if she feels a sudden coldness. Blackout.)

Scene Nine

SETTING: *Ghetto illusion.* NICKY *stands against brick wall.* WALTER *sits and listens to her. The song "Your Jingling Baby" by L. L. Cool J. plays in the background.* NICKY *jingles her earrings.*

NICKY: Yes, girlfriend, oh, yes, I heard Walter's dealing. Of course I'm going to pay him a visit. Girl, you know me. I'm proud to be a drug dealer's queen. Umhmm. Please, I don't care what they look like as long as what they got in their pocket is the right shade of green. (WALTER *puts a gold chain around her wrist.*) I'm good to go. Girl, stop, Walter's not ugly. And if he was, I'll put a paper bag right over his head when we're doing it. You're right, girl, when you say dealer, you see Nicky jump. Watch Nicky scream for more money, more money, more. What? Girl, look! Why does it have to be all about me using guys, though? Girl, I'm surviving. Besides, I like money. *(Pause.)* I mean, Walter.

(The music grows louder. Blackout.)

Scene Ten

SETTING: *Alley, same as Scene Four.* RAKIM *and* WALTER *look different, very different. They are wearing expensive outfits, particularly leather or name-brand sweats. Both have an extensive amount of jewelry. Not only is their appearance different but their attitude is harsher; vanity plays a part in their actions. The alley is also different. It is now a drugstore (but not the kind you get cough medicine at, unless you want to stop coughing permanently). There is a curtain stage left, in the shape of a little room. It seems to be hiding something.* RAKIM *is sitting on a carton counting money.*

WALTER: *(standing)* Yo, Rakim, don't forget to hold out some for the ice man. We owe him for cooking the coke.

RAKIM: *(Licks his fingers and keeps counting.)* No problem!

WALTER: *(Looks around, satisfied with what he sees.)* We hit it, man, we hit it. Ain't no way the D.T.'s would suspect we're back here.

RAKIM: *(still counting)* Of course not. This is the one and only "Little Rock Corporation."

WALTER: I like how that sounds. I'll use that on the customers.

RAKIM: That's if they ain't too high to remember it.

WALTER: I like them that way—means we feeding them good.

RAKIM: *(counting)* We got this to show. *(Shows money.)*

WALTER: Paid in full. Almost got enough to get my Mazda.

RAKIM: *(Mocks him.)* But what about helping out your mama, Little Walter?

WALTER: In time, in time. Let me treat myself first.

RAKIM: Word!

WALTER: Yo, we got enough to take two Skeezers for a ride.

RAKIM: We got enough for a whorehouse.

(Enter NICKY. WALTER laughs.)

WALTER: Speaking of the devil.

NICKY: Hi, Walter, I heard you were out here.

WALTER: Looking for me?

NICKY: I have to talk to you! *(Looks at RAKIM.)*

RAKIM: I ain't going nowhere—this is my corporation!

NICKY: Please, Rakim.

RAKIM: *(Gets up, puts money in pocket.)* I'll see you in the car.

WALTER: Why don't you go for a long ride, Rock. *(He winks at him.)*

RAKIM: *(Smiles.)* No problem! *(Exits.)*

WALTER: Well?

NICKY: Since the day I left your apartment, I was sorry. I couldn't stop thinking about you.

(WALTER turns his back to her, faces toward audience as she talks.)

NICKY: I realize it was love I was feeling. I needed the time to find that out.

WALTER: What about Darrell?

NICKY: I could care less about him. It's you I love.

WALTER: I heard he got busted. How long did he get?

NICKY: I don't know and I don't care! Walter, don't you feel the same for me?

WALTER: *(Smiles, turns back toward her.)* Of course, Nicky, I never stopped thinking about you either. *(She is delighted. You can tell by the big smile she shows.* WALTER *holds her.)* Nicky?

NICKY: Yes?

WALTER: I want to show you how much I care. Come with me.

(He takes her into the curtains stage left. She willingly goes. Blackout.)

Scene Eleven

SETTING: WALTER*'s kitchen, same as Scene Two.* TREY *and* ALBERT *are on the floor talking.*

ALBERT: Are you sure your father said I can help you?

TREY: Don't worry, man, me father don't mind.

ALBERT: What do I have to do?

TREY: After school me a go to me uncle house and pick up the white powder and put it in my book bag, then I take it for Papa.

ALBERT: White powder? You mean coke.

TREY: That's what me papa call it. You can help me.

ALBERT: Is that all you do?

TREY: Sometimes I deliver the powder to me papa friends.

ALBERT: That sounds easy. How much money do you get?

TREY: Twenty dollars a week.

ALBERT: That's it! I can't buy Air Jordans with that.

TREY: Ah good money.

ALBERT: Mama gives me ten dollars a week for doing nothing.

TREY: But that's all Pa give me.

ALBERT: Look, Treybag, I have to get my sneakers and soon. *(Pause.)* Wait, I have an idea. If I get the powder, do you think you can sell it to your pa's customers, we keep the money. *(Pause.)* I'll help.

TREY: Maybe, but where you going to get it from?

ALBERT: My brother. I know where he hides a whole bunch of that stuff. I've been watching him sell for a long time.

TREY: Whey?

ALBERT: In an alley, behind Rakim's apartment building. I followed them there two weeks ago.

TREY: Can we get it?

ALBERT: No one ever goes back there. They know my brother will kill them. He bought a gun last week.

TREY: Me papa got six rifle.

ALBERT: Can we get one?

TREY: Yeah, I can sneak it.

ALBERT: Good, we're a team, Treybag.

TREY: All right, Little Walter.

ALBERT: I like that name. It carries power.

TREY: Wha' we are wait fo', let's go get some white powder.

ALBERT: Yeah, but we run in when my brother leaves.

TREY: Cool, brethren.

(As they exit, MAMA *and* LATOYA *enter carrying bags.)*

MAMA: Albert, where are you going?

ALBERT: To the park with Trey.

MAMA: Okay, be careful.

ALBERT: 'Bye, Mama. *(They exit.)*

MAMA: Something about that Trey I don't like.

LATOYA: Me too!

*(*MAMA *goes into the kitchen and begins to unpack.)*

LATOYA: Mama, did you hear that new song about Walter?

MAMA: What, about our Walter?

LATOYA: It just has his name in it. *(Pause.)* Want me to sing it?

MAMA: Go ahead!

LATOYA: *(Begins to sing "Little Walter" by Toni, Tone, Tony.)* Hey, Little Walter, hey, Little Walter, listen. Hey, Little Walter, something's gonna get you, Little Walter!

(Doorbell rings. LATOYA *gets it.)*

LATOYA: Hey, Nicky, what's up?

NICKY: Nothing much, Toya. Walter here?

LATOYA: No.

MAMA: Hello, Nicole. Walter should be home from work in a few. You can take a seat and wait.

NICKY: You know Walter works?

MAMA: Of course, and I'm so proud of him, working in a law firm. He got a better job than me. Just wait until he gets out of high school. (MAMA *goes into the kitchen.*)

LATOYA: Mama gonna be waitin' a long time, ain't she? (NICKY *nods.*)

NICKY: *(to* LATOYA*)* I wish Little Walter would hurry up. I have something important to tell him.

LATOYA: Since when you started calling him Little Walter?

NICKY: That's what everybody calls him on the streets.

LATOYA: I thought it was just us that called him that.

NICKY: Not anymore.

MAMA: *(Yells from in the kitchen.)* Nicky?

NICKY: Yes, ma'am?

MAMA: You got some boyfriend there. Child, just last month I lost hope on my family's future. Then my child gets this job. All that hard work finally paid off. My baby's gonna take us places.

NICKY: *(solemn)* Yes, ma'am.

LATOYA: He's gonna take us straight to the morgue.

NICKY: *(nervous)* Latoya, don't say that! *(Pause.)* I wish he would hurry up. I got something important to tell him.

LATOYA: What?

NICKY: Excuse me. When did they name you Walter?

LATOYA: Well, for your info, we got two Walters in this house.

NICKY: Oh, and you're one of them, huh?

LATOYA: No, Albert is.

NICKY: What do you mean, Albert is?

LATOYA: Excuse me, but who gave you the right to barge in on Albert's business?

NICKY: Pardon me, honey child.

LATOYA: I'll let you pass this time, but don't make it a habit.

NICKY: *(less tense)* Okay. *(WALTER and RAKIM enter. NICKY rushes to them.)* Walter and Rocky, I have to talk to you.

WALTER: What are you doing here?

NICKY: Walter, this is important.

RAKIM: What?

NICKY: The guys that popped your cousin is out to get you.

RAKIM: What? Who told you that?

NICKY: Everybody knows. They've been asking around for you all over. They say you have something for them. I heard they found out where you keep the stuff at, and they are going to get it tonight.

(WALTER and RAKIM's attitudes change completely. Fear is on them.)

RAKIM: Shit, I knew this was gonna happen.

WALTER: I'm gettin' the tool.*

(WALTER rushes to the bedroom. MAMA notices.)

MAMA: Hi, Walter, back from work?

(No answer.)

LATOYA: *(Begins to sing.)* Hey, Little Walter. Hey, Little Walter, listen. Hey, Little Walter, something's gonna get you, Little Walter. *(She repeats.)*

WALTER: *(Runs in.)* I got it, let's go, get our stuff and break out!

(MAMA comes in.)

MAMA: Where are you going, Walter? I'm making a special dinner for you.

(LATOYA's still singing.)

WALTER: I'll be home in time for dinner. *(WALTER listens to LATOYA.)* What are you singing, Toya?

---

* gun

LATOYA: *(Pays no attention to question.)* "Something's gonna get you, Little Walter!''

(WALTER looks at LATOYA in awe.)

RAKIM: *(impatient)* Walter, come on, man!

(WALTER turns and runs out. NICKY follows. LATOYA runs into the kitchen and grabs her mother.)

MAMA: Toya, what's wrong?

(Blackout.)

Scene Twelve

SETTING: *The alley.* ALBERT *and* TREY *are filling up a paper bag with crack vials. The alley is dark, with a bright flash of light every five seconds.*

ALBERT: I hear something. Let's break out. *(They run out.)*

(Enter RAKIM, NICKY, and WALTER.)

WALTER: *(Checks behind the curtain.)* I can't believe it! Half the stuff is gone.

RAKIM: You mean they came already? That's it, man, I'm through with this shit. Yo, Walter, look!

(The flashes are flashing faster. There is a sound of a car door slamming.)

NICKY: Somebody's coming!

WALTER: Who is it?

(Sound of a car door slamming.)

NICKY: Oh, God, they have guns! *(She screams.)*

(Strobe lights. Everything has slowed down, like at a disco. Gunshots are heard. You see WALTER grab NICKY and push her to hide behind the trash cans. She does so. RAKIM appears to be hit several times and goes down screaming. Now WALTER is shot several times. He, too, goes down screaming in anguish. The shots stop. The automobile sounds as if driving off.)

WALTER: *(Rises up, bloody, in pain.)* There's no way they can stop us! *(He falls dead.)*

NICKY: *(screeches in tears)* Hey, Little Walter . . .

(Blackout.)

Scene Thirteen

SETTING: *The Reality. Funeral. The stage is empty and dreary. There is a casket center stage.* ALBERT *is dressed in expensive gear, as his brother once was.* WALTER*'s casket stands in front of them like a barrier.* MAMA *weeps. The song "What's Going On" by Marvin Gaye plays quietly. They stay like this.* MAMA*'s cries grow louder.*

MAMA: *(teary)* Nicky, I can't . . . *(Pause.)* Nicky, baby, take me to get a glass of water.

*(*NICKY *escorts* MAMA *offstage. As she does so,* MAMA*'s cries grow louder.* LATOYA *and* ALBERT *are left onstage.)*

ALBERT: *(hurt)* Aww, man. *(Hardens.)* I'm outta here. I got places to go.

LATOYA: *(Grabs him.)* Albert, what's going on?

ALBERT: *(Pushes her away.)* Yo, chill.

LATOYA: You think I don't know, but I do.

ALBERT: What you talkin' 'bout?

LATOYA: I know that you and Trey are doing the same thing Walter was.

ALBERT: Don't worry 'bout me, I'ma be aight.

LATOYA: That's what Little Walter thought too.

ALBERT: Yo, I got it under control.

LATOYA: I'll give you six months, Albert, and then you're gonna be dead, just like the rest of them. *(Pause.* ALBERT*'s facial expression hardens.)* Didn't Walter's death teach you anything?

ALBERT: Yeah, a lot, and I ain't going out like Walter did. I ain't going out like no sucker.

LATOYA: *(Backs up.)* What changed you? A year ago you was my brother Albert, now you're, you're—

ALBERT: *(Cuts in.)* I'm the new Little Walter, gettin' paid in full!

(LATOYA turns away.)

ALBERT: Man, Toya, you don't understand. You're too young to know that there's something in this world that brothers just got to do.

LATOYA: Like die! 'Cause that's the new in thing for brothers around the way, death!

ALBERT: *(justifying his actions)* Look, Toya, lately I've been getting bills that I ain't never seen that big in my whole life. I'm working with Trey's pops now and I'm going places. *(Pause.)* Toya, for generations we were poor, they took everything from us, but now we got something and they can't stop us. Toya, I'm gettin' paid! *(Silence. TOYA looks at him and sighs, then looks away.)* See, you too young to understand. I got things to do. I'm history. *(He exits. As he exits, he bumps into his brother's casket. He notices his brother's body and in a daze he backs offstage, staring at his brother in the casket.)*

LATOYA: You ain't lying.

(Enter MAMA and NICKY. The three stand and silently gaze into WALTER's casket. WALTER enters upstage center. He has money in his hands.)

WALTER: So now you know. Yeah, I got caught out there. Like I said, it just happened. For generations we were poor . . .

(Enter ALBERT stage right. He has money in his hand. He has come to do what he has been doing for a while now, dealing.)

ALBERT: *(justifying what he is about to do. Unknowingly he and his brother speak simultaneously.)* For generations we were poor. *(WALTER grows silent in disbelief at his brother's new presence.)* They took everything from us, but now we got something, and they can't stop us. Yeah, I'm getting paid.

(WALTER hides his head under his cap in shame. Enter TREYBAG stage right.)

TREY: Man, what's up?

ALBERT: Yo, you got the stuff from your pops?

TREY: Nah, man.

ALBERT: What?

TREY: I was thinking maybe we don't have to do this today, maybe we can go play some ball.

ALBERT: Play ball? Man, you must be kidding me.

TREY: But, Albert, me want to play ball. Remember our favorite game?

ALBERT: Man, get out of my face until you come to your senses.

TREY: Fine, Albert. Be that way. *(*TREY *begins to exit.)*

ALBERT: *(Holds on to the money tightly.)* It's Little Walter to you. *(He begins to count the money.)* Three hundred, four hundred, five hundred, six hundred, seven hundred . . .

WALTER: *(standing behind his brother, unable to touch him)* Listen, man, yo, can you hear me? Hey, look, don't! Please, man, what are you doing? why are you selling out? Can you hear me? Damn! *(Louder.)* Can you . . . *(*ALBERT *continues to count not noticing his brother.)* Hear me? *(*WALTER *notices his watch.)* Damn! Time to go pay the piper. *(As he exits, he sees* MAMA, NICKY, *and* TOYA *crying and takes one more glance at* ALBERT.*)* Damn! *(Exits.* ALBERT *continues counting.)*

ALBERT: One thousand, eleven hundred, twelve hundred, thirteen hundred, fourteen hundred . . .

MAMA: *(Wipes tears.)* Come on, girls, let's go.

NICKY: Are you ready, Toya?

LATOYA: Yeah. *(*NICKY *helps* MAMA *off, ahead of* TOYA. *Looks into casket.)* Hey, Little Walter. *(Pause.)* Something's got you, Little Walter.

(As she turns to exit, the song "Little Walter" begins to play. ALBERT *is left on stage counting money.)*

ALBERT: Two thousand *(kisses money),* twenty-one hundred, twenty-two hundred, twenty-three hundred . . .

CARLA DEBBIE ALLEYNE

(1990) Then . . .

I was born on November 4, 1971, in Port of Spain, Trinidad, and grew
up in Brooklyn. I am currently attending New York University, where I
am majoring in Dramatic Writing. I started writing plays in my freshman year of high school, when I saw a poster that read "Write a Play."
That poster started my career. It was put out by the Dramatists Guild
for the New York City High School Playwriting Competition. Since that
year I kept entering the competition, and each year I would place
higher than the past year. Until finally, in my senior year, I won first
place with *Hey Little Walter,* which went on to win the 1989 Young Playwrights Festival. Wow! Finally something I'm good at. The process of
actually having an Off-Broadway full production was invigorating. I had
a wonderful cast, a great director—Mark Brokaw—and an excellent
dramaturge—OyamO. I was set for a month.

About the Play

Hey Little Walter came to life in my sophomore year at John Jay High
School. Friends of mine were dying. I knew a lot of Nickys, Walters, and
Rakims. Dealing became the move for guys around my way, but death
quickly followed. I kept hearing myself saying, "Yeah, it's better than
making $3.35 an hour, but is a few bucks worth your life?" A young
African-American male named Walter began to live in my head. He
wanted to be heard. Thanks to the Foundation of the Dramatists Guild,
he was. So now what? Well, I just finished writing a new play that is an
African fairy tale. I'm working on a script for the CityKids Foundation
in New York City, and I can't wait to get started on a screenplay. My
goal is to raise the consciousness in the black community. It's time we
stop ripping, raping, and robbing each other blind. We must remove
our shackles and unite as a people, an African people.

Peace Out!

. . . And Now

After the 1990 Young Playwrights Festival

I knew I was indeed a playwright and it was a wonderful revelation.

So Now What Am I Up To?

Writing, writing, and more writing. I am in my third year in the New York University Dramatic Writing Program and I'm learning so much. I have just recently completed my first draft of my second screenplay, *Baby You Got It Goin' On!* (No, I have not deserted the theater. As a matter of fact, I'm working on a third draft of my play *Shackles in Nacirema.*)

Hey Little Walter on Broadway
(in the 1991 Young Playwrights Festival Tenth Anniversary Gala)

Was an unbelievable experience. I had a wonderful, enlightening dramaturge. Thank you for everything, you're truly a special person, Mr. David Henry Hwang. I had a wonderful cast and director from the Off Broadway production. You did it again, guys, thanks. So now who said I couldn't do Broadway before I was twenty-one?

Thank-yous

I want to take this time to thank all who have made this possible: God; the Foundation of the Dramatists Guild, Nancy Quinn, Sheri Goldhirsch (I'm proud to be a part of the family); Mark Brokaw, Allen Moyer, OyamO, David Henry Hwang; my cast: Lisa, Seth, Harold, Cynthia, Merlin, Natalia, and Sean; Wendy Lamb (thanks for your patience and *Hey Little Walter and Other Prize-winning Plays from the 1989 and 1990 Young Playwrights Festivals*); Grandma; John Jay High School; the Corbie family; Danielle; Richard Mason; Tajma Davis; New York University; Janet Neipris. God bless every last one of you. And if I could do it again, I wouldn't change a single thing.

Aight I'm out, 'cause me and Walter got things to do, places to go, and duckettes to make. Peace.

I'M NOT STUPID

by
DAVID E. RODRIGUEZ
(age eighteen when play was written)
New York, New York

∎

I'm Not Stupid was performed at Playwrights Horizons in New York City, September 24 through October 20, 1991. Seret Scott was the director, and Paul Selig the dramaturge. The stage manager was Liz Small. Sets were designed by Allen Moyer, and costumes by Elsa Ward. The lighting designer was Pat Dignan. Janet Kalas was the sound designer.

The cast:

ROGER . . . . *Curtis McClarin*
DR. GREEN . . . . *Peter Francis James*
MA . . . . *S. Epatha Merkerson*

Scene One

Scene begins with spotlight on ROGER. *He is sitting in a chair, rocking back and forth.*

ROGER: I was watching the Little Rascals on TV, they had a clubhouse . . . and I wanted a big clubhouse like the Little Rascals' . . . I'm not stupid! You need WOOD to build a clubhouse, and there is a lot of wood in the junkyard. I could get wood from the junkyard to make me a little house like the Little Rascals'. I was going to sleep in it, and Pa too. We were going to sleep in the clubhouse like the Little Rascals. I went to the junkyard and got a lot of wood . . . I'm not stupid! You need nails, I had a lot of nails . . . and you need a box, you build it like a big box, but it's turned upside down . . . I'm not stupid! I could make a clubhouse, you need a hammer for the nails. Pa had a hammer, he had a big hammer. Like this big. It was in the house . . . and I went into the house to get the big hammer. I asked Ma for Pa's hammer. She started to cry. She told me Pa wasn't coming back. *(Pause.* ROGER *begins to cry.)* I'm not stupid! I know Pa was dead. Sleep killed him. Sleep! . . . I was a bad boy.

(Lights come up revealing a doctor's office. DR. GREEN *is sitting behind a desk.)*

DR. GREEN: How were you a bad boy?

ROGER: I was bad. I was a bad boy.

DR. GREEN: How were you bad, Roger . . . Roger?

ROGER: Yeah?

DR. GREEN: Tell me, it's okay. How were you a bad boy?

ROGER: All I wanted to do was build a clubhouse *(pause)* . . . like the Little Rascals'.

DR. GREEN: Roger?

ROGER: Yeah? . . .

DR. GREEN: It's okay. . . . Okay?

ROGER: Okay!

DR. GREEN: Is it bad to build a clubhouse, Roger?

ROGER: Yeah!

DR. GREEN: Why? . . . Why?

(Pause.)

ROGER: I wasn't thinkin' about Pa. I wasn't thinkin' about Pa.

DR. GREEN: Roger?

ROGER: Yeah. You keep sayin' my name.

DR. GREEN: Was that bad?

ROGER: Yeah!

DR. GREEN: Why? Tell me. Why was that bad?

ROGER: I was supposed to be thinkin' about Pa. I didn't want to hear . . . hear that Pa was dead. All I wanted to do was build my clubhouse. I was supposed to be thinkin' about Pa. . . . That's bad. Why? Why she don't tell me after I make my clubhouse? I never finish the Little Rascal Clubhouse. I wanted Pa's hammer. I wanted Pa's hammer. Ma never gave me Pa's hammer, she never gave it to me!

DR. GREEN: Roger?

ROGER: Stop sayin' my name.

DR. GREEN: Do you want to talk more?

ROGER: No.

DR. GREEN: Do you want to be alone?

ROGER: I want to be alone.

DR. GREEN: Okay.

ROGER: Okay!

(ROGER exits. MA enters through opposite door.)

MA: *(sitting)* So, what did he tell you?

DR. GREEN: The usual.

MA: Bad things about me again?

DR. GREEN: Well, not exactly . . . bad.

MA: Oh . . .

DR. GREEN: Although, there were some things said that . . . concern me.

MA: Like bad things, right? That boy has always got something bad to say about me. . . .

DR. GREEN: Now, Mrs. Fletcher. . . .

MA: It's true. What did he say about me last week?

DR. GREEN: Well, the same thing he said for several weeks, the same thing he said today. . . .

MA: I'm not giving him the hammer.

(Pause.)

DR. GREEN: Why don't you give him what he wants?

MA: Isn't it enough that he got all the money?

DR. GREEN: Not all of it, Mrs. Fletcher.

MA: Oh, you're talking about my share. The third I get to take care of Roger with, and the rent, and the bills. . . .

DR. GREEN: You got what you were entitled to by law.

MA: What I'm entitled to and what I deserve are two different things.

DR. GREEN: We're here to talk about Roger.

MA: Why don't you buy him a hammer? You take care of his money.

DR. GREEN: It's not that simple. He doesn't want another hammer.

MA: I won't give it to him. He's taken far too much from me already.

DR. GREEN: Okay . . . Mrs. Fletcher, I know your late husband's will didn't come out exactly as you had hoped. . . .

MA: It's not only the money. . . .

(Enter ROGER.)

ROGER: Hi, Ma. I didn't say nothin' bad about you this time, Ma, I swear.

MA: *(to ROGER)* Why don't you shut up.

DR. GREEN: Mrs. Fletcher!

ROGER: That's okay.

DR. GREEN: Roger?

ROGER: Yeah?

DR. GREEN: Would you mind waiting outside?

ROGER: Yeah.

DR. GREEN: Please?

ROGER: Okay. I'll be right outside, Ma. Waiting right there. Ma. . . . Ma. . . . Bye, Dr. Green.

DR. GREEN: Good-bye, Roger. *(Exit* ROGER.*)* What was that?

MA: What was what? I don't know what you're talking about.

DR. GREEN: He's your son.

MA: No, he is not. He's no son of mine.

DR. GREEN: No? What is he to you, then?

MA: He's just this stupid, good-for-nothing that took everything I ever lived for!

DR. GREEN: That is not true!

MA: It's true! Since the day he was born I no longer had a husband. Now he's dead because of him.

DR. GREEN: It was a heart attack. Blaming Roger—

MA: *(interrupting)* Henry was strong! He worked day in and day out to pay doctor bills . . . *Doctor!* He'd come home tired every night. . . . So tired and pale, Dr. Green. How long do you think a man could last doing that without one day his body giving in? I saw it. I told him to stop. I told him to send Roger away so he wouldn't have to work so hard. But no, he loved Roger. That man gave more love to that idiot than he gave me in seventeen years!

DR. GREEN: I see. So what are you going to do now? Make him suffer? Treat him as if he were some kind of animal? What do you want?

MA: I want what I deserve!

DR. GREEN: And what is that? Money?

MA: I said it isn't about the damn money!

DR. GREEN: Okay. . . . What, then? . . . What?

(Pause.)

MA: If you don't like the way I treat him, why don't you have him sent away?

(Pause.)

DR. GREEN: *(They overlap for next few lines.)* This is all about the money . . .

MA: You're wrong . . .

DR. GREEN: We both know that if Roger is sent away, you'll be awarded his trust money . . .

MA: I want to go on with my life . . .

DR. GREEN: . . . I won't be able to provide services for him; thus I will no longer oversee the account . . .

MA: . . . I deserve some peace . . .

DR. GREEN: . . . making you the beneficiary of your husband's will, isn't that right? What else could it be?

(Overlapping ends.)

MA: You don't know everything, you have no idea!

DR. GREEN: Come now, Mrs. Fletcher, you said it yourself, he's not your son. All Roger is, is one big dollar sign.

MA: He's an idiot.

(Pause.)

DR. GREEN: Roger is very high functioning, he does not present a danger to himself or to others. He has proven able to cope with the everyday challenges, you are physically fit to care for him, and it goes on and on, Mrs. Fletcher, all that I can suggest to you is what I have requested in the past.

MA: No, I don't need a shrink.

DR. GREEN: You need to learn how to deal with Roger. I'm not going to diagnose you, or put you on any medication. We'll just sit down and talk—talk about your husband's death; most of all, talk about Roger, so you can get a better understanding—

MA: No, thanks.

DR. GREEN: I can help you.

MA: You know how you can help me!

DR. GREEN: Give it a chance. What do you have to lose? If you have one bit of love left in you for that boy, do it for him.

MA: No!

DR. GREEN: Do it for yourself, then?

MA: You think you know everything! You're so smart! You think you got everything all figured out!

DR. GREEN: I think you need more help than Roger. And I don't think I know everything. I don't know how a woman like yourself could be so full of hate . . . but if you continue on this path, one day it may very well lead you to break, and I don't think that's something for Roger to experience.

MA: *(exiting)* I've heard enough of your know-it-all talk. Good-bye, Dr. Green.

DR. GREEN: For your sake, listen to me!

MA: Whatever you say, doc. . . . Bye.

DR. GREEN: Before you go, just answer this, did you ever love him?

MA: Bye-bye.

(Exit MA. The lights fade to black.)

ROGER: *(as if holding a hammer)* Heavy. . . . Roger, hit the nail on top . . . if you don't, the nail will bend. . . . Look, Roger. . . . BOOM! BOOM! BOOM! . . . I hit it on top. BOOM! No, Roger. . . . BOOM! You're bending the nail! BOOM! Hit it on top! On top. . . . Boom! . . . On top! . . . Boom! Stop . . . it's bending, Roger! Try it. . . . BOOM! . . . I can't, Pa. . . . BOOM! . . . It's heavy. . . . BOOM! . . . Try it. . . . BOOM! I can't, Pa. . . . BOOM! . . . Hit it! . . . BOOM! . . . I can't. . . . Hit it, Roger! . . . I can't. . . . Hit it, Roger! . . . I can't. . . . On top! . . . BOOM! Again! . . . BOOM! *(Pause.)* Good boy, Roger, good boy. Good boy, Roger, good boy.

Scene Two

The Fletcher household, living room. We see MA *sitting in a chair watching television. There is a knock at the door. It is* DR. GREEN.

MA: *(drunk, but not noticeably so)* Dr. Green?

DR. GREEN: Good afternoon, Mrs. Fletcher. Please pardon this intrusion. I tried calling, but your phone is out of order. Roger didn't keep his appointment. Do you know where he is or if he left?

MA: He's at the junkyard.

DR. GREEN: This is most peculiar. All the years I have known him, he has never missed an appointment.

MA: Wait for him here. He'll be right back, and I do have to talk to you.

DR. GREEN: I see. Then I'll wait. *(He takes a seat.)* So, what is on your mind?

MA: I was thinking about that question you asked me, if I loved Roger. And I've been thinking; I love Roger. It's the kind of love you have for a pet . . . a dog, maybe. You give it a bath, feed it, clean up after it. Don't get me wrong, Dr. Green, did you expect me to love him as a son? How can I? He can't do anything, except eat and sleep, like a dog. I'm not mean. That does not make me mean. Did you ever wonder if a dog loves? I say that people say that dogs love, but that is just because you take care of it. They'll go back to sleep until they're hungry again, and then come back for more. They don't know where the food comes from, as long as it tastes good. They'll eat it, then they'll go back to sleep . . . Roger sleeps a lot. In a way, Roger isn't a person. He's a dog. You give him what he wants, and he stays happy, right? That's right! It's true! So why should I love him as a son, when he's a dog. Don't look at me like that, Dr. Green, you know what I'm saying is true. Why don't you just put away all that mumbo jumbo about a person is a person, and wake up and see that Roger is really a dog, that talks. A talking, walking, big ol' dumb dog, and maybe you could understand what I'm saying. So you can stop looking at me like that! I'm not stupid, I'm smart. Do you think I'm smart? I think I'm smart, this is my opinion. It is my opinion that Roger is a dog. So what? What's so wrong with that? Kill me, for cryin' out loud, but at least I loved him. I kept him happy. No, I mean, I love him and I keep him happy. Sometimes I mix words around, but I'm still smart, and he's still happy. So you see, there's nothing wrong. Roger would even tell you himself, and he will when he comes back, you'll see.

DR. GREEN: I can't believe you just said that.

MA: Why not? He's never going to get married and have kids. He's never going to have a job, much less take care of me when I get old. I'm lonely, even if Roger is around. Maybe . . . maybe I should get a real dog or something, what do you think? I'll bathe it, take it for walks, clean up after it. I have had years of experience . . .

DR. GREEN: You're drunk.

MA: So I'm drunk, what does that have to do with it? I'll still feel the same when I'm sober. I'll still want a dog . . .

DR. GREEN: Mrs. Fletcher, I think we ought to talk about this again, when you sober up. Obviously you're not yourself. Until then, I will look for Roger. If you will excuse me—

MA: No, stay here. Roger will come back. He's probably on his way, and it's so cold outside.

DR. GREEN: I appreciate your concern, but I think I really ought to—

MA: I gave him the hammer.

DR. GREEN: What?

MA: I did. After that, he went rushing out the door to the junkyard.

DR. GREEN: Well, that explains it. It was good of you, you know. You did something.

MA: I know I've been really hard on him for some time. You see, I'm not mean. I think I'm turning over a new leaf. I was just angry over Henry's death, that's all. Now, I'm over it.

DR. GREEN: Really?

MA: You say that as if you don't believe me. I may be drunk now, but this is the last time. I'm going to be a new woman, you'll see.

DR. GREEN: I see. A moment ago Roger was a dog.

MA: Oh, that. Really bad example, wasn't it?

DR. GREEN: I would say so, but—

MA: You know, I never knew what the "K" stands for in "Dr. K. Green."

DR. GREEN: Karl.

MA: Karl—that's a nice name. Do you mind if I call you Karl?

DR. GREEN: If you prefer.

MA: I would. I don't know, "Dr. Green" sounds so formal. Don't you agree? So distant, and I would like us to be closer, Karl. After all, you'll be treating me.

DR. GREEN: Treating you?

MA: Yes, didn't I tell you? No, I didn't, did I?

DR. GREEN: I don't believe so.

MA: Well, now you know. I've decided to take you up on your offer. I figured some treatment will do me some good.

DR. GREEN: I see.

MA: What's wrong, you don't want to treat me? I know, I'm blowing your mind, right? Oh, don't be surprised, Karl. I was on my bad side for a while like I said before, I'm over that now.

DR. GREEN: Well, then I think that Dr. Green would be more appropriate.

MA: Why?

DR. GREEN: I think it would make our relationship more professional. Now that you are under my care—

MA: Oh, don't be such a stiffy? Wanna drink, while you wait? Oh, I forgot, doctors don't drink, right?

DR. GREEN: I don't know about other doctors, I don't.

MA: That's good. I wouldn't want you to either, Karl. Oops, I forgot! I'm sorry.

DR. GREEN: That's all right.

MA: Since you're here, maybe we can have my first session right now.

DR. GREEN: You've been drinking.

MA: Never mind, I'm sobering up already.

DR. GREEN: Really, Mrs. Fletcher.

MA: Call me Margaret, or is that not professional enough?

DR. GREEN: That's quite all right, if you prefer, but as I was saying before—

MA: Yes, as you were saying, Dr. Green.

DR. GREEN: —I think it would be more appropriate if I asked my secretary to make an appointment.

MA: There you go again, Mr. Stiffy. Do you always have to do things by the book? There's no bending you, is there?

DR. GREEN: I don't know. What do you mean?

MA: You know what I mean. Didn't you do anything wild and crazy when you were young?

DR. GREEN: Like what?

MA: You know, like play a practical joke on your friends, or steal the neighbor's dog? Play a big trick?

DR. GREEN: I have. Not that in particular, but yes, when I was young.

MA: That's what I mean. Come on, loosen up. Let's get a session going here.

DR. GREEN: All right, if you insist.

MA: Great. So what do I do now, lie down?

DR. GREEN: Whatever makes you feel comfortable.

MA: I'm comfortable. What do I do now?

DR. GREEN: Tell me what's on your mind.

MA: Where do I start?

DR. GREEN: Anywhere.

MA: I don't know, I feel funny. Give me a suggestion.

DR. GREEN: All right, why the sudden change in you?

MA: I told you, I'm letting go of the past.

DR. GREEN: Why?

MA: Why not? I can't stay bitter for the rest of my life. Now that Henry is gone, I'm over it. Why don't I start a new life with Roger? Have a chance to be a mother to him? After all, he is my son, isn't he? Forget all that nonsense about him being a dog. I do love him. I guess I've been denying it for so long . . . Well?

DR. GREEN: Well, what?

MA: Aren't you going to say something?

DR. GREEN: Like?

MA: Well, like, I think that you're making a change for the better.

DR. GREEN: I think you're making a change for the better.

MA: You really mean that?

DR. GREEN: Honestly?

MA: Yes.

DR. GREEN: No, I don't believe one word you've said.

MA: What? I can't believe it!

DR. GREEN: I'm a psychiatrist, Mrs. Fletcher. I don't believe in miracles.

MA: But I'm telling the truth! I swear, I gave him the hammer, and he's at the junkyard! Who the hell do you think you are, calling me a liar!

DR. GREEN: When did you give him the hammer?

MA: Today! I gave it to him today!

DR. GREEN: What did you make him promise? What did he have to do?

MA: Nothing. Why are you doing this to me! I just wanted him to be happy.

DR. GREEN: How do you know he is at the junkyard?

MA: I took him there myself.

DR. GREEN: Really? Why?

MA: He wanted me to see him build his goddamn clubhouse!

DR. GREEN: Then why isn't he here now? Tell me! Why?

MA: What? What are you accusing me of? Do you think I'd go that far?

DR. GREEN: Go as far as what? GO AS FAR AS WHAT!!! WHAT DID YOU DO TO HIM?

MA: I'm changing, don't you see? I'm not lying! I swear!

DR. GREEN: I'm going to the junkyard.

MA: No!

DR. GREEN: Why not? I'm going, Mrs. Fletcher.

MA: *(Clings fiercely to him.)* Don't go—please, please don't go! He's there! Believe what I'm saying! He's there!

DR. GREEN: Let go of me! Let go of me!

MA: All right, all right, go then! Go!

(DR. GREEN *exits.*)

MA: You think you know everything! Go!

(Breaks down in tears on the floor. Lights fade to black.)

Scene Three

The Fletcher household. The lights are dim, one lamp is on. DR. GREEN *bursts in with the hammer in his hand.*

MA: I told you he was at the junkyard, but you didn't believe me. *(No response.)* Now do you believe me? You thought you knew everything. I'm a new woman, now. I've changed for the better. I gave him the hammer. *(DR. GREEN drops the hammer.)* I did it to make him happy. Why are you looking at me like that? He built the clubhouse, didn't he? You should've seen the look on his face. First time I've seen him smile since Pa died. I haven't seen a more satisfied look. I wasn't satisfied, though. No. . . . Sure, Roger got something else he wanted. He always gets what he wants, he's always satisfied! It was special this time. I've seen that look before. It was the time I took him to the city. Roger wanted to get Pa a birthday present. So did I. We were at the hardware store, and when Roger saw the hammer—there were hundreds of hammers—Roger wanted this one. I told him that Pa already had one, but Roger didn't listen. He went on and on about the stupid goddamn hammer! So, I smacked him real good, and he went running out of the store. I figured he'd come back, but after a long while, he didn't. Good! So I just took the bus back alone. I wanted him to stay in the city. I swear, I never wanted him to come back. I didn't see him for two days. Henry didn't notice. He would work day and night. I began to think, what happened to that dummy? I thought he'd come home. And I realized that I can't do such a thing. I may never see him again! Oh my god! What if he's starving, or cold? It wasn't my fault he left. That night I found myself in the city. "Excuse me, did you see my son? My son? My little boy? Did you see him? Are you blind? Are you stupid? How can you not see him?" And all around, I saw people walking, laughing, eating dinner, wearing warm coats. How can they have fun? Don't they realize what happened? I lost my son, don't they care? How can I have been so stupid? I said, "God, please God, if I find him I swear . . . I swear I won't ever touch him again. I'll give him anything he wants." And what was I going to tell Henry? And at that moment, I loved Roger more than anything in the whole world. "Just let me find him." I wasn't going back home without Roger. I'd been walking for five hours, and every alley I passed, I prayed and prayed that I wouldn't find him there, face down in the gutter. It's funny, how everybody started to look like him. Three blocks away I saw someone with the same stupid walk. I started to first walk faster and faster, then jog, then run faster and faster. "Roger! Roger! Roger!" I went up to him and it was a bum. It was Roger. Roger is a bum. Roger was, still is, and always will be a bum. AND THIS BUM HAD THE GODDAMN HAMMER IN HIS HAND! And the first thing he says is, "LOOK, I GOT THE HAMMER!" So what? And then the same look of satisfaction was there! And I wasn't satisfied. The same day, I beat the living daylights out of that boy, and I still wasn't satisfied. But I am satisfied for the first time in my life, right now. I'm satisfied. I don't care what happens now. He was like a pet. All I have to do now is get a dog, a big dog, then I'll be satisfied.

(DR. GREEN *advances violently.*)

DR. GREEN: HOW! HOW CAN YOU BE SO EVIL! He was doing so well. He had a chance!

MA: He wasn't a person, he was a dog! You saw him yourself, didn't you, in a doghouse?

DR. GREEN: I saw your son—your son—with a hammer in his head!

MA: He was your patient. That's all he was to you! That's all he was to you! You don't know what it was like!

DR. GREEN: I loved Roger as a son!

MA: A son? He didn't even know your first name, Karl. If he was my son, if he was a human being, I wouldn't have done it!

DR. GREEN: You actually believe it. You're not just calling him a dog. You actually believe it. I will have you committed for life! You will pay for this! You will rot in a cage where you belong!

MA: So you can get the money.

DR. GREEN: What!

MA: You brought the hammer. People saw you coming out of the junkyard. And you came here to attack me.

DR. GREEN: What are you talking about?

MA: Yes, Karl, because the neighbors heard you when you left, and when you came back. Now we are arguing because you killed Roger!

DR. GREEN: What?

MA: It's a lot of money, isn't it? Enough for a shrink to kill for!

DR. GREEN: You're insane!

MA: And now you want to blame it on me, and send me away, and call me crazy so you can get the money! You knew Roger for many years. He would go anywhere with you!

DR. GREEN: Stop it!

MA: And I'm saying this loud enough so all the neighbors can hear! No, don't hurt me! Dr. Karl Green, please don't hurt me, I'll give you the money! I'll give you what you want, don't kill me too!

DR. GREEN: *(Tries to shut her up.)* I said stop it! Shut up!

MA: Help! Help! He's killing me! Let me go!

DR. GREEN: *(withdraws)* All right! All right! I'm not touching you! Don't do this . . .

MA: *(lower)* You think you know everything, Mr. Know-it-all. I'm not stupid, Karl. A nice long trip to Mexico will do me some good. After all, I am a new woman. Don't look at me like that, Karl. I'm not a mean person. That doesn't make me mean. I just want to be satisfied.

DR. GREEN: You'll never get away with this!

MA: Like I said, Mexico. I'll leave after I get the money.

DR. GREEN: You'll never . . . How could you have done this?

MA: I'm not stupid. A poodle sounds real good right now.

DAVID E. RODRIGUEZ

(1991)

Right now I'm supposed to be writing a film script. Two hours ago was Christmas Day, and I have three more days to complete the script . . . tonight I don't sleep . . . tonight I don't work on the script . . . tonight I ask myself, "Why bother?" Something is eating away at my insides right now, and if I don't let it out, it'll devour me whole. I went home today after disappearing for a couple of weeks, locked up in my new apartment consisting of a chair, a desk, a computer, and a futon with sheets I've forgotten the last time I washed. My big disappearance occurred right after I quit my job and left college to write a film script which will start shooting next year, and to be around for a production of my first full-length play to open around the same time. I have no back-up plan if things should fall through. I've always made huge sacrifices in my life, and I often wonder if I should turn myself in for illegal moral gambling, not to mention some of the other stuff I've done as a kid growing up on the streets on the Upper West Side—a place where I found myself this evening, feeling slightly out of place. I didn't expect to recognize anyone, most of the friends I grew up with are either dead or in jail. I walked into my mother's apartment to find her laid out on the couch watching television with her eyes hardly opened. As soon as she realized there was someone towering over her, she greeted me, even though she didn't recognize me. I thought she was drunk. My mother is a recovering alcoholic. It turned out that she wasn't drunk at all, she was on some other drug prescribed to her to help with depression. She'd experienced violent fits of rage, and nonstop crying that pushed everyone away on Christmas Eve. . . . My mother told me this after I introduced myself as her son. She also told me that the origin of her depression lies in the fact that in a few months she could be living on the streets with my autistic little brother. I've read the documents from the welfare office; they were written in Recession. I remember spending one Christmas in a dumpy, smelly welfare hotel because my family was homeless when I was nine. And when I was ten, I remember spending Christmas without my father because he was shot dead in the street. I also remember spending Christmas in a state mental institution when I was fifteen. The rest of the years I spent the holiday working in restaurants. Today I am nineteen. I hate Christmas, I don't remember any other. This evening I walked into my old bedroom; my autistic little brother was in bed, and I sat on my old worn mattress on the floor, where I used to sleep. Next to the bed I used to have a small b/w TV set with a wire hanger sticking out of it as an antenna. I used to have to hold it to get any type of reception; me and my older brother would take turns. My older brother wasn't home that day. He also left school so he could get a job to save up money so he could represent the Dominican Republic in the 1992 Olympic games in Spain. The Dominican government doesn't have money. My brother holds local and state track records. He's also getting a job to help the family. Tomorrow I want to forget all this writing shit, and get myself a *real* job to help my family. They need me *now*, and all the time. As I was walking around my old neighborhood, I was surrounded by Hispanic laborers, many of them are poor, uneducated, and *have families to support*! And for just a split second I thought that the only way to succeed, or realize a dream, is to have money to begin with! As I was walking, I threw up my hands and yelled, *"I can't fucking afford to be a writer!"* I'm trapped, like the rest. So is my brother, and mother, who still bought me a Christmas present. There's something that stops me from giving up writing, I still haven't figured out what it is. Maybe it's rage, or maybe I'm destructive, or just plain crazy. I always say that one *has to* make huge, huge sacrifices to reach their goal. I won first prize in several competitions, I've opportunities to really grow as an artist and I'll be damned if I let myself be trapped, I don't want to kick myself in the ass ten years from now still living in the old neighborhood thinking about what I could have become. I realize that I will always keep writing no matter what. And this business with my family just gives me more reasons to make more sacrifices to write more.

I used to believe that life is nothing more than a product of all the decisions one has made. If a person has made bad decisions, they have a bad life, and if they have made good decisions, they have a good life, etc., etc., etc. I always end up relaying that message when I speak to an audience or write a letter to help a young person. Right now I don't believe that anymore, so this is the last time that I'll write it. I've learned today that people could make good decisions but still lead a bad life. I don't know what's in store for me in the future, but whatever it is, it will have everything to do with writing, and everything to do with my family. Now, I got three days to finish this script, I'd better start working. I feel a little better now.

I dedicate my success in the Young Playwrights Festival to my family.

WOMEN
AND
WALLACE

by
JONATHAN MARC SHERMAN
(age eighteen when play was written)
Livingston, New Jersey

■

Women and Wallace was performed at Playwrights Horizons in New York City, September 13 through October 8, 1988. The director was Don Scardino, and the playwright adviser was Albert Innaurato. Roy Harris was the production stage manager. Allen Moyer designed the sets, the costumes were by Jess Goldstein, the lighting designer was Nancy Schertler, and the sound designer was Lia Vollack. The music was composed and performed by John Miller.

The cast:

WALLACE KIRKMAN . . . . *Josh Hamilton*
MOTHER . . . . *Mary Joy*
GRANDMOTHER . . . . *Joan Copeland*
VICTORIA . . . . *Dana Behr*
PSYCHIATRIST . . . . *Debra Monk*
SARAH . . . . *Bellina Logan*
LILI . . . . *Jill Tasker*
NINA . . . . *Joanna Going*
WENDY . . . . *Erica Gimpel*

TIME:
1975 to 1987

"The great question that has never been answered, and which I have not been able to answer, despite my thirty years of research into the feminine soul, is 'What does a woman want?' "

—SIGMUND FREUD

For Maria, who justifies romance

Prologue

WALLACE *is standing to the left with a tomato in his hand and a crate of tomatoes at his feet.* NINA *is standing to the right, wearing a white dress. Pause.* WALLACE *lobs the tomato. It splatters on Nina's dress. (Pause.)*

WALLACE: I love you.

(Pause.)

Scene One

WALLACE: "Mommy." By Wallace Kirkman. Age Six. I love Mommy because she makes me peanut butter and banana sandwiches on Wonder bread and it tastes better than when I order it at a restaurant. And Mommy never looks at me funny like the waiters in restaurants do. And Mommy crushes aspirins and mixes them into jelly when I get sick. Because I can't swallow aspirins. They just sit on my tongue and wait for me to finish the whole glass of water. And then I spit them out. But when they're mixed into jelly, I hardly have any problem at all. I just eat the jelly and feel better. And Mommy washes my clothes, so I don't have to. And she does it so they all smell nice when they come out. They come out smelling clean. And they even smell a little like Mommy, because she folds them for me, and her smell rubs off onto my shirts. She smells like perfume. Not really sweet, like Billy Corkscrew's mother. Mommy smells like she's getting ready to go out to dinner. And Mommy's read every book in the library downstairs. I couldn't do that. She can read three books in a week with no trouble at all. Real books, not the Hardy Boys. Mommy's really smart. She can read and take care of me. Both. That's why I love Mommy.

Scene Two

The kitchen. MOTHER *is fixing a peanut butter and banana sandwich with a large knife. She puts it into a lunchbox on the table.* WALLACE *runs in.*

WALLACE: I'm going to miss the bus! Is my lunch ready?

MOTHER: All set.

(WALLACE *grabs the lunchbox and kisses* MOTHER *on the cheek.)*

WALLACE: 'Bye, Mommy.

MOTHER: 'Bye, Wallace.

WALLACE: *(to the audience)* I love the second grade!

MOTHER: Don't shout, Wallace.

(WALLACE runs out. MOTHER watches after him. She writes a note on a slip of paper and puts it on the table. She takes off her turtleneck shirt, so she is in her brassiere. She slits her throat with the large knife. She falls to the floor. Pause. WALLACE runs in.)

WALLACE: Mommy, I'm home! *(WALLACE sees MOTHER on the floor. He picks up the note.)*

WALLACE: *(reading the note)* "Cremate the parasite."

Scene Three

Wallace's bedroom. WALLACE *is lying on his bed.* GRANDMOTHER *walks in, holding a gift and a photograph.*

GRANDMOTHER: Here you are. Your teacher gave me this gift for you.

WALLACE: It's not my birthday.

GRANDMOTHER: Well, something bad happened to you. When something bad happens, you get gifts to make you feel better.

WALLACE: Why do I get gifts on my birthday?

GRANDMOTHER: Well, because you're a year older.

WALLACE: Being a year older isn't bad.

GRANDMOTHER: It adds up. Open your gift.

(WALLACE opens his gift.)

WALLACE: Peanut brittle.

GRANDMOTHER: Isn't that *lovely*—

WALLACE: I *hate* peanut brittle.

GRANDMOTHER: So do I. Don't forget to send your teacher a thank-you note.

WALLACE: Why should I *send* her something? I see her every day.

GRANDMOTHER: So *give* her a thank-you note.

WALLACE: But I *hate* peanut brittle.

GRANDMOTHER: So throw it at her during the pledge of allegiance. Just give her *something* in return for her gift. It's good manners.

WALLACE: Okay.

GRANDMOTHER: She's a very pretty woman.

WALLACE: I guess so.

GRANDMOTHER: Why aren't you downstairs?

WALLACE: Too many people. Why'd they all come back home with us?

GRANDMOTHER: I don't know. They didn't get enough grief out, maybe.

WALLACE: I think they just like free food.

GRANDMOTHER: You're probably right. They're all bunched together like a big black cloud of perfume and cologne, munching on little corned beef sandwiches. *Horrible.*

WALLACE: What's that?

GRANDMOTHER: What? *This?*

WALLACE: Yeah.

GRANDMOTHER: Oh, it's a photograph of your mother. The last one, as far as I know. Your father took it six days ago. I wanted to have it.

WALLACE: I wish Mommy would come back.

GRANDMOTHER: I know, Wallace, but for whatever reasons, she wanted to go—

WALLACE: She didn't want to.

GRANDMOTHER: What? Wallace—

WALLACE: I know she didn't want to, Grandma, I know. A pirate came in while I was at school and tore her open. He took everything inside of her and put it in his sack and escaped through the kitchen door. She didn't want to go, Grandma. And if I was here—if I pretended I was sick and stayed home—I could have saved her—

GRANDMOTHER: No. You couldn't have. Don't think you could have saved her, because I'm telling you, you couldn't have. Nobody could have. It was time for her to go. It'll be time for me to go soon, too. And someday, it'll be your time to go—

WALLACE: Not me. I'm going to live forever.

GRANDMOTHER: I wish you luck. You'd be the first person to do it.

WALLACE: I'm going to.

GRANDMOTHER: If anybody can, Wallace, I'm sure it'll be you.

WALLACE: And I'm going to find the pirate who did this. You wait and see.

GRANDMOTHER: I will, Wallace. I certainly will. *(Pause.)* You look very handsome in your suit.

WALLACE: Thank you.

Scene Four

The schoolyard. WALLACE *is sitting on a bench eating a sandwich.* VICTORIA *walks in.*

VICTORIA: Hi, Wallace.

WALLACE: Hi, Victoria.

VICTORIA: Can I sit down?

WALLACE: Free country.

*(*VICTORIA *sits down next to* WALLACE.*)*

VICTORIA: What you got for lunch?

WALLACE: Peanut butter and banana.

VICTORIA: Want to trade?

WALLACE: What do you have?

VICTORIA: Tuna.

WALLACE: No, thanks. Besides, I already ate some of mine.

VICTORIA: Peanut butter and banana's my favorite. Bet it's good.

WALLACE: It kind of sucks. My dad made it. Dads can't make lunch. You can barely *taste* the banana.

VICTORIA: *(pause)* I'm sorry about your mother.

WALLACE: Yeah. Me, too.

VICTORIA: She killed herself?

WALLACE: Who told you that?

VICTORIA: I don't know. Somebody.

WALLACE: She didn't kill herself. A pirate slit her throat, I think. I haven't finished checking things out yet.

VICTORIA: Uh-uh. That's not what they said. They said, "Suicide."

WALLACE: Who cares?

VICTORIA: I don't know. *(Pause.)* You want a hug?

WALLACE: *(quiet)* Yeah.

(VICTORIA hugs WALLACE for a few moments. He pushes her away suddenly, and she falls.)

WALLACE: Get away from me! *(Pause.)* I gotta go.

(WALLACE runs out. After a moment, VICTORIA walks over to WALLACE's sandwich and looks at it. She picks it up and takes a bite.)

Scene Five

WALLACE: "Broken Glass." By Wallace Kirkman. Age Thirteen. It's past four in the morning and I can't sleep. I go downstairs to get something to drink and maybe see what's on television. I open the refrigerator and take out the orange juice. I drink orange juice because I'm susceptible to colds. And because I heard that Coke rots your teeth. Whether it does or not makes no difference, because after you hear something like that, it stays in your brain. So I pour some orange juice into a glass and put the carton back in the fridge. And I drink. It goes down smooth and cold, and I just swallow it all without stopping. When I'm done, I look at the empty glass in my hand. My parents got a truckload of glassware for their wedding, and the glass in my hand is one of the set. It's older than me. Respect your elders, I think, but then I see her. She's laughing at me. She's inside the glass, laughing at me. I throw the glass against the refrigerator and hear it crash. I look at the shards on the floor. Like an invitation. I know that glass is made of sand, and I like walking on the beach, and I almost step toward the glass, but I don't. I think of blood. My blood. And I just kneel down and stare at the broken glass on the floor, watching for any reflection of the moonlight outside the kitchen window and waiting for my father to come downstairs, because he can't sleep through anything.

Scene Six

(Psychiatrist's office. PSYCHIATRIST *is sitting in a chair writing in a notebook.* WALLACE *walks in.)*

PSYCHIATRIST: You must be Wallace.

WALLACE: Yeah, I'm him.

PSYCHIATRIST: Pleased to meet you. Would you like to have a seat?

WALLACE: Can I lie on the couch?

PSYCHIATRIST: If you'd like.

WALLACE: It seems like the proper thing to do.

PSYCHIATRIST: Go right ahead.

WALLACE: I should *warn* you that I've had my head measured by a close friend, and if you shrink it by so much as a *millimeter,* I'm taking you to *court.*

PSYCHIATRIST: I don't shrink heads.

WALLACE: If I say "*I* do," does that make me insane?

PSYCHIATRIST: It's not that simple.

*(*WALLACE *lies down on the couch.)*

WALLACE: Nice couch. Where'd you get it?

PSYCHIATRIST: Bloomingdale's.

WALLACE: Really? I would have thought there'd be some store that would sell special couches for psychiatrists. It doesn't feel as good when you know that anybody with a few bucks can get one.

PSYCHIATRIST: Tell me why you're here, Wallace.

WALLACE: It was either this or a straitjacket, I suppose.

PSYCHIATRIST: Why's that?

WALLACE: Come on, didn't my father tell you all this?

PSYCHIATRIST: I'd like to hear what you have to say.

WALLACE: Can't argue with that. You see, I've been breaking glasses. In the kitchen.

PSYCHIATRIST: Any particular reason?

WALLACE: I like to live dangerously. You know, in perpetual fear of slicing the soles of my feet open. I don't know what it is, but ever since they cut the umbilical cord, I've been obsessed with *sharp* things. Especially knives. I'm attracted to knives. I'm *incredibly* attracted to *doctors* with knives. Do *you* have a knife, Doctor?

PSYCHIATRIST: No—

WALLACE: Do you want to *buy* one?

PSYCHIATRIST: No.

WALLACE: Oh.

(Long pause.)

PSYCHIATRIST: Tell me about your mother, Wallace.

WALLACE: She was like Sylvia Plath without the publishing contract.

PSYCHIATRIST: Do you remember much about her?

WALLACE: *Nothing.*

PSYCHIATRIST: Nothing at all?

WALLACE: Nope.

PSYCHIATRIST: Are you sure?

WALLACE: Why are you asking me this? Tell me, would you ask me this if my father weren't paying you?

PSYCHIATRIST: You're upset because your father made you come here.

WALLACE: No, I'm upset because he didn't pick a prettier psychiatrist.

PSYCHIATRIST: Was your *mother* pretty, Wallace?

WALLACE: *(pause)* Yeah, she was pretty. *Pretty* pretty. Pretty *suicidal.* And now she's pretty *dead.*

PSYCHIATRIST: You know, Wallace, you don't have to say anything you don't *want* to say.

WALLACE: Okay.

(Long silence.)

PSYCHIATRIST: What are you thinking about, Wallace? *(Pause.)* Wallace? *(Pause.)* Wallace?

Scene Seven

The park. WALLACE *and* VICTORIA *walk in.* WALLACE *is eating a Mallo Cup and drinking something pink out of a bottle.* VICTORIA *is eating Jujyfruits.*

VICTORIA: Good movie.

WALLACE: Yeah.

VICTORIA: I like the kissing stuff.

WALLACE: I like when the girl died.

VICTORIA: You want to sit down here?

WALLACE: Here?

VICTORIA: Yeah. Sure.

WALLACE: Yeah. Sure.

*(*WALLACE *and* VICTORIA *sit down on a bench.)*

VICTORIA: You want a Jujyfruit?

WALLACE: No, they stick to your teeth. You want a Mallo Cup?

VICTORIA: Chocolate makes you break out.

WALLACE: Oh.

*(*WALLACE *takes a bite out of a Mallo Cup and drinks from his bottle.)*

VICTORIA: What is that?

WALLACE: What is *what?*

VICTORIA: *That.* In the bottle. The pink stuff.

WALLACE: Oh. You don't want to know.

VICTORIA: Sure I do. Wouldn't ask if I didn't want to know.

WALLACE: Uh, well, it's Pepto-Bismol mixed with seltzer.

VICTORIA: *What?*

WALLACE: I've got this perpetually upset stomach, and drinking this helps. It isn't all that bad, actually. Want some?

VICTORIA: No, thanks. I'll pass. *(Pause.)* It's such a nice day.

WALLACE: Yeah, it's not bad.

VICTORIA: I don't want to go back to school. Do you?

WALLACE: Oh, I'm just *dying* to sharpen my pencils and do tons of homework every night.

VICTORIA: Do you think eighth grade is going to be any different from seventh grade?

WALLACE: Nah, no chance. It's all the same. I don't think it matters. They just keep us in school until we're safely through our growth spurts and all of the puberty confusion, then send us out to make the best of the rest of our lives. And we get so terrified of the real world that we pay some university to keep us for four more years or eight more years or whatever. It all depends on how terrified you are. My grandmother's brother is sixty-two; he's *still* taking classes up in Chicago. If they keep you long enough to get comfortable when you're young, they've got you for *life*.

VICTORIA: Not me, that's for sure. Once I'm out, I'm *out*. I'm not going to college, no *way*.

WALLACE: What are you going to do?

VICTORIA: Who knows? Sit on the beach and get a really solid tan. Watch a lot of movies. Dance.

WALLACE: Sounds pretty stimulating, Victoria.

VICTORIA: Don't tease me.

WALLACE: I wasn't.

VICTORIA: Yes, you were.

WALLACE: I swear, I was not teasing you. Why would I tease you?

VICTORIA: I don't know. *(Pause.)* You didn't like the kissing stuff?

WALLACE: Huh?

VICTORIA: You know, in the movie.

WALLACE: Oh, I don't know.

VICTORIA: Sure you do.

WALLACE: I was getting candy. I missed it. Leave me alone.

VICTORIA: You want to try?

WALLACE: Try what?

VICTORIA: *That.*

WALLACE: What's *that?*

VICTORIA: Kissing.

WALLACE: You mean, with *you?*

VICTORIA: Yeah.

WALLACE: You mean, *now?*

VICTORIA: Yeah.

WALLACE: Umm—

VICTORIA: Scared?

WALLACE: Yeah, *right.* Go ahead. Kiss me.

VICTORIA: You sure?

WALLACE: As Shore as Dinah?

VICTORIA: *Dinah?*

WALLACE: Forget it. Will you kiss me already?

VICTORIA: Okay.

(VICTORIA *takes out the Jujyfruit she was eating and throws it away. They kiss.*)

WALLACE: You didn't fade out.

VICTORIA: Nope.

WALLACE: I think I love you, Victoria.

VICTORIA: Really?

(WALLACE *grabs* VICTORIA *and starts kissing her with great passion, holding her in his arms. After a few moments she breaks away.*)

WALLACE: What's wrong?

VICTORIA: What's *wrong?* You're too *fast* for me, Wallace, *that's* what's wrong. (VICTORIA *walks out.*)

WALLACE: Too *fast?* (*Pause.*) I mistook love for a girl who ate *Jujyfruits.* (WALLACE *drinks from his bottle.*)

Scene Eight

Grandmother's kitchen. WALLACE *is sitting at the table.* GRANDMOTHER *walks in with a glass of milk and a plate of cookies.*

GRANDMOTHER: Tollhouse cookies, baked this morning especially for *you.*

WALLACE: Thanks.

GRANDMOTHER: You look wonderful. Such a *handsome* thing.

WALLACE: This is delicious.

GRANDMOTHER: Of *course* it is. Would I serve you anything *but?* The first batch went to Grandpa, so *terrible.* *(Pause.)* I'm so *happy* you came to visit.

WALLACE: I love to visit you guys.

GRANDMOTHER: That's like sugar on my heart. It makes me feel so good.

*(*WALLACE *points to a photograph in a frame on the table.)*

WALLACE: Who's this?

GRANDMOTHER: That's Grandpa's second cousin, Jerry. He just died. That's the last picture of him, taken *two minutes* before he went. He was at a wedding there, sitting at his table, in between two pretty young girls—you see? The photographer snapped this picture, Jerry was joking and flirting with these young girls—he was like that, Jerry, so *bad.* Two minutes later he just *shut his eyes. (Pause.) Gone.* But still smiling.

WALLACE: *(pause)* Nice picture. *(Pause.)* Grandma, can I ask you something stupid?

GRANDMOTHER: If it makes you happy, I don't see why *not.*

WALLACE: What was your first kiss like?

GRANDMOTHER: My first *kiss?* You really have faith in my memory, don't you?

WALLACE: You don't have to tell me.

GRANDMOTHER: No, no, no. Let's see. It was with Grandpa, and we were—

WALLACE: Your first kiss was with *Grandpa?*

GRANDMOTHER: Sure. We were steadies in *high* school, you know.

WALLACE: I just never really thought about it. *(Pause.)* Was it nice?

GRANDMOTHER: I was petrified, but he made me feel comfortable. Still petrified, but in a comfortable way. Comfortably petrified. It was on a Saturday night, in 1936, I think. We were in Wentworth Park, about four blocks from here.

WALLACE: Wow.

GRANDMOTHER: I remember thinking he kissed really wonderfully. I mean, we were just in high school, and kissing him made me feel like the movie stars must have felt. I almost fell *backward,* I was so taken away. Then I got suspicious, asking myself where'd he *learned* to kiss like that. When I asked him—

WALLACE: You *asked* him?

GRANDMOTHER: I *asked* him, and he told me he had been practicing on his pillow for almost five years. That made me feel better. Besides, with those eyes, I couldn't help but believe him. *(Pause.)* I was sixteen then. Generations are different.

WALLACE: Yeah.

GRANDMOTHER: Each generation changes. It either improves or declines.

WALLACE: Yeah, trouble is, you can't tell one from the other. I mean, what *your* generation calls decline, *mine* calls improvement. It's so confusing. Along with everything else.

GRANDMOTHER: Don't waste your time thinking of it. I will say one thing, though. Hair is important. Secondary, but important nonetheless. Find a girl with *hair.*

WALLACE: *Hair?*

GRANDMOTHER: Sure. I mean, I can't run my fingers through Grandpa's hair. All I can do is rub his scalp. *(Pause.)* Which some say brings good luck.

WALLACE: I think that's when you rub *Buddha*'s scalp.

GRANDMOTHER: Well, Grandpa's certainly not *Buddha.* And I'm certainly not *lucky.*

WALLACE: *(pause)* Do you ever miss Mommy?

GRANDMOTHER: All the time.

WALLACE: *(pause)* Me, too. *(Pause.)* All the time.

GRANDMOTHER: *(pause)* Drink your milk. It's good for your teeth.

Scene Nine

WALLACE: "My Mother's Turtlenecks." By Wallace Kirkman. Age Sixteen. My mother loved my father and hated her neck. She thought it was too fleshy or something. If I hated *my* neck, I'd have it removed, but my mother never trusted doctors, so she wore turtlenecks. All the time. In every picture we have of her, she's wearing a turtleneck. She had turtlenecks in every color of the rainbow. She had blacks, she had whites, she had grays, she had plaids, she had polka dots and hound's-tooth checks and stripes and Mickey Mouse and even a sort of *mesh* turtleneck. I can't picture her without a turtleneck on. Although, according to Freud, I *try* to, every moment of every day. We have a photograph of me when I was a baby wearing one of my mother's turtlenecks. *Swimming* in one of my mother's turtlenecks is more like it. Just a bald head and a big shirt. It's very erotic, in an Oedipal shirtwear sort of way. It's a rare photograph, because I'm smiling. I didn't smile all that much during most of my childhood. I'm taking lessons now, trying to learn again, but it takes time. I stopped smiling when my mother stopped wearing turtlenecks. I came home from a typical day in the second grade to find her taking a bath in her own blood on the kitchen floor. Her turtleneck was on top of the kitchen table, so it wouldn't come between her neck and her knife. I understood then why she had worn turtlenecks all along. To stop the blood from flowing. To cover the wound that was there all along. They tried to cover the wound when they buried her with one of her favorite turtleneck dresses on, but it didn't matter. It was just an empty hole by then. My mother wasn't hiding inside. *(Pause.)* She wrote a note before she died, asking to be cremated, and I asked my father why she wasn't. He said my mother was two women, and the one he loved would have been scared of the flames. *(Pause.)* I look at that photograph of little me inside my mother's shirt all the time. It's the closest I can get to security. There are no pictures of me inside mother's womb, but her turtleneck is close enough.

Scene Ten

Wallace's bedroom. WALLACE *and* SARAH *are sitting on the bed.* SARAH *is reading something on a piece of paper.*

SARAH: Oh, I *really* like it.

WALLACE: *Really?*

SARAH: *Really.* It's very good.

WALLACE: *Why?*

SARAH: Well, it's funny, but it's also *sad.* It's really *sad.* And it's so *true.* I mean, there's so much of *you* in there. I mean, if I didn't know you, I'd *know* you after I read this. You know what I mean? I think it's really talented work. What's it for?

WALLACE: *For?*

SARAH: I mean, is it for English class or something?

WALLACE: No. I just sort of *wrote* it. Not really *for* anything. For me, I guess.

SARAH: You should submit it to the school newspaper. I bet they'd publish it.

WALLACE: I don't think I want the whole school reading this.

SARAH: Why not? I mean, you shouldn't be *ashamed* or anything—

WALLACE: I'm not *ashamed.* It just seems a little *sensationalist,* you know?

SARAH: I don't know. I guess so.

WALLACE: *So. (Pause.)* What do you want to do?

SARAH: Oh, I don't know.

WALLACE: We could go see a movie.

SARAH: Sure.

WALLACE: Or we could stay here.

SARAH: Sure.

WALLACE: Well, which one?

SARAH: Whichever.

WALLACE: Come on, I'm horrible with decisions.

SARAH: So am I.

WALLACE: Sarah, you're the valedictorian of our *class* for Chrissakes. If you can't make a decision, who can?

SARAH: Umm, do you want to . . . stay *here?*

WALLACE: Yes.

SARAH: Okay. Let's stay here, then.

WALLACE: Settled. Do you want something to drink?

SARAH: Umm, sure.

WALLACE: What do you want? Some wine? A screwdriver?

SARAH: Oh, you mean something to *drink.* I don't drink.

WALLACE: Oh. *(Pause.)* Do you mind if I drink something?

SARAH: Oh, no, don't let me stand in your way.

WALLACE: I'll be right back.

SARAH: Okay.

*(*WALLACE *walks out.* SARAH *looks around the room. She looks at a photograph in a frame by the bed.* WALLACE *walks in, sipping a glass of wine.)*

WALLACE: In vino veritas.

SARAH: Who's this?

WALLACE: It's my mother.

SARAH: She was beautiful.

WALLACE: She was okay. I'm going to light a candle, okay?

SARAH: Sure.

*(*WALLACE *gets a candle. He takes a lighter from his pocket.)*

WALLACE: My great-grandfather was lighting a pipe with this lighter when he died. It's a Zippo. Pretty sharp, huh?

SARAH: It's very nice.

*(*WALLACE *tries to light the lighter. It won't light.)*

WALLACE: I think it has to warm up. *(Pause.* WALLACE *tries to light the lighter a few more times. It won't light.)* Uhh, I guess my great-grandfather forgot to *refill* it before he died. It's just as well. I hate candles. They're so *clichéd. (Pause.)* You want to listen to some music?

SARAH: Sure.

WALLACE: What do you like?

SARAH: Oh, *anything.*

WALLACE: You like James Taylor?

SARAH: Sure.

WALLACE: Let me just find the tape. *(WALLACE looks for the tape.)* I don't know where I put it. Maybe it's out in the car. I can go check—

SARAH: That's okay. We don't *need* music. Do we?

WALLACE: Uhh, *no,* I guess *not. (Pause.) Well.*

SARAH: What was your mother like, Wallace?

WALLACE: What was she *like?*

SARAH: Yeah.

WALLACE: She was like Sylvia Plath without a Fulbright scholarship.

SARAH: What do you mean?

WALLACE: I mean—I don't know what I mean, I'm *sixteen. (WALLACE drinks his glass of wine.)*

WALLACE: Would you mind if I kissed you?

SARAH: The wine works fast.

WALLACE: No, *I* do. Can I?

SARAH: Umm, can't we *talk* for a while?

WALLACE: I don't *want* to talk, I want to *kiss.* Can I kiss you?

SARAH: I'd really feel better if we just—

WALLACE: Oh, come *on. (WALLACE kisses SARAH long and hard.)*

SARAH: Maybe I should go.

WALLACE: What? Oh, come on—

SARAH: No, I mean, maybe this wasn't such a good idea.

WALLACE: Don't you *like* me?

SARAH: Very much, Wallace. But I don't want this to be just—I don't know, a lot of *stupidity.* Just kissing and nothing else. I wanted to *talk* to you, you know?

WALLACE: Yeah, whatever.

SARAH: Oh, Wallace, don't do that—

WALLACE: Just go, please.

SARAH: What?

WALLACE: You said maybe you should leave, so leave. I don't want to —I just don't want to *deal* with this, okay?

SARAH: But—

WALLACE: But *nothing.* Just, please, go, okay?

SARAH: I—*fine.* 'Bye, Wallace.

WALLACE: Yeah, yeah, *see* you—

SARAH: I'm sorry this didn't work out. *(Pause.)* I'll see you in school on Monday. Okay? *(Pause.)* Okay, 'bye.

(SARAH walks out.)

Scene Eleven

Wallace's bedroom. WALLACE *is sitting on his bed, talking on the phone.*

WALLACE: Yeah, I wanted to see if I could make a song request and a dedication. . . . Umm, "Something in the Way She Moves" . . . by James Taylor. . . . You *don't?* I mean, it's on "Greatest Hits." You see, I'm trying to right a wrong, as they say. . . . I don't know, it's an expression. . . . Umm, do you have any, I don't know, like, Cat Stevens or something, somebody *close* to James Taylor? You know, one man and a guitar, that sort of thing. . . . Only top forty? . . . Who's *in* the top forty? Anybody named James? . . . No, that's not really appropriate. . . . Umm, could I just make a dedication, then? . . . Well, I *know* it's supposed to be for a song, but you don't seem to have the song I *need,* so if I could just maybe make the dedication and then you could maybe not play anything for about three minutes in *place* of the song I need and that way— hello? *(Pause.) Shit.* (WALLACE *hangs up the phone.)*

Scene Twelve

Sarah's front door. SARAH *inside,* WALLACE *outside.*

SARAH: Wallace.

WALLACE: Sarah.

SARAH: What are you doing here?

WALLACE: I wanted—umm, I wanted to *apologize.*

SARAH: You don't *have* to—

WALLACE: Yeah, I do.

SARAH: Okay. *(Pause.)* So?

WALLACE: You know, I just—it's funny, you know, sometimes I just wish I were a little kid again, when "sorry" was okay, you know?

SARAH: Yeah, well, we're not little kids, Wallace.

WALLACE: We're *not?* Umm, no, no, we're *not.* We're *certainly* not. Umm—*okay. Well.* I was acting *really* stupid before, I mean, just very —*stupid.* It was—I was being, umm—

SARAH: Stupid.

WALLACE: *Yeah.* And it was *wrong,* and it was—you know, it made you —it was *unfair.* And I *apologize.*

SARAH: Okay—

WALLACE: And I thought maybe we could try *again.*

SARAH: Again?

WALLACE: Yeah, you know, maybe I could come *in*—

SARAH: My parents are sleeping.

WALLACE: Oh. *(Pause.)* I could try to be quiet.

SARAH: It's kind of *late.*

WALLACE: Umm, well, you know, maybe you could come back over to my house and we could start from the *beginning.*

SARAH: *Wallace*—

WALLACE: I mean, I know it *sounds* like a stupid idea, but trust me, I'll behave this time, I know what to do. We can *talk.* We can have a *conversation.* We don't even have to kiss, we'll just *talk* and then you can go. *(Pause.)* Or we can just sit in *silence* for a while. We don't *have* to talk.

SARAH: I don't think that's a very good *idea,* Wallace.

WALLACE: All I'm *asking* for is another chance, Sarah. Don't make me beg.

SARAH: There's no need to *beg,* Wallace, I just don't think—

WALLACE: Okay. I'll beg. *(WALLACE drops to his knees.)*

WALLACE: I'm *begging,* Sarah, give me another shot.

SARAH: Wallace—

WALLACE: I'll be *good.*

SARAH: *Wallace*—

WALLACE: Look at the moon, Sarah. It's *full.* It's *romantic.*

SARAH: Wallace, get off your knees.

WALLACE: *(pause)* That's okay. I kind of like it down here. *(Pause.)* I was going to bring a guitar and maybe *serenade* you, but I can't sing. And I don't play the guitar. I did have Romantic Thoughts, though.

SARAH: That's very sweet, Wallace. *(Pause.)* I really should go back *inside*—

WALLACE: Yeah, I understand. You know, I tried to dedicate a song to you on the radio, you know, something by James Taylor, and they didn't *have* any James Taylor. Can you *believe* that?

SARAH: That's pretty funny.

WALLACE: Yeah. Pretty funny world.

SARAH: Sure is.

WALLACE: So, umm, you wouldn't want to maybe try again, say, *next* weekend? A movie or—

SARAH: *Wallace.*

WALLACE: No, I understand. Okay.

SARAH: I'm *sorry,* Wallace.

WALLACE: Yeah, no, *I'm* sorry.

SARAH: *(pause)* Are you going to *stay* down there?

WALLACE: For a little while, yeah. If you don't mind.

SARAH: No, I don't mind.

WALLACE: Thanks.

SARAH: Yeah, well, okay. Good night, Wallace.

WALLACE: 'Night.

SARAH: 'Bye.

WALLACE: 'Bye.

(SARAH *walks out, closing the door behind her. Pause.* WALLACE *looks up at the moon.)*

WALLACE: Thanks a lot, Moon. You really came through for me.

Scene Thirteen

Psychiatrist's office. PSYCHIATRIST *is sitting in a chair, writing in a notebook.* WALLACE *walks in.*

PSYCHIATRIST: Hello, Wallace. It's been a long time since I've seen you.

WALLACE: About five years.

PSYCHIATRIST: Yes. Nice to see you again.

WALLACE: I'll bet.

PSYCHIATRIST: Would you like to have a seat?

WALLACE: No.

PSYCHIATRIST: Okay, then. What's on your mind?

WALLACE: Lots. *(Pause.)* I came here last time because my father made me, but now I'm here because I want to talk to you. You see, I'm confused. My mother makes me a sandwich for lunch. I take it. She, in turn, slits her throat. And after the funeral, when I go back to school for the first time, my *father* makes me a sandwich for lunch, or at least he *tries,* so as not to screw up my daily routine any more than it already has been. And I'm thinking, all day while I'm in school, that *he's* going to be lying on the kitchen floor when I get home. It's the same thing, you see, because I *took* the sandwich. If I didn't *take,* I think, they'll be okay. But I *take,* and that kills them. And when I came home from school and he *wasn't* on the floor of the kitchen, but instead sitting in his study, *alive,* I was disappointed. Let down. Because my system didn't work. It *failed* me. Everything was *failing* me. And when I *expected* my father to fail me, he failed me by *not* failing me. He was just sitting there in his study. Alone, deserted by the woman he loved and planned to—I don't know, move to Florida with, and he can manage to stay alive, to go on living. *How?* And, I mean, Victoria, this thirteen-year-old *girl*, is *sitting* there, practically *begging* me to kiss her, I mean, she would have been on her *knees* in a second, in more ways than one, that's how it seemed, and when I finally let down and actually *do* what she's been *asking* me to do—I *kiss* her and *bang*—all of a sudden, *I'm* too goddamn *fast* for her. I told her I *loved* her, and she runs off, *skipping*, and the next week she's kissing somebody else, and I heard he got up her *shirt*, and *he's* not too fast, *I'm* the one who was too *fast*. So I get this reputation that scares the hell out of me, because, not only will no *decent* girls *look* at me, I can't even think about any of the *in*decent girls, because I'm scared to death of having to live up to my own reputation. And, now, I mean, when my big mistake has always been talking too much, so I try, finally, on this girl I *really* like, okay, I mean, *bright, pretty*, actually *nice, caring*, I try not to screw it up by talking too much, and I go *right* for the kiss, and she won't ever see me again because I didn't talk too much. I mean, I can't *win*. They *desert*. Women *desert*. And I know it all stems back to my fucking *coward* mother, and if she hadn't *offed* herself, I'd have no problems, but what I'm trying to say is I don't know what the hell to *do* about all of this, Doctor, and it's my life, so can —you know, can you give me some *advice* or something, Doctor? *(Pause.)* Doctor? *(Pause.)* Doctor?

Scene Fourteen

WALLACE *and* PSYCHIATRIST.

WALLACE: "Tyrannosaurus Rex." By Wallace Kirkman. Age Eighteen.

*(*PSYCHIATRIST *gets up and starts to walk out.)*

WALLACE: Don't go. I need *help* with this one. Stay right there. Please. You'll like this. It's very *Freudian*. In fact, it's a *dream*.

(The lights change rather dramatically. PSYCHIATRIST *sits, and* WALLACE *walks out. He walks in a moment later with a crate of props.)*

WALLACE: I need a *mother*. *(Pause.)* I need somebody who can *act* like a mother.

(VICTORIA *walks in.*)

WALLACE: You'll do. I always wanted to be a dinosaur when I was young. Young*er.* I have a lot in common with Tyrannosaurus. We both walk on two legs, we both eat meat, and we both occasionally answer to the nickname "King of the Tyrant Lizards." Anyhow, the recipe for this dream is something like two parts *Oedipus Rex,* two parts Freud, and nineteen parts me. In the beginning, the eventual parents are both thirteen years old.

(WALLACE *pushes* PSYCHIATRIST *and* VICTORIA *onto their knees.*)

WALLACE: And Jewish.

(WALLACE *pulls two pairs of gag glasses out of the crate of props. He puts one —with a plastic nose—on* VICTORIA *and the other—with a plastic nose and a plastic mustache—on* PSYCHIATRIST.)

WALLACE: They get bar mitzvahed and bat mitzvahed on the same day and sleep with each other on the same night. Kids today. God bless 'em. On with the dream. The girl gets pregnant, as girls will do.

(WALLACE *pulls a baby doll out of the crate of props and hands it to* VICTORIA.)

WALLACE: She wants to get an abortion so the baby won't get in the way of the seventh grade, but neither of the partners got any cash for their *mitzvahs,* only savings bonds. *Lots* of savings bonds. So, they pack several pairs of underwear and go to stay with the girl's grandmother, a mentally ill fortune-teller from Boston.

(GRANDMOTHER *walks in—a grand entrance—wearing a turban.*)

GRANDMOTHER: This baby is *trouble.* He's going to fight with you and *shtoop* you.

VICTORIA: *Shtoop?*

PSYCHIATRIST: How do you know the baby's going to be a "he"?

GRANDMOTHER: I'm a fortune-teller. Give me a break.

WALLACE: When the baby is born, they immediately sell it on the black market.

(VICTORIA *tosses the baby doll to* WALLACE. WALLACE *pulls a packet of play money out of the crate of props and hands it to* VICTORIA.)

WALLACE: They use the money to pay a few months' worth of rent on a Beacon Street apartment.

(WALLACE *takes the packet of play money from* VICTORIA *and replaces it in the crate of props. He pulls a pair of boxing gloves out of the crate of props and hands them to* PSYCHIATRIST, *who puts them on.*)

WALLACE: The father starts taking boxing lessons. The mother spends her spare time in their spare apartment reading spare Japanese literature.

(WALLACE *pulls a Mishima paperback out of the crate of props and tosses it to* VICTORIA.)

WALLACE: They earn rent money and grocery money and boxing-lesson money and Japanese-book money by becoming kiddie porn stars.

(PSYCHIATRIST *and* VICTORIA *look at one another in horror.*)

WALLACE: *Cut.* And, at this point, the dream leaps ahead about seventeen years or so. The father is a very popular amateur boxer.

(WALLACE *pulls* PSYCHIATRIST *up off her knees so that she is standing.* WALLACE *pulls* VICTORIA *up off her knees so that she is also standing.*)

WALLACE: The mother is about to commit ritual suicide.

(WALLACE *pulls the large knife* MOTHER *used to slit her throat out of the crate of props and hands it to* VICTORIA.)

VICTORIA: I've tried and tried and *tried.* And I'll just *never* be Japanese.

(VICTORIA *plunges the large knife into her bowels and falls to the floor. Dead.* WALLACE *stares at her for a moment, then tosses the baby doll into the crate of props and pulls out a pair of boxing gloves. He puts them on.*)

WALLACE: The son is a boxing necrophiliac who masturbates. A lot.

(WALLACE *approaches* GRANDMOTHER.)

WALLACE: Hello.

GRANDMOTHER: *Shalom.*

WALLACE: *(to the audience)* I *hate* when people say "Shalom." I never know whether they're *coming* or *going* or just a *pacifist.*

GRANDMOTHER: How may I serve you?

WALLACE: I'd like to know my fortune.

GRANDMOTHER: Easy. You're going to fight with your dad and *shtoop* your mom. Ten bucks, please.

WALLACE: This is *horrible.* I don't want to fight with Dad. I *love* Dad.

GRANDMOTHER: Ten bucks, please.

WALLACE: And I don't want to *shtoop* Mom. Because Dad would get mad. And we'd fight.

GRANDMOTHER: Ten bucks, please.

WALLACE: And I don't want to fight with Dad. I *love* Dad. Boy, this makes me tense. I need some *release*.

GRANDMOTHER: Ten bucks, please.

(WALLACE punches GRANDMOTHER and knocks her out.)

WALLACE: I wonder if there's anything good over at the *morgue*.

(WALLACE looks at VICTORIA.)

WALLACE: She's *beautiful.* She's *everything.* She's *dead. And* she's a nice Jewish girl. I wonder where her bowels are.

(WALLACE leaps onto VICTORIA, kisses her madly for a few moments, then rolls off onto the floor.)

WALLACE: It's time to *box.*

(WALLACE approaches PSYCHIATRIST.)

WALLACE: You want to fight?

PSYCHIATRIST: Sure.

(A bell rings. PSYCHIATRIST punches WALLACE and knocks him out.)

PSYCHIATRIST: Ten, nine, eight, seven, six, five, four, three, two, one.

(PSYCHIATRIST slaps WALLACE's face and he comes to.)

WALLACE: Did I win?

PSYCHIATRIST: Nope.

WALLACE: *Shit.*

PSYCHIATRIST: Come on, I'll buy you a beer.

WALLACE: I'm underage.

PSYCHIATRIST: You don't have a fake ID?

WALLACE: I was always too busy *masturbating* to buy one.

PSYCHIATRIST: Oh. *(Pause.)* Come on, I'll buy you a ginger ale.

WALLACE: Yeah, okay. You're on.

(PSYCHIATRIST helps WALLACE up, and they walk a few steps.)

PSYCHIATRIST: One beer and one ginger ale, barkeep.

WALLACE: Excuse me for a moment, I've got to go to the bathroom.

PSYCHIATRIST: But you haven't had anything to drink.

WALLACE: *(pause) Excuse me for a moment, I've got to go to the bathroom.*

PSYCHIATRIST: Oh. Sure, go right ahead.

WALLACE: Be right back.

(WALLACE *walks out. He runs in a few moments later, without the boxing gloves on, his hands covering his eyes. He is* screaming. GRANDMOTHER, PSYCHIATRIST, *and* VICTORIA *clear the stage and walk out. The lights change back.* WALLACE *takes his hands off his tightly closed eyes, opens them, sees nobody around, and stops screaming. He yawns, as if waking up.)*

WALLACE: I've been having this dream every night for the past two months. It's always pretty much the same, although sometimes it's in color and sometimes it's in black and white, and once the black-and-white version was colorized, which pissed me off. I mean, it's more or less my life story, and who wants their life story *colorized?*

Scene Fifteen

Wallace's dormitory room. WALLACE *and* LILI *walk in.*

WALLACE: This is my room.

LILI: How did you get a single room your first year?

WALLACE: I had a psychiatrist write the school a note saying essentially that if I had to live with another person, I'd probably kill them.

LILI: Seriously?

WALLACE: Not really. But the school believed it. *(Pause.)* You must be tired.

LILI: Why?

WALLACE: Well, I mean, you were onstage for practically the entire time.

LILI: It's an important part.

WALLACE: And you did it so well. *Really.* The whole thing was—*beautiful.*

LILI: The choreographer's pretty talented.

WALLACE: I mean, who would ever think to do *Catcher in the Rye* as a *ballet?*

LILI: The *choreographer* would.

WALLACE: I—well, I mean, I *know,* but it's just—*wow.* You know, I never realized there was so much stuff about *lesbians* in *Catcher in the Rye.*

LILI: It's all in the *subtext.*

WALLACE: Yeah. But I think, you know, having *you*—you know, having a *woman* as Holden Caulfield really made everything *quite* clear.

LILI: I'm glad you liked it. *(Pause.)* You're very *cute,* Wallace.

WALLACE: *Me?*

LILI: Yes, you. I'm really *drawn* to you, you know?

WALLACE: Umm, *sure.*

LILI: What are you waiting for?

WALLACE: Huh?

LILI: *Kiss* me.

WALLACE: Umm, are you—umm, *sure.*

(WALLACE kisses LILI.)

WALLACE: How was that?

LILI: That was nice. Do you want to sleep together?

WALLACE: *What?*

LILI: Do you want to *make love?*

WALLACE: Umm, with *you?*

LILI: *Yes,* with *me.*

WALLACE: Umm, sure, yes, yeah, *sure. (Pause.)* What do we do?

LILI: Are you a *virgin?*

WALLACE: Umm, *technically,* no.

LILI: What do you mean, "technically"?

WALLACE: Well, what is the definition of male virginity?

LILI: Is that a rhetorical question?

WALLACE: A male virgin is a male who has never had his thing inside a female's thing. Right?

LILI: Anybody still calling it a "thing" is probably a virgin, I know that much.

WALLACE: Well, when I was born, I had a thing. A very tiny, bald thing, but a thing nonetheless. And I entered this world through my mother's thing—the infamous "tunnel of love." Therefore, my thing has been inside of a female's thing, although it had to share the space with the rest of my body. In fact, pretty much all men are born nonvirgins. The only exceptions would be men born cesarean style.

LILI: You're saying you lost your virginity—with your *mother*?

WALLACE: Yeah.

LILI: You're pretty weird, Wallace.

WALLACE: Thank you.

LILI: So, will this be your first time having sex with somebody outside your immediate family?

WALLACE: You've got me there. Yes.

LILI: I'm *honored*.

WALLACE: I'm *terrified*.

LILI: It's simple. Don't worry, you'll be fine. Before we get started, do you have any protection?

WALLACE: Umm, no.

LILI: Here, take this.

(LILI *hands* WALLACE *a condom.*)

WALLACE: You really come prepared.

LILI: I don't want to even joke *around* with AIDS, you know?

WALLACE: I know. Remember when Ayds was just a dietetic candy? There's a stock that must have done *real* well. Can you picture the president of the company right before the end? "Call the thing Dexatrim, it's a *superb* name for a disease!"

LILI: You don't have to make jokes, Wallace, everything's going to be fine. *Better* than fine.

WALLACE: How did you know I was nervous? I thought I was covering it pretty well.

LILI: A woman knows.

WALLACE: Hey, tell me something.

LILI: Yeah?

WALLACE: What can you possibly see in me?

LILI: What do you mean?

WALLACE: I mean, how did I end up here with *you*? You're a beautiful senior, I'm a nervous little freshman.

LILI: You've got great eyes.

WALLACE: I *do*?

LILI: Really intelligent eyes. Like they've seen a *lot*, that's what they look like.

WALLACE: You're here with me because of my *eyes*?

LILI: Yeah, sort of.

WALLACE: The brochures don't do college justice.

LILI: Let's get on the *bed*, Wallace.

WALLACE: Let me just hit the lights.

LILI: No, keep them *on*, I want to *see* you.

WALLACE: You keep the lights on with a guy named Biff who pumps iron and gasoline. With a Jew from Jersey, you do it in the dark.

(WALLACE *flips the light switch. Blackout.*)

LILI: *(pause)* Why do you wear so many *layers*?

WALLACE: Wearing layers of clothing keeps you warmer than wearing one *thick* garment.

LILI: But it's not cold out.

WALLACE: All right, so I hate my body. I'm too skinny. Is that such a crime?

LILI: You've got a nice body.

WALLACE: In the *dark*, maybe. You're so *sweaty*—

LILI: I want to *see* you, Wallace, I want to see *all* of you. Can't you turn the lights on?

WALLACE: If the lights go on, I go in the closet.

LILI: Do you have a candle or something, at least?

WALLACE: I *hate* candles. *(Pause.)* Am I doing okay?

LILI: You're doing *fine.* Just *fine.*

WALLACE: *(pause)* Why did the chicken cross the road?

LILI: This isn't the *time,* Wallace.

WALLACE: Sorry.

(Long pause. WALLACE *flips the light switch. The lights come up. They sit up in bed together.)*

WALLACE: *Wow. (Pause.)* You know, I always wondered what this would be like, I always tried to imagine, and it's just—now it's *actual.* Now it's *real.* Now—I just slept with an older woman. An older woman who *dances.* Billy Corkscraw would never believe it.

LILI: *Who?*

WALLACE: This kid I was friends with growing up, Billy Corkscraw. He talked about sex all the time. He told me everything, little Mister Know-It-All. You know, told me that the only way to *really* satisfy a woman was to put Spanish fly in her drink, and if you were dating a girl who spoke French instead of Spanish, you had to get your Spanish fly "translated," which Billy said could only be done at the French embassy and it cost a lot of money, and he said we would probably just be better off paying professionals. *(Pause.)* He moved to Arizona when we were eleven. Last I heard about him, he couldn't find a date for his senior prom.

LILI: *(pause)* You have to meet my little *sister.*

Scene Sixteen

Wallace's dormitory room. WALLACE *and* NINA *are sitting on the bed. She is looking at a photograph in a frame by the bed.*

NINA: Is this your mother?

WALLACE: Yeah. She's dead.

NINA: Oh. I'm sorry.

WALLACE: For what?

NINA: For asking.

WALLACE: I don't mind. I mean, I've lived without her for so long—it's not all that bad, really.

NINA: What was she like?

WALLACE: Like Sylvia Plath without talent.

NINA: She killed herself?

WALLACE: Yeah. When I was six.

NINA: That's too bad. How'd she kill herself?

WALLACE: You really want to know?

NINA: Yeah. If you don't want to talk about it, though—

WALLACE: No, I do. It's just that it freaks most people out. *(Pause.)* She slit her throat with a kitchen knife.

NINA: Oh, God. I never understand why people don't just take pills and die painlessly.

WALLACE: I guess if you hate yourself enough to want to die—it's just like if you wanted to kill someone else. If you hate something, you want it to die painfully. I mean, I guess that's what it is. I know that pain belongs in there somewhere.

NINA: How did you deal with all that? I mean, how'd you get through it?

WALLACE: I used to break glass.

NINA: Huh?

WALLACE: I used to break glasses on the kitchen floor. That helped a little. It was destructive, but it eased the pain.

NINA: How *sad*—

WALLACE: It's no big deal. I mean, I guess it made me who I am today, and who knows what I would have been if she was still alive. Maybe I'd be somebody I'd hate, you know. Sure, there are times I'd kill to have her back, just for a day. So I could show her something I've written, or talk to her about my thoughts, or just even to see her smile when I did something silly.

(Long pause.)

NINA: What are you thinking about?

WALLACE: I don't know. About my mother, and about how you listen to me talk, and—and about how I'd love to kiss you right now.

NINA: So why *don't* you?

WALLACE: What? Well, umm, Nina, do you—did your sister tell you—

NINA: I know. You and my sister were—*together.*

WALLACE: And it doesn't *bother* you?

NINA: A little. Not much. I mean, you were *drunk*—

WALLACE: *What?*

NINA: And all you did was *kiss,* right?

WALLACE: Umm—umm, *yeah.* Just a few drunken kisses, that's all it was.

NINA: A *few?* She said *one.*

WALLACE: Well, I mean, there were a few *within* the one. But we never pulled our lips apart, so technically, I guess, yeah, just *one.*

NINA: Okay. *(Pause.)* Well?

WALLACE: Well what?

NINA: *Kiss* me.

WALLACE: Nina, I think I *love* you. I know it sounds stupid, but—is that okay?

NINA: Sure.

WALLACE: Okay. I'm going to kiss you now, okay?

NINA: Okay.

WALLACE: Okay.

(They kiss.)

Scene Seventeen

Wallace's dormitory room. WALLACE *and* WENDY *are sitting on the bed, kissing.*

WENDY: Are you sure we should be doing this?

WALLACE: Why not?

WENDY: Well, what about your girlfriend?

WALLACE: What *about* her?

WENDY: Well—

WALLACE: I'm drunk, you're drunk, we don't know what we're doing. Right?

WENDY: Umm, *right.*

WALLACE: *Right.* Give me a kiss.

(They kiss.)

Scene Eighteen

WALLACE *in a spotlight.*

WALLACE: I fucked up. Mommy. I fell in love—*really*—for the first time. I mean, it wasn't romance for the sake of romance. It was romance for the sake of—*somebody. Nina.* Nina listened. And I got scared. I ran away. To somebody else. What do I do? Mommy. It *hurts. (Pause.)* I want my—I *need* my mother. *(Pause.)* I'm not asking for much. I just—all I want is to take the knife away from her. To go back and take the knife away from her. All I want to do is change history.

(The lights come up on the kitchen. MOTHER *is fixing a peanut butter and banana sandwich. She is peeling the banana.* WALLACE *looks at her. He looks at the audience, then looks back at her. He walks past the table, picking up the large knife as he goes by. He walks out.* MOTHER *finishes peeling the banana and fixes the sandwich, breaking the banana up with her hands and spreading the peanut butter with a spoon. She puts the sandwich into a lunchbox on the table.* WALLACE *runs in.)*

WALLACE: I'm going to miss the bus! Is my lunch ready?

MOTHER: All set.

*(*WALLACE *grabs the lunchbox and kisses* MOTHER *on the cheek.)*

WALLACE: 'Bye, Mommy.

MOTHER: 'Bye, Wallace.

WALLACE: *(to the audience)* I love the second grade!

MOTHER: Don't shout, Wallace.

(WALLACE runs out. MOTHER watches after him. She writes a note on a slip of paper. While she is writing the note, WALLACE walks in and quietly watches her from the side. She puts the note on the table. She takes off her turtleneck shirt, so she is in her brassiere. She wraps the turtleneck around her neck and pulls it taut, attempting to strangle herself. The lights on the kitchen slowly fade, and WALLACE is in the spotlight again.)

WALLACE: *(after a moment, to the audience)* In countless science fiction stories about time travel, the moral is quite clear. When you go back in time, if you so much as step on an ant, the course of history will change drastically. Don't try to change history. It's dangerous. *(Pause.)* In my experience, trying to change history isn't really dangerous. It's just a waste of time—a futile, frustrating exercise where you exert yourself and use up boundless energies and—and everything stays exactly the same. With small technical differences, perhaps. One more dead ant. If you take a razor away from a man who wants to kill himself, he'll *still* kill himself—he just won't be clean-shaven. The will is all that matters. If the will is there—*(Pause.)* I should dwell on the future. Dwelling on the past is hopeless.

Scene Nineteen

Wallace's dormitory room. WALLACE *is standing. There is a knock on the door.*

WALLACE: Yeah.

(NINA walks in.)

NINA: Hey, there.

WALLACE: Sit down.

NINA: What's wrong?

WALLACE: Sit down.

NINA: Okay.

(NINA sits on the bed.)

NINA: What's the matter?

WALLACE: You deserve better.

NINA: Huh?

WALLACE: I'm not good enough for you.

NINA: What are you talking about? You're the *best*.

WALLACE: I'm the *worst*. You should *hate* me.

NINA: Why?

WALLACE: You don't want to know.

NINA: *What* don't I want to know?

WALLACE: I've been with somebody else.

NINA: *(pause)* What?

WALLACE: I was with somebody else.

NINA: *(pause)* Who?

WALLACE: Wendy.

NINA: Wendy. *(Pause.)* I think I'm going to be sick.

(NINA *runs out.*)

WALLACE: *Nina. (Pause.)* Women *desert*.

(WALLACE *picks up a glass. He holds it in his hand, looking at it. He starts to throw it so that it will break against the wall.* NINA *walks in.*)

NINA: Don't you dare break that glass or I'll turn right around and I won't come back.

(WALLACE *stops. He puts the glass on the bed and looks at* NINA.)

WALLACE: You came back. *(Pause.)* You should hate me.

NINA: I do. But I also happen to love you, and I'm not going to lose you without a fight.

WALLACE: You came back.

NINA: Do you want to work through this? I'll tell you right now, it's not going to be easy.

WALLACE: I know.

NINA: You betrayed me.

WALLACE: I know.

NINA: I know you may have been scared or whatever, but I swear to God, if you ever do this again, both you and her—*whoever* she is—will be lying on the street, okay?

WALLACE: Okay. *(Pause.)* You came back.

NINA: You want to work through this?

WALLACE: Yes.

NINA: Okay. Then we will.

WALLACE: You came back.

(WALLACE *goes to hug* NINA. *They hug. After a few moments she breaks from the hug and slaps him, hard, across the face.)*

NINA: Don't you *ever* do that to me again, understand?

WALLACE: You came back.

Scene Twenty

GRANDMOTHER *'s kitchen.* WALLACE *and* GRANDMOTHER *are sitting at the table.*

GRANDMOTHER: And you *really* love her?

WALLACE: I *swear.* At least, I think I do. I mean, I know I do. And I was running away from her. You know, I was so terrified that she'd leave me, I wanted to leave first so I wouldn't have to deal with the pain. You know, I *wanted* to get caught with this other girl, Grandma, I *had* to tell her about it right away. It all made sense when I told her. Too much sense. She said she was going to be sick and walked out of my room. And something in me clicked. Something in me had been expecting it. Had been expecting her to leave me. And it made sense. And it was complete. *(Pause.)* And then she came *back.* That's what threw me for a loop. And right then I said, There is no way I am going to lose her. I am going to do everything in my power to keep her. Because she came *back.* And it terrifies me that I almost lost her because Mommy killed herself. I mean, my mother deserts me for whatever reasons, but she almost made me lose the one girl I've ever really *loved.*

GRANDMOTHER: *(Pause.)* You can't *blame* her until you die, you know.

WALLACE: What?

GRANDMOTHER: Your mother. I mean, sure, you can invoke her name once in a while to clear up a messy situation, but you've got to be responsible for *something* eventually. A dead mother does not give you *carte blanche* for a lifetime of screwing up. You can *do* it—you can screw *up,* go right ahead, but don't keep blaming her, or you'll just go through life fooling yourself and you'll die a blind man. *(Pause.)* Understand?

WALLACE: I think so. I'm not sure.

GRANDMOTHER: It's okay. You're still young. *(Pause.)* Are they feeding you enough up at school? You look thin.

WALLACE: They're feeding me fine, Grandma.

(Pause. WALLACE *points to a photograph in a frame on the table.)*

WALLACE: Who's this?

GRANDMOTHER: Oh, that's Gertrude Mawsbaum, we grew up together. She just passed on. This picture was taken three weeks before she died.

Epilogue

WALLACE *is standing to the left with a tomato in his hand and a crate of tomatoes at his feet.* NINA *is standing to the right, wearing a white dress. Pause.*

NINA: Well?

WALLACE: *(pause)* I don't want to ruin your dress. *(Pause.)* I don't want to ruin your beautiful dress.

(Pause. The lights slowly fade.)

JONATHAN MARC SHERMAN

(1988) Then . . .

I was born in Morristown, New Jersey, and grew up in Livingston, New Jersey. I dropped out of Livingston High School in my senior year and now attend Bennington College. I started writing plays when I got a typewriter for my twelfth or thirteenth birthday, I don't remember which. My last play, *Serendipity and Serenity*, was given a staged reading in the Sixth Annual Young Playwrights Festival, and *Women and Wallace* was fully produced in the Seventh Annual Young Playwrights Festival. It's tough to communicate exactly what I got out of the experience. I met some interesting people and saw my words brought to life. The preliminary reading of the play, in May 1988, directed by James Lapine, with Robert Leonard as Wallace, was enormously helpful to me and remains a treasured memory. The production of the play in September and October 1988, directed by Don Scardino, with Josh Hamilton as Wallace, was more than I could have ever hoped for. The first time I heard the play draw out wonderful laughter from the audience. The shock I had while doing a rewrite when I realized I was writing Wallace with Josh's voice in my head and not my own. The blast of energy unleashed by a group of six young men at Show World Center the night the play finished its run at Playwrights Horizons. These are a few of the strange, inexplicable but meaningful memories I have. I won't know if I've learned all that much until the next one, which is coming up right behind you. Watch out.

. . . And Now

I've got to sum up the past two years of my life, so bear with me. Thanks.

I graduated from Bennington College and dropped out of the Yale School of Drama.

Women and Wallace was broadcast on public television's *American Playhouse*. I'm still writing plays. *Veins and Thumbtacks* was produced at the Los Angeles Theatre Center. *Jesus on the Oil Tank* won the 21st Century Playwrights Festival Competition. *Sons and Fathers* and *Sophistry* have been given a bunch of staged readings at different places, including the Los Angeles Theatre Center, the Manhattan Theatre Club, and

Playwrights Horizons, and eventually I'll finish both of them and everything will be hunky-dory.

I knew I'd slip *hunky-dory* in here somewhere.

Last summer I drove across America and back with Josh Hamilton (who played Wallace) and Ethan Hawke (who *didn't* play Wallace) in a car that almost exploded, went to Paris for the first time, and finally finished a screenplay called *Wonderful Time*.

I don't think it would be a good idea to say what I'm working on now. Zeus might punish me for my hubris.

I take great comfort in the fact that Beckett was forty-two when he wrote *Waiting for Godot*, but have difficulty forgetting that Orson Welles was only twenty-five when he made *Citizen Kane*. I'm twenty-three. I hope when I'm seventy, I can show this book to my grandchildren and smile.

If you bore with me, you win! Take this purple ticket stub to the gentleman with the goatee behind the counter to claim your exciting prize!

Oh, yeah, one last thing:

"Actions speak louder than words" is a silly thing to *say*, if you know what I mean.